T0265597

THE UNSPOKEN
MORALITY OF CHILDHOOD

the
UNSPOKEN MORALITY OF CHILDHOOD

FAMILY, FRIENDSHIP, SELF-ESTEEM AND THE WISDOM OF THE EVERYDAY

KRISTEN RENWICK MONROE

ANTHEM PRESS

Anthem Press
An imprint of Wimbledon Publishing Company
www.anthempress.com

This edition first published in UK and USA 2022
by ANTHEM PRESS
75–76 Blackfriars Road, London SE1 8HA, UK
or PO Box 9779, London SW19 7ZG, UK
and
244 Madison Ave #116, New York, NY 10016, USA

British Library Cataloguing-in-Publication Data
A catalogue record for this book is available from the British Library.

Library of Congress Cataloging-in-Publication Data
Names: Monroe, Kristen Renwick, 1946– author.
Title: The unspoken morality of childhood : family, friendship, self-esteem and
the wisdom of the everyday / Kristen Renwick Monroe.
Description: New York, NY : Anthem Press, [2022] | Includes bibliographical
references and index. | Identifiers: LCCN 2021063022 | ISBN 9781839982392
(hardback) | ISBN 9781839982408 (pdf) | ISBN 9781839982415 (epub)
Subjects: LCSH: Families—Moral and ethical aspects. | Child rearing—Moral
and ethical aspects. | Self-esteem. | Identity (Psychology) | Ethics,
Modern—21st century.
Classification: LCC HQ519 .M66 2022 | DDC 306.85—dc23/eng/20220104
LC record available at https://lccn.loc.gov/2021063022

ISBN-13: 978-1-83998-239-2 (Hbk)
ISBN-10: 1-83998-239-X (Hbk)

Cover image: Photo of the author with her daughter, on the author's 50th birthday,
taken by Trudi Monroe.

This title is also available as an e-book.

"[W]e are well advised to keep on nodding terms with the people we used to be, whether we find them attractive company or not. Otherwise they turn up unannounced and surprise us, come hammering on the mind's door at 4 a.m. of a bad night and demand to know who deserted them, who betrayed them, who is going to make amends. We forget all too soon the things we thought we could never forget. We forget the loves and the betrayals alike, forget what we whispered and what we screamed, forget who we were."

Joan Didion. "On Keeping a Notebook"
Essay in Slouching Towards Bethlehem

For my children,
Chloe, Nicholas and Alexander
In memory of Prem Chadha, their much-loved Nani,
and for Trudi Monroe, the best grandmother in the world

CONTENTS

ACKNOWLEDGMENTS

FROM BABYSITTERS TO ELEPHANTS AND JOHN STUART MILL'S ADVICE FOR CHILDREN[1]

We moved to California from New Jersey in 1984, Alex, my husband and I. There is always a lot to do after a move and my husband agreed to take care of shifting the car registrations from New Jersey to California. "There is a form you can fill out and donate money to the wildlife fund in California. You pay a bit extra, but you then can choose a special license plate. You know, have your initials on it or something like that. Would you like me to do that for you? I'm going to pay to have my initials put on mine."

"That sounds like a good idea." I was intrigued.

"Well, what do you want me to put down for your vanity plate?" he asked.

I thought a moment. "I know! J. S. Mill, for John Stuart Mill." I replied. Then reflected, "Oh, but I'm sure someone else already has it. It's an obvious choice."

My husband raised his eyebrows but said nothing. When he returned home that evening, having been to his new office and to the Department of Motor Vehicles (DMV), he tossed me a package of forms. "Well, you got your wish. You have your J. S. Mill plates. They'll be here in a couple of weeks." He paused, then shook his head. "Hard to believe that out of all the people in the state of California, you are the only one who wanted to have John Stuart Mill's name on your license plate."

"Yeah, it's kind of amazing, isn't it?" I said, so struck by my good luck that I failed to recognize my husband's sardonic wit.

This exchange reflects a wonderful reality: How differently we all see the world, and seldom recognize it. I have become aware over the years that my own viewpoint is idiosyncratic; this book may perhaps reflect that eccentricity more than is usually the case in my writings. So let me provide a bit of background for the book's inception, as a way of thanking a few special people who showed me new ways of seeing the world, thinking about reality and, as part of this, suggested that perhaps others might find some little of what I say of interest.

One of those people is Chuck Myers, a generous and caring book editor. I had published one book with Chuck as editor and had sent him the final manuscript in what had grown into the last volume in a trilogy on moral choice. (*The Heart of Altruism* 1996, *The Hand of Compassion* 2004 and *Ethics in an Age of Terror and Genocide* 2012.) This last book was the most difficult one I had ever written. It was completed just after my divorce, when my children were flying off into their own new worlds and I was ending a research project that had begun more than 20 years earlier. Completing this project thus was infused with that sense of loss we often feel at relinquishing something—raising children, ending a marriage, writing a series of books—which we have lived with for a long time. No matter how natural or how good it is to complete the project, there remains a sense that something important and of personal value is passing out of your life. Beyond that, this particular book—*Ethics in an Age of Terror and Genocide*—contained my thoughts as a senior scholar who had spent over 20 years pondering how people make their moral choices and was now trying to pull it all together into a theory that made sense to me, and perhaps to others.

For whatever the reasons, I felt more than usually vulnerable, hoping someone I respected would like the book. I thus was unprepared for Chuck's reaction when we met at the meetings of the American Political Science Association to discuss the manuscript sent to him in July 2011.

"What is the audience for this book, Kristi?" Chuck asked.

"Academic. It's an academic book," I replied.

"Well, what I'd like you to do is to write something that's a popular introduction to ethics. You have such an unusual way of looking at things. I'd like you to try to capture that for a broader audience."

I was crushed. "So, you don't want this book?" I asked.

"Oh, no. I want the book," Chuck reassured me. "I just want you to do something different as well, something for a more general audience interested in ethics."

I had no idea what Chuck meant or how this would play out. I was simply relieved that Chuck wanted to publish the book I had sent him. But something in Chuck's words must have struck home, for over the next 10 years I found myself jotting down little bits and pieces of stories, random thoughts almost, prompted by things that happened—or were remembered—in my own private world.[2] Chloe having a babysitter, a beautiful Korean girl, tiny and delicate and so sweet she would allow herself to enter Chloe's imaginary world. I often would find them both squished into a closet, hiding from some dragon or other make-believe villain. Chloe was four at the time, so the closet was fine for her. But the babysitter was a college girl at the University of California, Irvine (UCI), and I used to give the two of them lectures on how there must be no babysitter abuse. "No one must ever abuse a babysitter by making a grown person hide in the closet or under the bed, even in a game," I would tell them, trying not to laugh at the absurdity of this particular scenario.

One day Chloe was playing with Lily in the family room, and I asked Lily if she had a boyfriend.[3] (I am embarrassed to admit how patronizing this now feels.) "I did, but my parents made me break up with him because he wasn't of my race," Lily explained. "He was only part Korean, and part Filipino. I'm pure Korean, so I need to marry a pure Korean," she continued. I said nothing and there was a long pause as I—at least—pondered the question of a pure anything. Lily may have picked up something in my silence.

"How would you feel if Alex or Nik [Chloe's older brothers] came home with someone not of their race?" Lily asked.

"You mean like an elephant?" I replied. Lily said nothing, but I could smell the wood burning as she thought about the implications of my reply.

In another event, I remembered how I was driving home one day in Princeton, NJ, with both boys in the back seat, Nik then five and Alex nine.[4] I heard Alex tell his younger brother, "Don't you know, Nik, you can do just about anything you want to do as long as you don't hurt yourself or someone else?" I can remember laughing to myself, thinking: "From John Stuart Mill to me to my children's ears, and not a bad ethical mantra to pass on."

So this is essentially a book of stories, highly personal ones. I don't expect them to mean anything to anyone else. My experience is neither a template nor exemplary; the stories reveal a fallible human being, one who does not always get it right and is far from a role model in any way. Beyond this, it is important to acknowledge that publishing any kind of memoir raises disconcerting ethical questions for the author. Is it fair to tell stories about friends and families, even loving ones? Does memoir inherently exploit personal lives for professional reasons? Even when we recognize—and acknowledge publicly—that we all view situations from our own, often eccentric perception, are we doing harm—however inadvertently—to the people we discuss, simply by opening our views of mutual interactions to public scrutiny? What are the ethics of possibly violating the privacy of loved ones in order to better understand something in our mutual lives, and in the hope of sharing that understanding with others?

These are only some of the perils and pitfalls of memoir. So why cast ethical discussions in that context? After many years spent trying to understand human beings, using a variety of social science methods, I find the human brain wired for narrative. We think in terms of stories, stories that constitute a valuable path into our inner lives. Although I begin with individual reflection, I try to combine real life stories with scholarly work, in as honest a fashion as I can. I have disguised identities, used composites, or given no names at all whenever a story might reflect badly on someone; I also have tried to recount events fairly although I recognize that everyone inevitably sees the world primarily from their own perspective. Above all, I hope I have recounted anecdotes of dear friends and family members in a way that shows my love and respect for them, as well as—perhaps—their minor foibles. In discussing ethical issues with students over the last 30 years, I have learned how difficult it is to be vulnerable, how much strength it takes to refrain from hiding behind intellectual sophistication and the professorial objectivity of discussing others' work. But it is often this very vulnerability, the willingness to open one's own life experience and ask how our mistakes can help us learn, that encourages and facilitates a mutual process of self-discovery. Sharing personal stories helps provide students the skills, and both the intellectual and the emotional strength, to do the same with their own life history. That process of self-examination lies at the core of ethical growth. I have tried to marry real life accounts—things that could and do happen to most of us—with more general ethical theories and academic writing. Woven into these essays—little vignettes of family and friends, and my thoughts on them—are some concepts that people who think about ethics might want to consider. Stories are, after all, a long-respected way to convey thoughts on ethical concepts.[5] I am especially grateful to my friends and family—especially my children—for their willingness to let me share my thoughts on their lives.

The first chapter discusses our nostalgia for a simpler time, and links that to politicians who exploit this yearning, turning it into bigotry and prejudice against strangers. This chapter was written before the advent of Donald Trump into American politics but seems doubly prescient since then. Chapter 2 tells how we can learn about important things in life—in this case the pitfalls of fame and the nature of politics and its ability to corrupt—from people we don't even like very much. Chapter 3 deals with forgiveness and Chapter 4 presents some incomplete thoughts on how we can deal with those innocent bystanders who are affected by our relationships with those we cannot forgive. Chloe's experiences (Chapter 5) while traveling in Europe showed me the importance of agency, even for a young girl, and Chapter 6 reveals what an irate 11-year-old can teach us about "differences." It asks why we accord ethical and even political significance to some differences (gender, race, religion) but not to others (musical ability, creativity or personality traits such as arrogance). Chapter 7 tells what I learned from my son, Nicholas, about the moral imagination and how important that is to our ability—as a society and as individuals—to conceptualize our way out of difficult problems. Chapter 8 deals with passion and what to do once it passes, and Chapter 9 considers unconditional love. Chapter 10 asks about loss and kindred spirits. It suggests how frequently there is little we can do to help those we love the most, and how important loss and failure can be for our emotional growth and understanding. Chapter 11 describes a very uncool mother deluding herself about how adult and mature she is as she sends her beloved daughter off to college. Chapter 12 contains the last lecture I gave to a very special class at UCI and ends by making the point with which I began this introduction: We all need others in our lives to show us who we are, to help us see our potential when we ourselves may be unaware of it.

So, we all need people like Chuck Myers, people who challenge us and help us grow by moving us out of our comfort zones. I can thank only a few of the people who did this for me. I am grateful to Lloyd and Susanne Rudolph, who introduced me to political psychology and narrative analysis. The Rudolphs effectively gave me permission to use literature in my social science courses and taught me that if we can understand one person, that this knowledge can inform our whole world, even though that knowledge is not collected "systematically" or following the rules and procedures of behavioral science.

Joe Cropsey taught me to always think about the foundational assumptions of our disciplinary approaches and, although it may not have been consciously imparted on Joe's part, this idea was critical in my slowly coming to appreciate the importance of identity for our treatment of others. As another student remarked at a celebration of Joe's work, "He reminded us to always think about who we are when we are with others, and who we are when we are by ourselves." Surely this admonition lies somewhere near the heart of ethics.

Rose McDermott has a wonderfully infectious joy and humor in her incredibly well-rounded worldview, and I was fortunate enough to be able to write one of these essays ("Nicole's father is NOT German!") with Rose. In this volume, most of the technical discussion of differences has been relegated to the endnotes, with only the gist of the article remaining.

Other friends and colleagues were kind enough to read all or parts of the manuscript in draft form. Jennifer Jones, Elaine McDevitt, Adam Martin, Kay Monroe, and Rebecca Morton offered specific advice that was immensely helpful. The final product has benefitted enormously from their criticism. Beyond that, I am grateful to the following people for specific comments and for more general emotional support in publishing essays that are far more revealing of the author personally than is the case with most of my academic work: Andrada Costoiu, Barbara Dosher, Lynda Erickson, Lily Gardner Feldman, Jennifer Hochschild, Rose McDermott, Elizabeth Mitchell, Sandra Morton, Phyllis Osaben, Cheryl Nichol Hawkins, Laura Scalia, Etel Solingen, Kay Schlozman, and Lawrence Sporty.

Perhaps my greatest debt, however, is to my children: Alexander Hart Lampros, Nicholas Monroe Lampros (aka Nik) and Chloe Wilmot Lampros-Monroe. It was Alex who truly started me on the road to thinking about ethics as a professional topic. When he was born people kept giving me good advice. "Never take a baby into bed with you," one young mother told me. "You don't want them to get used to human warmth." Other advice included: "Just let the baby cry himself to sleep. It's good for him."

None of this resonated. Why would I not want someone—especially this cherished child—to get used to human warmth? Wasn't that what it was all about? And letting anyone cry when I could so easily comfort them just felt wrong, especially for a child, my child.

I suspect it's toughest for the first born. We parents are so new, so ignorant and unsure of ourselves, and the poor kid has to help us learn on the job, as it were. I fear I was often too insensitive, too caught up in my own worldview, trapped by a superego that said I should do X, because that is how I had been raised. I probably tromped around my children's psyches, unaware of my inadequacies as I ignored the effect of my gaucherie on my poor children. Chloe brought someone named "Mom-Mom" into the house, as when she would hold up her hand to halt me when I started to talk too soon. "Mom! Mom!" Chloe cautioned, reminding me to listen more and speak less. Had "Mom-Mom" been there sooner, perhaps the first two children might have found a mother more closely attuned to their needs.

Life often gifts us with lessons too late for the learning. I can hope only that my children will forgive my clumsy ineptitude. I have learned as much from them as they have from me, and I have shown each of them this book in manuscript form, so they can excise anything they find too personal, or just simply ask me to not include them here. I'm not sure they actually *read* the manuscript, but I did show it to them and offered them the opportunity to censor parts concerning them. With one exception, they have generously given their consent.

Finally, the last chapter of this book is entitled—as indeed was the book initially—"Chloe, Nicole and the Elephant in the Parlor" since so many of the stories begin with Chloe and Nicole, Chloe's dearest friend, discussed in detail in the chapter entitled "BFF: Best Friends Forever." I send special thanks to Nicole and her family for their friendship and for being a part of our lives. On that note, I end with a word of explanation about the choice of the chapter title.

Chloe is my much-cherished daughter. Nicole is her best friend. The elephant in the parlor is our identity, our character, our sense of who we are. It is the most precious and enduring item any of us ever will possess. Guard it well.

REFERENCES AND FUTURE READINGS

D'Aulaire, Ingri and Edgar Parin. [1992]/2002. *D'Aulaire's Book of Greek Myths*. New York: Delacorte Press.

———. *D'Aulaire's Book of Trolls*. 2006. New York: New York Review Children's Collection.

———. *D'Aulaire's Book of Norwegian Folktales*. 2016. Minneapolis, MN: University of Minnesota Press.

Mill, John Stuart. 1859. *On Liberty*. London: John W. Parker and Son.

Singer, Peter and Renata Singer (eds.). 2005. *The Moral of the Story: An Anthology of Ethics Through Literature* (first edn.). New York: Wiley-Blackwell.

PREFACE

WE TELL OURSELVES STORIES IN ORDER TO LIVE[1]

I sometimes think of legacy. Not in terms of money but more a concern about what I am leaving behind for my children, for my students, maybe for the world. This is not a new phenomenon for me. Always a self-serious little girl, I focus—overly dramatically, I have long realized—on the big questions. I remember riding my bike when I was nine, stopping on the little pier overlooking Pine Lake, looking at the lake and wondering if I deserved to live. For some reason, I decided that if I could think of one good act I had done for someone else, not for self-aggrandizement or praise but simply and generously to help that other person, then I would deserve to live. If not, I would throw myself off the pier and be drowned in Pine Lake. In fact, the pier was certainly no more than five feet above the water. I was an excellent swimmer, and the water was between three and maybe four feet deep at that particular place. All that would have happened is that I would have scrapped my legs, gotten wet and had to explain to my down-to-earth Midwestern mother what in the world was going through her daughter's melodramatic head. Fortunately for all concerned, I thought of one good deed. I cannot now recall what that deed *was* but it was as if a box were checked. *"Am I a good person, worthy of living? Check! Asked and answered. Move on to the next thing."* The tendency to think about myself in the universe and where I stand thus is not a new one.

A far more modest variant of that question perhaps remains relevant here, as at the beginning of any book: what do I have to say in this book that is of any interest to anyone else?

I have learned a few things over the years, especially about writing and teaching. First, many of us write for ourselves. We write to help us puzzle out and understand what is going on around us, to realize what just happened, to discover what sense we can in a world that too often confounds. To figure it all out and determine what role we play in it. *"To remember who we are. That is always the point."*[2] Second, we don't really teach anyone else. We can help them learn, but it is the students who have to work out things for themselves, whether that be a particular topic, a discipline of study, or even life itself. This is especially true for students and for our children when you deal with ethics, as I have done now for over 30 years. You better be sure you don't just make yourself feel good by giving a great lecture. You have to do whatever you can to make certain the students really get it, that they are thinking about the questions you raise for them to ponder. (That old adage from college. I can hear my political theory teacher cautioning me now: *"Plato did not tell us the <u>unexamined</u> life is not worth living. A more accurate translation is that the <u>un-examining</u> life is not worth living. It is you who has to examine your life. My examining it for you won't do the trick."*) One way to do this—perhaps the best way, certainly a way that is too often overlooked today—is to have the student engage with their own lives. To think about what it means to live a life, not just inhabit it. The introduction elaborates on this idea, providing lots of good reasons why I believe ethics, in particular, is often taught best through stories. But just for a moment, I want to answer a question I usually avoid, since I mainly write for myself and am always surprised whenever anyone tells me they actually read or enjoyed my work.

Why *should* you read this book? The stories here are those of a scholar and a mother. I'd like to think they are stories of a life well lived but I'm not really sure what that means. Certainly they are stories of a life lived fully, by someone who enjoyed it immensely and botched it up a lot but nonetheless always did try to do her best, for her children, her students, herself and all the others she met. Someone who was too idealistic, demanding, proud and unbending when she was young but who got enough of that kicked out of her by life to cherish the solace of humility, compassion and the quiet joys of friendship and family. Someone who still cares deeply about all those old-fashioned but eternal values—truth, justice, decency, kindness, and fairness—but who has had to accept how little she can do to change the world or make others happy; someone who has slowly recognized the necessity of living life in cameo.[3] Someone who spent a professional lifetime listening to other people's stories, only to gradually recognize the tremendous value of stories—narratives—in reaching people.

Stories help construct an emotional connection. They provide the context necessary to give meaning to abstract principles, such as never lie or love your neighbor as yourself. It is this connection that stories provide which plays a critical part in thinking about who you are, about understanding how your character, your identity, sets and delineates the choices you find available, not just morally but cognitively. I have learned that my students, as they ponder who they are and what they want out of life, need to be able to walk around inside the head of someone they know well and with whom they have forged an emotional bond. Someone they trust. Learning comes best when there is an emotional connection. Affection helps. Social scientists—academicians in general—tend toward the analytical, not the emotional. We don't like talking about love or affection or emotional ties. Yet, as I hope these stories will reveal, the case could be made that learning important life lessons comes most easily when we have an attachment to the person whose life we study. When we can see that we are not unlike the older person, or the famous person, or even the person who has hurt us or the villain in the piece of fiction. Most of us are simply doing the best we can to compose a life that makes sense to us. Good stories do that. They present a complex, multifaceted character to whom the reader can relate, and then share and learn from the journey the character takes with the reader.

Each chapter in this book thus opens with a story, usually the story of one person: primarily a scholar and a mother, but also a friend, a daughter, a wife who failed in a marriage, someone who disappointed and was let down in turn, but someone not unlike you in taking chances as she tried to figure out how to compose a life in which she could take pride and find meaning and joy. The central theme that runs through these stories is identity, of course, and how the characters we construct come back to bite—and warm—us later. I hope I have rendered these personal stories universal, for the stories themselves touch on timeless themes: how we find self-respect, how we suffer and grow through loss, how we figure out the delicate balance between work and play, between what we give to others and what we hold for ourselves, how we learn to laugh at ourselves when we do something absurd or disappointing or just human. (Remember that self-serious little nine-year old, melodramatically contemplating throwing herself off a bike into a lake unless she decided she deserved to live.) By writing essays in the form of a memoir, I hope to take my experience as someone who thinks about ethics, and who has raised children, and filter my scholarly knowledge through the particular lens of a parent and a scholar who cares deeply about what we give to our children and our students, not in the form of money or financial security or degrees, but in the things that really count in the end.[4]

REFERENCES AND FUTURE READINGS

Didion, Joan. 1979. *The White Album*. New York: Simon and Schuster.

———. 2011. *Blue Nights*. New York: Vintage Books of Random House.

Dunne, Griffin, Annabella Dunne, Mary Recine and Susanne Rostock. 2017. *Joan Didion: The Center Will Not Hold*. Netflix Documentary.

Sandel, Michael J. 2012. *What Money Can't Buy: The Moral Limits of Markets*. New York: Farrar, Straus and Giroux.

THE MORAL OF THE STORY

TEACHING ETHICS THROUGH STORIES

We can define ethics—or moral philosophy; the two terms are often used interchangeably—as the moral principles that govern our behavior, the study or the branch of knowledge that asks how we ought to live. There are many ways to teach ethics. Instructors frequently lecture about the great works, describing the critical texts that address major themes in ethics, introducing the student to the canon: Plato, Aristotle, St. Thomas Aquinas, Machiavelli, social contract theorists, moral sense theorists, Utilitarians, virtue ethics and so on. Ethics is often also taught via religious instruction, in which students discuss the messages and values of various religions, from the Abrahamic Judaism, Christian and Islam to non-Western religions, such as Buddhism, Confucianism, Hinduism or the myriad other names given to faith by various groups over the centuries. Another approach emphasizes the Socratic dialogue; here students are posed hypothetical situations and asked to work their way through important moral issues. Is it always wrong to lie? Most of us would initially say yes. But what if the Nazis come and ask if Jews are hidden in your home? Would lying be the ethical thing to do then? Or, to consider another complex ethical situation, should society expend thousands of dollars to keep alive one premature baby or an elderly person, soon to die anyway, or instead spend the money on mosquito netting to keep alive hundreds of other small children? How do you decide this question if you are a Utilitarian? A Kantian? If it is your child? Your parent?

Each of these approaches carries value and worth. But this book takes another tack. It introduces the student to ethics through the use of stories. In particular, we ask how people use stories to weave thoughts about their lives into the moral choices they confront. Where do we get our moral values? Our ethical beliefs? How much of it comes from the stories we are read as children, the books we later read ourselves, the shows we watch on TV, or via novels, plays and short stories, such as those in *Aesop's Fables*? By the narratives created by adults to explain critical events in our lives, such as the death of a grandparent or a divorce?[1]

The term *moral* comes from the Latin *morālis* and denotes a message or a lesson that is conveyed or learned from a particular story or event. The particular moral derived from the story or the event is left to the readers or viewers of the event to figure out for themselves although sometimes the lesson may be more explicitly encapsulated and framed as a maxim. So, for example, children are told the Aesop fable of the sour grapes, where the fox attempts to jump up and get grapes which are too high on the tree for the fox to reach. Eventually, the fox gives up and walks away, muttering as he does so that the grapes are probably sour anyway. The moral of the fox and the sour grapes story conveys a psychological truth: when faced with failure, many of us downgrade our loss by saying that the prize we failed to achieve probably wasn't really all that great anyway. Using stock characters—such as the fox—presents the moral of stories in a simple way which minimizes complex issues and lets the reader—in this case, young children—grasp the moral message easily.

Stories can be more complex and convey important, multifaceted, intricate and ambiguous moral messages. Witness Shakespeare's plays, such as *Macbeth*, which is often viewed as a caution against the pursuit of power. Yet *Macbeth* also forces us to ask why we strive to achieve things in life, and what happens to us when the people we care about no longer exist, or no longer matter to us, as when Macbeth realizes all the plotting and scheming, the drive for power, no longer matters to him after his wife dies, and he is left to face "tomorrow and tomorrow and tomorrow" alone, and all for what? Or *King Lear*, which warns of the foolishness of age but which also cautions against vanity and falseness, in ourselves and in those we love and trust. Both plays also capture the cost of self-knowledge and ask whether that self-knowledge is worth the pain.

Stories can teach ethics in a happier vein, as when Jane Austen's *Pride and Prejudice* charts the pitfalls in the dance to the altar while instructing us on the value of good character, social decorum and family ties. Indeed, much of great fiction not only entertains; it also instructs, often through forcing the audience to think about complex moral issues in thoughtful and fresh ways that intrigue our sense and our sensibility—to borrow from Austen—while engaging both our intellectual and our emotional intelligence, all in a context that provides depth and meaning to the story, giving it some of the eternal even while making it relevant for our own lives.

Stories thus are a time-honored way to let us think about moral issues in a complex world. What is the right thing to do? What is the wrong thing? What do those concepts mean? How do we come to believe certain acts are "good" and others are "bad" and what do those terms mean for and to us? Is ethics about behavior? About character? About how we live and what we hold dear? About what we hold fast to during the dark nights of the soul that come to each of us at some point in our lives? Stories help us think about these issues in contexts and situations that hold meaning for us. They touch on the cultural context of ethical precepts. Indeed, the specificity of their context can bring home the message of the story even as the story itself touches on something ever-present in our human nature.

This book contains stories—part memoir, part essays—that helped me think about some of the ethical issues I confronted in my own life. The particular context is specific, of course, dealing with an academic raising children in twentieth- and twenty-first-century America, but the themes addressed here are universal and enduring. How do we think about who we are as we grow and move from one geographic place to another, transitioning from a child to an adult? How do we address our own parents, separating and forming our own person and finding a new equilibrium—perhaps even friendship—with people who once constituted our entire world, and who ran that world with varying degrees of success and kindness? How do we deal with loss, with betrayal and disappointment? How can we learn something from that loss and help build our character? How can we laugh at our own fallible nature, and learn to forgive ourselves and others? These are timeless themes, addressed by stories throughout the ages.

I developed these essays over the course of 10 years, during which time I taught many different types of courses on ethics. I have given what I thought were well-organized and thoroughly researched lectures on the great thinkers in ethics. I have enjoyed the Socratic dialogue, in which students are pushed a bit to examine their own presuppositions about ethics and morality through a series of staged situations. In some of the courses I've taught, we discuss the difference between ethics and morality as concepts, too. I have found that the best way to teach a course in ethics, however, is to engage the student's emotional intelligence, as well as the more academic intellect. This, I find, is done best through raising difficult issues in a format to which the students can relate, and then after discussing critical aspects of the problem, assigning students writing of their own on these issues.

One year, for example, I asked the students to study Kant's categorical imperative, one of the most important ethical writings in the last thousand years. I paired it with *Invisible Man*, a book published in 1952 about a Black man in America. The author—Ralph Ellison—designed the book to reveal "*the human universals hidden within the plight of one who was both black and American ....*"

The essay assignment that week asked students to consider both of these works—Kant's and Ellison's—and to write about a time when they were made to feel invisible and a time when they made someone else feel invisible. One student came to my office hours, concerned about her essay.

"I understand the assignment but don't see how it relates to Kant."

"Well," I replied, "what are you writing about?

"Part of my essay describes how I felt after my parents divorced. My mother was giving me really nice presents, and that made me feel she knew I was upset and was trying to make it up to me in some way. My father did the same thing." She paused. "But then I realized Mom was really just giving me the presents to make Dad feel bad, and Dad was doing the same to her. Neither one of them was truly concerned with how I felt. They just wanted to make each other feel bad, and that made me feel they didn't see me. They didn't know or acknowledge how bad I felt. It was like I was invisible to them."

"Good. That sounds like an excellent start. So, what's the problem?"

"I don't see what that has to do with Kant," was her honest response.

"Well, what does Kant's theory say?" I asked.

"He says you should think before you take an action, and only do that act if the world would be better if everyone did that." She hesitated a bit. "It's kind of relevant but I don't get how it relates to feeling invisible."

"Is there anything else in Kant's theory that might be relevant here?" I asked, fearful she had missed the entire second part of Kant's magisterial work.

She squirmed a bit, then said, "He says something about how you should never treat people as a means only …" Her eyes flew wide open. "Oh, my god! That's what he's saying. We shouldn't use people, should not treat them as means to an end." She hastily clarified. "It's okay to ask them to do something for you, to use them as a means to an end. But if that's the *only* reason you are being nice to them, then you are denying their existence as people. You're making them a tool for your own desires, not people in their own right. That's what you meant by invisible. That's what my parents were doing to me!"

The words flew out of her mouth at a rapid clip as she wrapped her mind around the deep meaning in Kant. Perhaps I was overly optimistic and naïve, but I believe that young woman understood Kant in her bone. I am willing to bet she never will treat anyone as a means only, precisely because this assignment helped her learn how bad it makes one feel to be treated that way. (Another important ethical concept: empathy.) I don't think the student would have gotten the same deep, pit-of-the-stomach, intimate understanding of Kant had we just read his work in class, or engaged in some hypothetical discussion of Kant's ideas. The story, her personal story, is what hit home the message for my young student.

Sometimes we watch a movie. Woody Allen's *Crimes and Misdemeanors* tells of a well-known ophthalmologist who has an affair with a stewardess. The stewardess slowly becomes more and more demanding, eventually threatening to write the man's wife, telling of their affair. The ophthalmologist is in agony, plagued by his conscience and fearful he will be caught. He solves the problem by arranging for someone to kill the woman and, after that is done, deteriorates into agonies of self-recrimination, terror and fear of being caught for that dreadful deed. At this point in the story, the standard ethical interpretation would be for the man's conscience to so trouble him that he would confess, make restitution and take his punishment. But this does not occur. Instead, time passes and the man realizes he has gotten away with murder—literally—and is safe. He goes back to enjoying his old life. He has neither grown nor changed from his ordeal. He learned no moral lesson. What do students think of this? What if good does *not* triumph in the end? What if ethics simply hobbles us with needless rules that trip us up? There is much evidence of this occurring in the world, after all. What does the student think?[2]

Still other times students are asked to do an extensive interview with someone they admire, asking them about their life and about how they dealt with ethical choices that confronted them. This assignment carries surprising consequences. One girl asked her grandmother if she could do an oral history with her. They were in the car, backing out of the garage when the student made the request. The grandmother got so excited she plowed the car into the mailbox. Yet another grandmother called my student's mother—the grandmother's daughter—after the interview. The grandmother was crying, saying "I didn't realize anyone in the family cared that much about me." There are numerous illustrations of such reactions to this simple oral history. All the students always enjoy the interview, although they are remarkably anxious in advance.

I have taught ethics courses using this more personal model at both UCI and Harvard. At both institutions, I find students respond well to the approach, telling me that it at first feels uncomfortable to have to think about their own lives as they discuss ethical concepts. But in the end, they often describe it as the best course they ever took, one that changed their lives. (This is what professors live for!) One student wrote on her final exam that she had never had a course prove relevant so quickly. In that term we had discussed the process by which children recognize the weaknesses in their parents and then come to accept their parents as humans, flawed and yet still worthy of love. We did this by reading Harper Lee's two published books. In *To Kill a Mockingbird* (1960), the father is a hero, a magnificent, loving, larger-than-life lawyer who takes on racism in a noble way, fully deserving of his young daughter's adoration. *Go Set a Watchman* is the first draft of *Mockingbird* although published much later (2016), as Lee had retreated into memory loss and her new literary executor allowed the much inferior but still important first draft to be published. In *Watchman*, the narrator is not the young Scout. It is a grown woman in her 20s who returns to her home in The 1960s south from a more liberal New York City, only to realize her father is a racist or, at best, someone who has learned to make comfortable accommodation with southern bigotry and racism, accepting it rather than combating it in an idealistic fashion. We used these two books as a backdrop for discussing an important topic, one disturbingly germane for most college students: how they deal with their own parents. The young woman—I'll call her Jessie—who wrote this particular note at the end of her exam told me that just as the quarter was ending, there had been a family crisis. It seems that Jessie's stepfather made sexual advances to Jessie's best friend one evening. When Jessie told her mother about this, the mother at first was supportive of Jessie and her friend. But slowly the mother shifted her allegiance to her husband, disbelieving the friend and Jessie, her own daughter. Continuing her note, Jessie told how upset she had been by what she considered a betrayal on the part of her mother. Her suitcase packed, ready to leave home, Jessie said she then remembered our class discussion of Harper Lee's books and how difficult it could be to realize and accept that one's parents were flawed human beings. Jessie decided to stay and try to work through things with her mother. Jessica wrote, two years after this class, to tell me she was trying to salvage her relationship with the mother but refusing any interaction with her stepfather.[3] I was an outsider, hearing second-hand of a family in crisis and making no judgment. But I was gratified if anything we did in my course helped the student navigate a difficult ethical dilemma. Ethics should be about that. It should not be all head, and it should help in our own lives, not just be lessons recited for a final exam or carried around as abstractions.

For teachers interested in this approach, I provide suggested readings at the end of each chapter. I also am happy to provide course syllabi upon request: Department of Political Science, Social Science Plaza A, UC Irvine,

Irvine, CA, 92697. I hope these syllabi, plus the stories in this book, can help provide a template for how to teach moral and ethical theory through the use of stories.

REFERENCES AND SUGGESTED READINGS

Bloom, Harold. 2020. *Take Arms Against a Seas of Troubles: The Power of the Reader's Mind over a Universe of Death*. New Haven, CT: Yale University Press.

Ellison, Ralph. 1952. *Invisible Man*. New York: Random House.

Lee, Harper. 2002. *To Kill a Mockingbird*. New York: Harper Perennial.

———. 2016. *Go Set A Watchman*. New York: Harper Perennial.

Nussbaum, Martha C. 1986. *The Fragility of Goodness: Luck and Ethics in Greek Tragedy and Philosophy* (second edn.). New York: Cambridge University Press.

Shakespeare, William. 1992. *Macbeth*. Wordsworth Classics. Ware: Wordsworth Editions.

———. 1994. *King Lear*. Wordsworth Classics. Ware: Wordsworth Editions.

Singer, Peter and Renata. (Editors). 2005. *The Moral of the Story: An Anthology of Ethics Through Literature* (first edn.). New York: Wiley-Blackwell.

CHAPTER 1

WALNUT

Bismarck supposedly quipped that when the end of the world came, he wanted to be in Weimar because everything happened 30 years later there.[1] I feel the same way about Walnut.

When the terrorists hit the Twin Towers on 9/11and all the airlines were grounded, my oldest son had no way to return to college in Chicago. Even after the planes were allowed to recommence flying, we were apprehensive. Then I remembered that the train from California to Chicago ran through Princeton, Illinois. Using a logic only a frightened, muddled mother could embrace, I decided my son should return by train. Even in a national emergency, I figured he could get off the train, follow the tracks till he got to Princeton and then find someone to get him to Walnut. Once in Walnut, he would be safe.

The world could be falling apart. The United States could be invaded by terrorists who hated our way of life and would stoop to nothing to harm us, as the media kept intoning. But it would take them at least 30 years to find Walnut.

I'm not sure why I felt this way. Walnut was a little town, declining rapidly in population even when I knew it. The high school had been torn down, despite the best efforts of my mother and my uncle Marvin. But with the demolition of the high school, the heart would go out of the town. Or so my family feared.

Instead, the town endured. Just a few houses—how many? Maybe 200? 300?—surrounded by rich farmland. The Walnut Café (pronounced caff by the locals who would have no truck with fancy French words) flourished. The farmers still seemed to come to town—"come ta' town" the locals said—for their midmorning coffee and pie. For a while the café owners served Greek salads and the Greek owners (new arrivals to town) would go home to get real feta cheese whenever my mother came to visit, Mother being one of the few people in Walnut who appreciated the real feta.

The movie theatre had long since closed, doubtless because of its policy of charging no admission for a movie on Tuesday evenings, when everyone—including my grandmother—would be sure to go. Likely the movie theatre staggered on as long as it did because people like Grandma Tuts (pronounced toots as in "toot toot tootsie goodbye") would loyally also attend a paying show, just to demonstrate her support.

Jack McCarthy had owned the local grocery store for as long as I could remember and it, too, had survived his death for many years. But eventually it was sold and turned into a pizza hut, complete with plastic chairs and video games. The video games delighted my young sons on their annual visits, but the closing of the McCarthy's grocery store left only the 7-Eleven store at the edge of town, and that was where we purchased groceries whenever we visited, which was not often, as my mother was wont to point out.

Mother, in contrast, was loyal, going every Fourth of July for a big family picnic and outing, complete with what can only be described as unhealthy Midwestern farm food: bacon and eggs for breakfast—what my English ancestors would have described as a big fry-up—plus the white flour gooey things that passed for Danish pastry in much of the Midwest. This repast was followed by hot dogs, potato salad and coleslaw for lunch and some kind of chicken fried for dinner. Plus pie and the most disgusting mess of soggy green beans soaked in Campbell's onion soup and topped with French fried onion rings out of a can. Truly "englopsulating."[2]

It was always too hot in Illinois on the Fourth of July for my taste. I hate the heat; well, actually, I think it was the heat plus the humidity that did me in. I was born in Illinois—Princeton, to be exact; not New Jersey, but Illinois—and was brought home to Walnut to live with my grandparents since the father I did not meet until I was six months old was still in the Far East hearing war crimes after World War II ended.

So I grew up in the Midwest. I thought the hot summers were an inevitable part of life, something to be suffered through, like chicken pox or measles or scarlet fever, all of which I also endured as a child. I remember the moment I discovered summers did not have to be hot and miserable. It was the first summer I spent in Vancouver when I realized I had put in more than enough time in the July heat to return to the Midwest that particular time of year. It was kind of a revelation, that sudden realization that one did not have to suffer from the humidity and heat.

As a child, of course, I had no such insight, believing that everyone must live much as we did. There was no home air conditioning in the 1950s, at least not in my world, so I would swim in Pine Lake during the late afternoons and lie in the hammock and read books in the shade during the rest of the day. In extreme heat, my brother and I would sleep on the cool tiles of our home, usually in the living room. I remember several times the humidity got so great that the tiles actually were wet, covered with a shallow film of water from condensation, and we had to keep from sliding and slipping on the wet floor.

It was a safe childhood, if a bit boring for a young girl living too far out of town to have easy access to friends. (Mothers did not ferry children to playgroups in the 1950s, at least not in the 1950s which I inhabited.) I read a lot and dreamed a million daydreams of a time when life would begin. (One thought contribution was to figure out a way to bank time, as one banked money. I figured if I could spend my time as a 12-year-old washing my hair, I then would not have to do it later, once life truly got going in earnest, and I could pull out of the time bank account all those wasted minutes in washing hair.) So life was sheltered if a bit lackluster on Pine Lake.

Walnut was different. It was small enough for a child to walk everywhere, and I was liberated once I hit eight or nine and was permitted to roam by myself. My favorite walk was to journey down the little street on which my grandparents lived. Streets in Walnut had no names in those days; now the block where my grandparents' house resides is called Second Street but back when I was young, everyone just knew who lived where and gave directions by "Go ta' the right when you hit the Hopkins house."

I would walk to the end of the street, just past the Hopkins house. Dr. Hopkins had been the family doctor since before I was born; his father— Dr. Sam—had been the town doctor before him. The Hopkins house was next door to Grandma and Grandpa's, and it had a sunken garden which intrigued me. How did they get the dirt scooped out? How did they get all those boulders down there to plant flowers around? We could see into Myrtle Hopkins's kitchen window from Grandma's kitchen window and there was a big tree at the corner of the street just before the high school. Then the vista opened up through the high school football field and one could view the beginning of Main Street, the only street I remember as having a name. The joke used to be that the only kids later to high school than the Renwick kids were the Hopkins kids, a joke that was funny only once you realized that the Hopkins house was just across the street from the high school and the Renwick house was two doors from the high school. The Hopkins children must have done well despite their perpetual tardiness, however, because Mom was fond of telling how Donny Hopkins had perfected some kind of rare medical operation while he worked as the doctor on an Indian reservation in North Dakota, and the other son ended up a doctor at the "U of Illinois," the be all and end all of education for my mother, who counted as a continuing source of regret the fact that her daughter did not attend Mother's *alma mater* for any part of her education. (My brother and many of my cousins did attend the U of I, as it was affectionately called, and one cousin even set aside money for his child's college education, beginning when his son was only a baby.)

For me as a child, the Hopkins house was the turning point before crossing the huge football field, empty all summer except for the August period when the team began its practice. Or for baseball games that occurred in the hot summer evenings, social events to which everyone in the surrounding area attended, farmers and children alike. But during the day, the field was wide open, and I used to enjoy perambulating slowing across the field, usually on a diagonal, until I came to the farm machinery supply shop at the other end of the field. At that point, I was in the "downtown" area and I would cross the street toward the abandoned movie house. I was always intrigued by the fact that the sidewalk was raised slightly and was fascinated by the metal loops embedded in the elevated sidewalk, where one could hitch one's horse. This was a short block, filled—if memory serves—with small shops, perhaps an antique shop (read secondhand store) and an insurance office. None of this mattered. What was located on the diagonal from this short block was the prize: the Federated store. In my younger years, when I apparently knew more history than I did grammar and, never being a detailed-oriented person anyway, I used to refer to it as the "Confederated Store" until one of my relatives informed me that I was "up north, honey chile, and that's *federated* not *con*-federated."

It did not matter to me. It was freedom. I would roam the aisles of the Federated Store gleefully, often with the five or ten cents Grandma would slip me, wondering what magical thing I could buy for myself. There was always candy, a penny a pop, sometimes two cents apiece or—better—two for a penny. But usually I was after bigger game. Maybe a bottle of nail polish, something glamorous and grown up, probably pink or even red. I can't remember actually ever buying anything but that was not the point. I had the dough. I had the goods right in front of me. And it was freedom, baby. Freedom big time! No one to tell me to hurry—no one EVER hurried in Walnut—and no one to supervise, to scoff or criticize my potential purchases. I felt grown up and on my own in Walnut.

I also was with my grandparents a lot since Daddy usually stayed in Collinsville to hear court cases, and mother was usually off with her sister. Aunt Beverly lived just outside town. For a while she lived in town. But her husband was a contractor who kept building nice houses and then selling them and building her another one. Her last house was more in the country, on a road called Lovers' Lane. In the last decade of his life, Grandpa's driving deteriorated and he plowed into a young couple parked on Lovers' Lane, practicing for their honeymoon the week before their wedding. As Grandpa slowly lumbered back toward the car he had hit, he was relieved to find they both were fine, though he was a bit concerned that he seemed to have knocked both the young people into the back seat of the car and that their clothing seemed a bit disheveled.

Beverly's third house thus was out in the country. In fact, it was probably only half a mile out of town. Distances felt longer in those days, especially to a child. This third house was built overlooking a little brook and had a huge oak tree which the house and the drive curved around. Years later, when I drove out to Walnut one weekend while in grad school in Chicago, I parked at Aunt Beverly's, under the big oak tree. Mindful that people in the country did not lock their cars, as I had learned to do after living for two years in the south side of Chicago, I left the car unlocked and went into the house. My cousin, Kathleen, came in soon after, and chided me for having become so distrustful and suspicious after living in the big city too long.

"Why?" I protested, knowing what she was referring to. "I didn't lock the car." "No. But you didn't leave your keys in the car."

"Well, no. I didn't." I remained clueless.

"What if someone wanted to borrow your car? How could they do that without the keys in the ignition?" Kathleen retorted.

I was speechless.

But this was all later. In my youth, Aunt Beverly lived in town. Aunt Beverly's first house was a little green house, nestled into the side of a hill. Then her family—cousins Moneta and Kathleen, then later Rob—moved into a rather non-descript ranch house, with a nice big yard and an interesting dining room that had some kind of intricate ceramic tile on a counter. Aunt Beverly and Uncle Walt gave great parties. Lots of food, lots of liquor. And even though Aunt Beverly was not the best housekeeper, she always was a lot of fun and always seemed very busy whipping up some kind of decadent meal, often from a recipe in *The Ladies Home Journal*. She also made lots of clothes and handy little items that my mother never would have attempted. What I'd probably call *tchotchkes* now but which then were associated in my mind with items that would be described in magazines like *Woman's Home Companion* or *Woman's Day*. I don't remember the names. They were not magazines my mother read and I spent most of my time at Aunt Beverly's playing World War II songs on her piano or devouring her ladies' magazines like a junkie who had been too long deprived of her cheap lady-magazine thrills.

Grandma also subscribed to some of these magazines and my summer reading would first be to consume all of them I could get my hands on. (Who wanted to read *Foreign Affairs* or *The Nation* or *Daedalus*? At 10, I was far beyond the boring leftist literary fare with which my parents cluttered up our house.) My favorite summertime magazine was *McCall's*, in those days—is it still published? I haven't a clue—it was a long magazine. Tall, not an 8×10, more oblong. Big and glossy. Most important, on the back of many of the *McCall's* magazines was a full-page photo of a woman, dressed in a glamorous ball gown, standing tall and slim and oh so elegant in front of a grand piano in a Parisian window with the long French doors, all paned glass and open to a beautiful balcony. (I just knew the drawing room was Parisian. It had to be Parisian.) The picture reeked class, style and elegance, with a touch of romance. (All the things I was not, as a skinny 10-year-old with huge glasses and stringy, straight hair.) The continuing caption was always the same: "Modess because […]." I had no idea what Modess was, my knowledge of female hygiene lying far in the distant future. But my knowledge of English grammar was perfectly honed and I knew that three dots meant something was omitted and to be continued, with four dots denoting that there was an end to the sentence. I searched frantically, but always in vain, for the continuation of that intriguing sentence. The picture was on the back of the magazine, which confused me. Presumably I had to turn to the next page, which logic dictated was the first page of the magazine. But that did not make sense. Worse, I never found any story that fitted the beautiful and oh so alluring photograph. It was years before my knowledge of Madison Avenue and feminine hygiene caught up with me and I realized the whole thing was just a slick ad for a sanitary napkin.

It was but one of many future disillusionments in life.

I'd been born in a hospital in Princeton, Illinois, but Walnut was my first home. The war had ended. My father, however, was still in China, doing war crimes, as I used to say until my mother finally corrected me. "You know, when you tell it that way, it sounds as if your father was running around committing war crimes. He was involved in the trials of people accused of war crimes. You might want to make that clear."

As usual, Mother was right. Daddy had a checkered history with the army. Practically blind, Daddy was hardly someone whose physical attributes would strike fear into the hearts of any enemy. At one point, I think he had been put into the special forces because he knew how to type. (Special forces, as mother explained it, was for entertainers, and Daddy's bunkmate on the boat to India had been Melvyn Douglas, the actor married to Helen Gahagan Douglas, the so-called Pink Lady later maligned by Richard Nixon in his 1950 bid for the Senate.) Daddy had edited the ship's newspaper on the boat to India, where he served under General Stillwell, before being transferred to the China theatre.

Daddy was to fly over the Hump, as they called the Himalayas. Daddy was concerned that he might lose his beloved typewriter if the plane were to crash. (The typewriter actually was Mother's. Daddy had caged it from her when he went into the army.) He wrote Mother that he had figured it out, however. He would hold his briefcase in one hand and the typewriter in the other. The army had fitted him with a parachute in case of emergency and Daddy figured that if the plane were to crash, he could simply parachute out holding the briefcase in one hand and the typewriter in the other. He'd pull the rip cord for the parachute with his teeth. When he wrote this to Mother, and she reported her husband's plan to her brother, Robert, a trained parachutist, Robert just roared with laughter.

"What's so funny?" Mother demanded.

"Well, first of all, you can't pull a parachute cord with your teeth and secondly, once the chute is activated, there's such a powerful counter-pull to gravity that Jim would be left holding two handles cause the tiny wire loops holding the handles to the typewriter and the briefcase would break!"

Fortunately for Mother's typewriter—and her husband's health and well-being, if not the American war cause in Asia—the plane did not crash, and Daddy made it safely to China. Luckily for all concerned, Daddy didn't do much fighting, as far as I was told, though he apparently would sleep through many air raids. (Daddy was a champion sleeper. After the war, however, he suffered from bad dreams, probably what we might now call PTSD-induced. He often would throw himself on top of Mother, yelling to run or telling her to stay still, that he would protect her. And so he did, for the most part.) His only wartime injury was an infected finger from a sliver from his desk in the China theatre.

So being a lawyer kept my father out of harm's way, all things considered. But it also meant he was asked to stay on to take part in the trials of crimes associated with the war. Some of these were war crimes, and Daddy was eventually given a ceremonial sword by the Japanese general he had been questioning. Daddy was a lowly captain and the British officer of higher rank, and greater arrogance, was in charge of the actual interrogation. The Japanese general had been in charge of a prisoner of war camp and the Allies badly wanted any records that might be available. They suspected the general had hidden them, to cover up any misdeeds.

Each day, my father followed the Brit as the two officers went to retrieve the general. Each day, they took the Japanese general to be grilled. Each day, the Japanese general gave them nothing. The Army high command finally despaired of ever getting any information and transferred the Brit off the case, leaving it in the hands of the lowly Yank. Shortly after that, the Japanese general must have gotten a ceremonial sword smuggled into his cell and committed suicide.

"*Hara-kiri*," my father told me. "It's a ritual suicide involving honor."[3] The same day that the general was found dead in his cell, all the documents for the prisoner of war camp were delivered to my father, along with the general's ceremonial sword.

Daddy never could figure out why the general had entrusted him with the documents. He speculated that it might be perhaps because Daddy had always held the door open for the general, on their daily treks to and from the cell to the interrogation room. Daddy also helped the Japanese general into his chair each day, treating him to what my father considered the normal human courtesies. The Brit always walked through the door first and treated the general with a kind of generalized contempt.

It was one of my first lessons in the importance of ordinary human decency and respect.

So my father was in China when I was born. Shanghai, I believe. He later told me he had a house boy who used to get very excited that Daddy was a new father. "Cap-i-tain have baby girl," he would say. "Cap-i-tain have baby girl!" Daddy didn't come home until December! the year after I was born so I was raised for the first six months of my life by a very nervous mother and my grandparents.

Mother was always a "good little girl," one of those people who always wanted to do everything right. She supposedly had a baby book that she followed faithfully, and Grandpa Bob—a telephone man—was not allowed to hold me unless he put on a white coat. At some point, I developed colic and while I apparently was fine during the day, the nights were a nightmare. (Even now, I do not sleep well, and am writing this at 3:30 a.m. after a few fretful hours of sleep. Eventually this was diagnosed as restless leg syndrome, something I inherited from my much-loved grandpa Bob, and which is now easily treated with a small pill called ropinirole. But for years it was a nightly horror.)

As a baby, I'd begin to cry around midnight and my poor mother would try everything to get me to sleep. Walking with me. Singing to me. Cuddling me.

But the baby book said to just let me cry, so Mother also eventually resorted to this. One night I was upstairs crying and Mother was sitting, dejected, at the bottom of the stairs, fighting off tears herself, alone, not knowing if her husband were coming back from a war that had long since ended for everyone else and feeling overwhelmed and insufficient to the task of motherhood.

Grandpa woke and staggered down the hall, following the noise. "Listen," he told his daughter sternly, Grandpa never being one to mince words. "You have five minutes to pick up that baby or you can pack your bags and your mother and I will raise that child."

That one incident captured Grandpa's attitude toward me, indeed, toward all his grandchildren. Lots of what Mother always referred to as common sense, certainly no nonsense, and extremely loving.

Grandpa Bob had been raised in Lacon, Illinois, where his father was an alcoholic who mistreated Great Grandma Annie MacIntee and whom Grandpa Bob finally threw out of the house. Although he was only in his teens, Grandpa took on the responsibility for his family at that point, dropping out of high school to support his mother and sister.

Grandpa must have been a bit of a hellion at one point, however, since we heard lots of great stories about his riding the rails, going out to the West Coast, surviving by his wits. He'd apparently blow into a new town on a freight train with the other hobos—that was the word for them then, not homeless people—and Grandpa would proudly tell how he always kept two bits saved for a shower and a shave.[4] He'd get dressed up in his clean suit and, union card in hand—Grandpa was big on unions and belonged proudly to the electricians' union—he would go see if he could find work. He usually could.

Grandpa was a good worker. He was a telephone lineman for most of the time I knew him, and founded the union in Walnut, an act that got my Uncle Marvin fired by the irate telephone company and led to Marvin's having a good career with Commonwealth Edison in Western Illinois.

Grandma Tuts used to tell how Grandpa had blown into Walnut on a motorcycle, looking quite the dandy on a very racy little machine called a Tomahawk. He met my grandmother and stayed. Both of them were well liked and well respected in the little town. Grandma had grown up in Walnut, was a favorite of the neighborhood children, and was quite outgoing, belonging to all the local social clubs. As a telephone man, plus an electrician, Grandpa knew and was popular with lots of people, from the female operators to the men on his crew. He installed phone lines in the country around Walnut and told me great stories about the Depression and the war.

Indeed, it was Grandpa who first made the Depression come alive for me, explaining that during the Depression you could always figure out which families had given up and gone to California to find work. "They'd always leave their lights on," Grandpa told me. "They were embarrassed at leaving and somehow thought that if they didn't officially leave, if they just snuck out at night, leaving the lights on in the house, the neighbors wouldn't know they had gone." Grandpa would shake his head then. The Depression had been tough on the farmers, he'd tell me. "There were millionaires in Chicago who lost everything and jumped out of the windows rather than sell apples on the street. Can you imagine that?" he'd relate, in one of his many repeated stories. But then he'd follow it up with his favorite Roosevelt story. "This guy in a wheelchair told us we had nothing to fear but fear itself." Again, Grandpa would shake his head in disbelief. "Here he was, sittin' there in a wheelchair, and he could say that to us! Well, I just figured if a cripple could say that, then maybe the rest of us could keep on goin' too."

So Grandpa was not broken by the Depression. Indeed, there was always food for the hobos at the Renwick house. Grandma used to say that the hobos marked a house in some way. They left some sign. "Don't stop here. They're skin flints." Or "Stop here. They'll give you a hot meal."

Grandma always had something to give to others. One time a man came by without a coat, just as winter was closing in on the prairies. Grandpa was always extremely careful with his belongings. Items were stored, cleaned, carefully packed away so you would know where they were when you needed them. Shoes were meticulously polished and put on with a shoehorn to ensure fit and not damage the backs of the shoes.

Grandpa was especially proud of his World War I gear and had kept the long coat he'd been issued in France, where he—fortunately for us—had been kept far from the front, stringing phone line with some engineer from Yale. Grandpa loved this World War I coat. But when he saw this fellow without a jacket, he told Grandma to give the man his coat. He did ask her to cut off the buttons and sew on new ones, so he could keep the original buttons as a souvenir. But the coat went, in what was one of the many quiet, unannounced acts of kindness done spontaneously and without any fuss.

This Midwestern common sense and decency were traits inherited by my mother.

During the summer vacations spent in Walnut, Mother would clean Grandma's house. (Scrubby Dutch, they'd call her.) I guessed traits skipped generations for I resemble my grandma in many ways. My home is far too cluttered, something that especially annoys my eldest son. I enjoy puttering around, cooking with young children though, in fairness, my mother was like this too. Each holiday grandchildren made dozens of Christmas cookies, and pies! My cousin Tommy—not allowed to mess up his mother's pristine kitchen—made his first pie with my mom. Mother said the kitchen looked as if a white tornado had hit it, but Tommy returned home happy, and announced that he was moving in with Aunt Trudi.[5]

Both Grandma Tuts and I were good with flowers. Grandma always had African violets on the ledge in the kitchen window, above the big sink and countertop.[6] She claimed they loved the moisture from the kitchen. Grandma had a huge vegetable garden, and also planted beautiful flowers in the yard of her home. Grandma was a natural cook. That is, she cooked without regard for recipes or directions, a trait I also inherited, to my mother's chagrin. Mother— like my own daughter—followed recipes to the letter. Not Tuts! She would dump in a bit of flour, walk around the kitchen, preoccupied with something else, then stir it a few times, then be off onto something else. Her cooking tended to the farm food end of the continuum and there was always a pie or cake for dessert.

Once Grandma had made a big sheet cake. The delivery boys came with the groceries and she told them to help themselves to a piece of cake, thinking they would each take a piece. They did, but they did so by cutting the cake into half and each taking one HUGE piece, not the normal size Grandma had anticipated when she made the offer. Grandma just laughed and whipped up another cake.

Grandma was short and plump, with the kind of bosoms that did well with babies, serving as nice hot water bottles on which the babies could snuggle and fall asleep. Tuts loved children and had four, giving birth to her last one after she had an appendectomy seven months into her pregnancy. Both she and my uncle Marvin survived. (His siblings were allowed to choose his name and supposedly found Marvin Elmer from the phone book.) This was the same summer Grandpa dragged the whole family on a trip to Minnesota in an old Model T. Tires were pretty primitive in those days and they kept having blowouts that Grandpa had to repair. Once, just after they had passed some Indians on horseback and carrying guns, the spare tire blew from the heat. Grandma was convinced the Indians were shooting at the family, but it was only the spare tire exploding in the summer heat.

Grandpa was a tease, not his best trait, and he constantly teased my grandmother. She was afraid of mice and, although the family had many cats, the cats were not allowed inside the house. Hence there were mousetraps everywhere. Grandma refused to empty them, and Grandpa was not averse to chasing her around the house with a dead mouse in hand. He also told me, with delight, how one night they had gotten into bed. He had his arm under her pillow. She felt it and misinterpreted her husband's thick arm hair for kitten fur. She was convinced there was a kitten in the bed with them. Grandpa let her think it was so until she caught on.

Fortunately, Grandma had a good sense of humor, herself. When her brother boasted of his chickens laying an extraordinary number of eggs, Grandma began to send over the children to slip in an extra egg or two into her brother's henhouse. Soon her brother's boasting of the many eggs his chickens were laying resulted in articles written about his hens for *The Walnut Leader*, the local newspaper. All the farmers around town were asking Uncle Harold how he did it. "What did he feed the chickens? When did he take the eggs? Did he talk to the hens?"

Harold was delighted with all the attention until his daughter spilled the beans. "Oh, Daddy. Don't you know it's Aunt Tuts who's putting eggs in our henhouse?"[7]

One time her daughters—my mother and her sister, Beverly—decided they would get their mother a brassiere that would make their mother more modern. They pooled their money and bought her the kind of bra only a zaftig Mae West would have worn, and Grandma's sumptuous and otherwise rather comfortable bosoms were suddenly lifted and sculpted into something majestic to behold. Grandma thought it was so hilarious that she put on an old pair of Grandpa's long underwear, grabbed a ballet tutu she was making for my mother and came dancing into the living room dressed only in these, plus her new rather overwhelming bra. Grandpa creased up with laughter, but his mother— Grandma MacIntee—was living with them and she thought her daughter-in-law had gone nuts. "Good God, Vernie's gone crazy," she kept intoning, crossing herself as she whipped out her rosary beads. Annie MacIntee was gone long before I came along but Mother tells she used to think Grandma Annie was wealthy, counting her money every night, only to later learn it was the religious, Irish grandmother saying her rosary before bed.

I did experience Grandpa Bob's famous teasing as a young child. The worst jest concerned toast crusts. I had red hair, which I detested as a child. Worse, my hair was straight. My mother had gorgeous black hair, naturally curly and I— like so many little girls—wanted to look like my mother. "Eat your toast crusts," Grandpa would say. "It will make your hair curly."

I'd diligently dig into the crusts, then Grandpa would add, waiting just long enough so that I had swallowed the first bite and knowing full well how tormenting a dilemma this would pose for me, "Of course, the crusts also make your hair red."

Later, as we aged, he would laugh at the dinner table, pointing to one child or another, peacefully drinking their milk, "Look at my grandchildren. None of them can drink their milk without sticking their noses in the glass!"

It was my brother Jamie who fixed Grandpa. Jamie came prepared with a straw, and Grandpa had to take the one-ups-manship with the good grace he usually showed when bested by someone.

Teasing was considered a Midwestern "thing," just something one did to keep people from taking themselves too seriously, or becoming too pretentious. Being cut down to size was a big thing in the Renwick family, too. It was only later, after I had my own children, that I realized how mean and ugly teasing actually can feel, and I tried to correct for the past tendency to engage in such sport. With rare exceptions, teasing's not funny. Teasing's mean, nasty and cruel.

Grandma Tuts was not the best housekeeper. That role fell to my mother, who would assiduously clean all of Grandma's closets, dust the shelves and generally make her mother miserable by doing this each summer on her extended visit. After she had finished this, however, Mother would be free to hang out with Aunt Beverly, a more laid-back version of my grandma Tuts. Mother and Jamie would leave each evening after dinner to visit with Beverly.

Beverly had three children. Moneta was Jamie's age, and a beautiful blonde, dressed in very girlie clothes, at least as I recall her. Kathleen was a couple of years younger and was a little fireball of energy. I liked Kathleen a lot. Still do, and found her feisty, tomboy approach to life much more copacetic than Moneta's little lady-like behavior. But Jamie, Moneta and Kathy were close enough in age to enjoy each other's company. I would sometimes play with Kathy but mostly I was odd-man-out, being so much older, so I usually stayed at home and hung out with my grandparents. Indeed, one of my strongest memories of Walnut summers is sitting on the front porch, after dinner, with Grandma Tuts and Grandpa Bob.

Grandpa would smoke his cigar, sitting in the corner in his favorite chair. Grandpa was a man of moderation. He smoked one and only one cigar a day. Had one and only one cup of coffee with his meal. It had to be WITH the meal, not after the meal. Breakfasts were huge, including cereal with real cream, eggs and bacon and toast then finished up with a slice of pie left over from dinner the night before.

Grandpa loved gooseberry pie and tried to get me to taste a serving of it. I preferred cherry, and refused. (Kids are the world's natural conservatives.) But one night I came in from the kitchen and proudly announced I had found a delicious piece of white cherry pie. It was the slice of the gooseberry pie saved for Grandpa's breakfast, of course. Grandpa just laughed, and welcomed me to the gooseberry pie club. For lunch Grandpa liked a full meal. Meat and potatoes. There would be a vegetable of some kind but if Grandpa had to eat salad it had to be smothered in vinegar, or else—I was later told—he wouldn't eat the lettuce and tomatoes. Grandpa always ate spinach covered with vinegar. When he eloped at 88, after my grandmother had been dead for ten of the most miserable years of Grandpa's life, he and his new wife drove to Vancouver to visit me on their honeymoon. I served Grandpa what I believed was his favorite meal: salmon, potatoes and spinach served with vinegar.

"Kristabelle," he sighed, "I have to tell you. I hate spinach."

"I thought it was your favorite, Grandpa," I said, confused. "Mother always had it whenever you came to visit us in Collinsville."

"I know she did. She'd make it for you kids and when I said I didn't like it she said that if the kids had to eat it, so did I. So I always drowned it in vinegar, to kill the taste. But I truly hate the stuff. I ate it only cause your mother made me."

Another insight into Gertrude's managerial propensities.

But the cigar and the coffee were real pleasures for my grandfather. As was sitting on the porch after dinner in the summer. Grandpa always sat in the corner on a kind of wooden camp chair; my grandmother on a softer, more comfortable chair that had been brought from the house. I sat next to Grandma, on a larger sofa.

As the soft night descended and the crickets began their friendly chirping, Grandma and Grandpa would sit quietly, watching the street, commenting on who went by. Then began the gossiping about the neighbors.

A red car would drive by, fast. "There's a Johnson. Probably goin' home ta' see his mother. He's a good kid, though he did get into trouble once while in high school, ya' remember?"

Grandma would reply like a seasoned tennis pro returning the soft volley, warming up to the familiar game, filling in the details of the long-passed event.

"His grandfather was a Hofstadter. They're hard workers, I tell ya'. And scrubby Dutch clean. His grandmother used ta' shine the kitchen till it fair sparkled."

One person had a farm outside of town. Another had gotten his girlfriend "in the family way" when he was a wild youngster but he had since married her, settled down and become a good farmer. The fabric of small town life was etched and sewn back and forth in the evening musings, with a quiet and soothing tenderness that gave me, as a child accustomed to a far more exciting outside world, a sense of the eternal, of life going on much as it probably had forever in small farming communities, whether on the River Nile or in the Pennsylvania Dutch Country from which my grandma hailed, or the rural Scotland of the border country near Melrose, when Grandpa's family had been weavers in the mills of Selkirk, near Sir Walter Scott's home.

Most people long to know where they come from, the kind of folk that bred them. They crave a sense that they belong somewhere.[8] They need not choose to stay there. My mother had not. She had gone to the University of Illinois and flown off into the Spanish literature of *Don Quixote*. Indeed, assigned *Don Quixote* one summer during college, Mother requested it from the interlibrary loan, since the little Walnut library did not have any copy of the book, let alone one written in Spanish.[9] The state of Illinois apparently possessed a seventeenth-century copy of the masterpiece, brought from Mexico and written in the Spanish of that period. The librarian in Springfield simply mailed it to Mother, packing the three-hundred some year-old book only in brown paper. After Mother finished reading it—in the original Spanish—she carefully wrapped it in an old grocery bag, cut down for mailing and returned it, again uninsured, to the State of Illinois in Springfield.

Mother had left this safe world behind. She had fallen in love with my father and never looked back, jumping headfirst into his world of politics and poetry and classical music. She relinquished *McCall's* in favor of *The American Scholar*.[10]

But part of her always remained rooted in Walnut, in the quiet traditions of the sweet summer nights, as her parents told her daughter about their world, a world that was safe, comforting and sheltering.[11]

I think some of what Mother and I found in Walnut is what many people today hunger after, perhaps what people at all points in time have cherished and yearned for. It's a kind of nostalgia for the past. It's why books like *To Kill a Mockingbird* or *Cranford* strike such a deep chord. They evoke a childhood innocence and a time when life felt gentler, safe.

Politicians often exploit this longing for a simpler time, when rules seemed to be known and grandparents watched over us and life felt as if it moved to a slower, more secure rhythm. They can play on this desire, turning it to their political advantage by telling us that if we only elect them they will be tough on crime, keep out all the immigrants who are ruining our lives with their strange, foreign ways, restore our country to what should be our national grandeur. They will be the big people protecting us. This I find ironic—and disturbing—especially since the desire to be safeguarded, to find a simpler past is as ubiquitous and universal as family love. It's the perverted shape politicians and demagogues give to it that should be mistrusted and rejected.[12]

The attachment to home—and the security evoked by the memory of a less complicated time that is represented by home—is one all human beings share.[13] That bond, that connection, that desire itself is not a bad one. Home should be like that; it should be a sanctuary, somewhere we can return to—if only in our minds—when life in our own reality becomes too jarring, too threatening, too confusing or overwhelming. We should all have some clear-cut blueprint of how life could be, a mythic vision, not a real one perhaps, of how safe life once was for us all, whether we are born in Walnut or New York City, Damascus or Shanghai or anywhere else.

At some level, we all crave the sense of security that comes from knowing there are big people out there who will protect us from all the fearful things in the outside world. A place where we can walk alone to the Federated Store with our nickel or dime, and feel rich beyond our wildest dreams of avarice, with all the splendid possibilities of life still waiting for us, before returning home to the comfort food offered by grandparents who have nothing more important to do than to show us how to live life in miniature.

I think this is the role played by grandparents. I know my own children experienced it with my mother and her home on Pine Lake.[14] It's the craving for an easier, less demanding time, for a world where grandparents are champions who fight for their right to spoil and indulge you, their right to love you unabashedly and without regard for how your future character develops.

The house in Walnut is still there. My cousin Bruce owns it now. Before my mother died, she spent every Fourth of July there with Bruce's family, including his grandchildren. The big oak tree that stood beside the front steps is now gone, as is the pine tree to the right of the large screened-in front porch. Grandma's snowball bush has died back, as have most of the flowers she tended so carefully each year. The house has knob and tube wiring that needs to be redone. The skylight in the bathroom upstairs—installed by Uncle Marvin and my mother once they inherited the house—leaks and needs to be replaced.

But the little closet in the upstairs bedroom on the left still has its tiny, pink roses on the wallpaper, and the roses still welcome the children who want to camp out in their sheltering embrace. I can still remember snuggling with Grandma Tuts in her big double bed, reading her ladies magazines with all the wonderful, sappy stories in which the heroine always came out happy. The coal cellar still has the shelves for canned peaches or pickles, or whatever else grew well that summer in the garden. And at least part of me still believes that if a disaster occurs in this wonderful country of ours that it will take at least 30 years before it finds its way to Walnut.

REFERENCES AND FUTURE READINGS

There are many books that address the themes in this essay. Rousseau's work on demagogues and how they rise from populist and democratic movements via their capturing and embodying the will of the people is one text from political theory. (See Jean-Jacques Rousseau's *Discourse on the Origin of Inequality*. Translated by Donald A. Cress. Hackett Publishing, 1992.) Robert Penn Warren's novel—allegedly modeled on Huey

Long—depicts the foibles of an American populist grown into a demagogue. *All the King's Men* was published by Warren in 1946 (Harcourt Brace and Company). Two movies have since been made of it.

There are many novels that capture our nostalgic love of a simpler time. *Cranford* is a sweet novel by the nineteenth-century English writer Elizabeth Gaskell, and describes a quiet village as it is affected by change. Published in eight installments, between December 1851 and May 1853, in *Household Words* (edited by Charles Dickens), it appeared in a slightly revised version in book form in 1853.

Lark Rise (1939), *Over to Candleford* (1941) and *Candleford Green* (1943) are Flora Thompson's depiction of English country life at the turn of the twentieth century. Based on Thompson's childhood experiences, the stories trace three closely related Oxfordshire communities—a hamlet, a village and a town—and the townsfolk who live there. Each of these stories of a gentle rural past have been depicted in BBC/PBS dramas. Thomas Hardy's novels depict the same time period but in far less gentle or nostalgic terms. *Far from the Madding Crowd* (1874 Harper & Brothers) is one of my favorites.

I have painted a rather idealized picture of small-town America. A darker portrait appeared in *Main Street*, a novel by Sinclair Lewis published in 1920. It focuses on the rigidity, narrow mindedness, conformity and mediocrity of early twentieth-century small-town America. Mother told me she was struck by how close to home Lewis's social satire struck. Analogous works exist in other countries, such as Thomas Mann's *Buddenbrooks* (1901) which traces bourgeois life in Germany and *The Forsyte Saga* (1922) by John Galsworthy, which chronicles the life of a large upper-middle-class English family. Both Mann and Galsworthy received the Nobel Prize in Literature, in large part for these works.

Possible questions / written assignments for students if this essay is used in a class. Describe a time from your childhood. What moral values, attitudes or beliefs did you pick up as a child? Which individuals influenced you? What did they teach you? Did you change your views as you became older and moved out into the world? If so, how and what caused you to change? Are you happy you did change? What would you teach your children?

REFERENCES

Cervantes Saavedra, Miguel de. 1605-1615/1949. *The Ingenious Gentleman Don Quixote of La Mancha*. Translated by Samuel Putnam. New York: Viking Press.
———. 1991. *El Ingenioso Hidalgo Don Quijote De La Manca*. Madrid, Espana. Akal.
Galsworthy, John. 1922/2008. *The Forsyte Saga*. Oxford: Oxford University Press. Oxford World's Classics.
Gaskell, Elizabeth Cleghorn. 2011. *Cranford*. Oxford: Oxford University Press.
Mann, Thomas. 1901/1994. *Buddenbrooks: The Decline of a Family*. Translated from the German by John E. Woods. New York: Random House.
Maurois, Andre. 1931. "The Three Ghosts of America". *Scribner's Magazine*. August 23, 1931.

Rousseau, Jean-Jacques. 1992. *Discourse on the Origin of Inequality*. Translated by Donald A. Cress. Indianapolis, IN. Hackett Publishing.

———. 2002. *The Social Contract and the First and Second Discourses*. Translated by Susan Dunn and Gitz Mary. New Haven, CT: Yale University Press.

Thompson, Flora. 1945. *Lark Rise to Candleford, a Trilogy*. New York: Oxford University Press.

Warren, Robert Penn. 1953. *All the King's Men*. New York: Modern Library.

CHAPTER 2

J. O.

He was a newspaper publisher, a state senator and a son of a bitch.

He was also my grandfather.

A relatively short man—5′6″ if memory serves—with a shock of gorgeous white hair and translucent blue eyes, J. O. was an attractive person, bright, intensely intellectual and interested in everything around him, gregarious, with the kind of charm needed by both politicians and newspapermen interested in ferreting out the story. Much of my knowledge of my grandfather comes from my mother who was not, I believe it is safe to say, her father-in-law's greatest fan. Mother's stories often carried a whiff of the Apocrypha but in this case, at least, her version of her father-in-law's life captures enough of what I personally knew to be true of my grandfather that I tend to believe it.

Whatever the case, it is verified fact that the Monroes came from southern Illinois, somewhere around Mount Vernon, Illinois, where they were what could only be termed poor dirt farmers. The original family came to what were then the American colonies around 1720, if family lore is correct. Somewhere in the DNA is a Spaniard, for when my uncle Karl developed a rare blood disease we were told it was odd to find it in him, given his background, since the disease usually affected Basques.[1] We figured this possible link came from a Valentine Sevier, known as the Huguenot, who left southern France—somewhere near Navarre—in the late seventeenth century and fled to England, fearing religious persecution. This Valentine begat another Valentine, who apparently came to the new world and the Sevier family moved from its initial landing somewhere in Virginia. Eventually the Seviers came to rest in Tennessee, where a John Sevier became the first governor and supposedly fought a duel with Andrew Jackson.[2] (One family tale has Sevier and Jackson both giving away the same land parcels to their followers; another version holds that Sevier insulted Jackson's wife. Both accounts end with the two good Tennessee gentlemen deciding to go have a few drinks before the duel and the whiskey doing in each of them. Whatever.

The Monroes never were great drinkers.) John Sevier was the famous one; we descended from his younger brother.

My Aunt Olive, J. O.'s sister who retired to Collinsville after working for many years in what was then called an insane asylum, one night rattled off the history of who married whom. "A Sevier married a Landrum, who married ..." I got lost in the names and the speed of dispatch with which this family lore was transmitted, and never did get it straight. But I do remember Aunt Olive saying that the family was working in the Underground Railroad in Tennessee before the Civil War.

> The night riders—precursors of the Klan—found out about it and they came one night and burned down the barn. They said they'd be back the next night and if the family was still there, they'd burn down the house. So, the family hitched up the wagon, piled on as many of their things as possible and headed north. There was a two-year-old, so they took a cow to provide milk. Well, the horse went lame, and they had to hitch the cow to the wagon to pull it, so her milk went dry and the two-year old died.

Olive also said another child in the family later fell into the fire and was burned to death, further evidence that life was hard in those days, and that people had to be both tough and lucky.

To my mind, all the Monroes were smart and reasonably well educated, certainly for their day. J. O.'s sister Ruth was tall and redheaded. She supposedly wanted me to be named after her since I had red hair at birth. (Mother's sense of humor ran to the cheeky and she allegedly described my hair color on the birth certificate as "fire-engine red." Auburn is probably more like it, but it certainly felt like the dreaded red when I was a child.) Ruth tried to bribe Mother by promising to leave me all her money if I were named Ruth. This was not an idle gesture since Ruth had married a wealthy doctor and spent many years attending Veiled Prophet Balls and living on the periphery of St. Louis society before she died of cancer, some 10 years after I was born. I don't remember Ruth well but, in her photos, she indeed was pretty, and highly stylish.

After Ruth's death her home—a townhouse near the St. Louis Cathedral in what then was the fashionable West end of St. Louis—went to her two sisters: Olive and Sal. The house I do remember, and it was lovely, with two downstairs parlors, both with grand pianos, as I recall, and a back staircase, something I had never seen before. Ruth was elegant, smartly dressed and seemed quite sophisticated to my untutored eye. When she died, all her money and her house went to Aunt Sal and Aunt Olive, who hated Aunt Sal so much she refused to be buried in the family plot with her and wrote that request into her will.

Aunt Olive was smart but certainly not pretty, resembling a bit of a smushed mushroom. She tended to wear skirts and plopped down quite ungracefully into chairs, legs spread wide apart to cushion her descent into a chair too low, thus exposing her undergarments to the world in the process. A widow and probably sexually frustrated, my father said—Daddy being the only one in the family who would say such things out loud to children—Olive was fascinated with JFK's sex life and used to cut out small items about it and stick them on her wall with a straight pin. Obviously, this slightly bizarre behavior would elicit the desired: "What in the world is that, Aunt Olive?" This simple request then would allow Aunt Olive to launch into a diatribe about what a cad and roué the president was. I wish only that Aunt Olive could have lived long enough to savor the Clinton–Lewinsky sex scandal or Donald Trump's sexual behavior. What fun Aunt Olive would have had with the prurient details provided by a press much freer at discussing presidential sexual peccadilloes!

I knew Sal briefly. She lived in Ruth's home for many years, renting rooms to St. Louis University Med students and occasionally inviting my cousins Kay and Becky and me for an overnight in the big city. I seem to remember Sal would pick on one of us, taunt us about being fat (which none of us was) or for having straight hair. (Guilty as charged.) But she could occasionally do kind things for us. She gave me a perm when I was 10. Unfortunately, I had very long hair and left shortly after the perm for summer camp, where we swam twice a day. Mother said when she and my father picked me up, I had my long hair in a ponytail, and looked like some kind of wild woman with a huge wad of frizz residing behind a rubber band on top of her head.

I don't think Sal and Olive much liked their brother, my grandfather, named James Oliver but called J. O. by everyone. The immediate family did not run to close ties of affection. There were other children among my grandfather's siblings, but I met them only rarely and they did not signify in my young life. J. O. was the *pater familia*, the oligarch wannabe.

Smart, J. O. was, and he had gotten an education at what I was told later became Illinois Normal University. According to Mother, one of J. O.'s professors was my great grandmother, Elizabeth Habermas Koch, who had been educated in Germany before emigrating to the United States. Great Grandmother Koch was supposedly a strong individual, who divorced her husband—a railroad man—once she learned he was keeping a family at the other end of the line. Mother always said J. O. liked and respected the old lady and married her daughter, Frieda, because of that.

I never knew my grandmother Frieda. She died in 1945, before I was born, but my father must have loved her for he kept a small photo of her always in his study and spoke kindly of her, telling me how beautiful she was, how much she liked to read. When I was eight or nine, Daddy came in one July and gave me a radio, saying it was his mother's birthday and he was missing her, so he thought he'd do something nice for me in her honor. I was touched by that, and always treasured the radio because of my father's gesture and his opening up about his loneliness for someone he loved and had lost.

Mother said Frieda was a large-boned woman who always seemed overwhelmed by the demands of motherhood, better suited to the life of the mind than to the running of a small household of five children plus her own mother and a difficult husband. Apparently, Frieda used to retreat to the bathroom, where she would read to her heart's content, undisturbed by her offsprings. (Bathroom reading seems entirely sensible to me, even without a hoard of children bearing down upon me, and my bathrooms always have several piles of books or magazines scattered nearby.)

After college, the story goes, J. O. worked as a journalist and wanted to have his own newspaper. He heard there was a paper for sale in Carlinville and got on the train from southern Illinois determined to buy the paper. Like most of the Monroes, J. O. could fall asleep anywhere and he dozed off on the warm train, sleeping through his stop. He woke as the conductor yelled out, "Collinsville. All out for Collinsville." The towns sounded similar to J. O.—Carlinville, Collinsville—so my grandfather figured he'd check to see if Collinsville had a newspaper for sale. There was a certain logic in this. (That's how all the Monroes approached life. They had the ability to step outside the circumstance and convention to view life afresh, if somewhat eccentrically. I include myself in that dubious category.)

The newspaper actually was for sale although it had not yet been publicly advertised as being on the market. But—Mother's story went—the newspaper editor had come home late one night, after putting the paper to bed, a term I imagine is now archaic but which then indicated the process of putting the stories up from the typewriter to the linotype machine and then rolling out the presses and checking to make sure everything was done correctly as the giant presses whirred and hummed, happily putting all the news that was fit to print— and some that was not—onto the paper.

As the editor approached his house, he noticed a light on in his bedroom window. By the time he reached the bedroom, however, the light went off and, as he entered the room, his wife asked him to please not turn on the light since she had a dreadful headache. The editor complied, undressed in the dark and climbed into bed. After a few moments, however, his wife begged him to get dressed and go the pharmacist and get some aspirin for her headache. Dutifully, the editor again obeyed, putting on the pants draped on the chair and grabbing his jacket as he left the dark room. He went to the pharmacy, woke the pharmacist and asked for some aspirin for his wife. As he reached into his pants pocket to pay, he realized the pocket contained a huge roll of bills. The editor examined the pants. They were not his. The editor said nothing, paid the pharmacist, returned home, gave his wife the aspirin and went to sleep.

The next morning the editor went to the newspaper office and wrote an ad for the lost and found column. "Found, in my wife's bedroom. One pair of pants with a large wad of bills in the left pocket. Owner may identify the pants and claim the money at the newspaper office."

Everyone in town knew the banker was notorious for carrying wads of money in his pockets. Everyone in town also read and laughed about the ad, including the banker, who was far less amused than were his neighbors. The banker called in the debt on the newspaper, the editor could not pay it, and hence the *Collinsville Herald* came to J. O. It was a fitting beginning.

J. O. cared a lot about the news and the *Herald*—as the *Collinsville Herald* was always affectionately known—became a first rate bi-weekly paper, winning prizes for its coverage and well respected in the local community in down-state Illinois, just across the river from St. Louis. One of my boyfriends joked that the paper should sponsor a group of Christmas carolers called the angels, so that "Hark! The Herald Angels could sing." Nothing ever came of this tomfoolery, but the *Herald* was well regarded in the local area, and did a superb job of raising important local issues, as good newspapers did in bygone days. I suspect much of this quality and affectionate respect associated with the *Herald* was due to my Uncle Karl, who dutifully agreed to run the paper, while his father devoted his time to politics.

If J. O. was a good newspaperman, he was far less of a businessman, suffering from the malady that seems to have afflicted the entire family: a lack of interest in money. It's not that the Monroes are hostile to money. Nor do they denigrate or mitigate what money can go in the world. They just personally don't find it very interesting.

When my own father went on the bench, he gave his checkbook to my mother to balance. His secretary had done it while he was in private practice as a lawyer, Daddy explained, but it would be neither right nor proper for his court reporter to do so now that he was a judge. Mother—herself meticulous with money, as with everything in her life—agreed. Once she took the checkbook, however, she realized there was nothing written in the check recorder. (I'm so like my father in this regard I don't even know the word for the place where you record what you have paid out via checks.)

> "Jim!" Mother called to her husband, exiting the room. "There's nothing written down here. How did your secretary balance the check book?"
>
> "Oh, it's no problem," Daddy reassured her. "The bank sends you a statement each month telling you how much money you have so you just use that."

Another time Daddy was driving to St. Louis. He had to cross what was then called the Eads Bridge and pay a toll of what was then either ten or fifteen cents. Daddy explained to the gentleman manning the bridge's tollbooth that he had forgotten his cash. He had no money at all; not even ten cents in his pocket. But, Daddy assured the man, he would write him a check. After some discussion, the toll taker agreed. Daddy then went to write the check, only to find that he had no more checks left in his checkbook. Daddy then assured the by-now bemused toll taker that Daddy was a lawyer and that it was legal to accept any kind of piece of paper with a legal signature. The bank would honor it, Daddy confidently guaranteed the toll taker. By this time, I imagine the poor tollbooth keeper figured this story was worth the ten cents he would be out for letting this noodlehead cross the bridge without paying, and he agreed to take my father's check for ten cents, written and properly signed on a piece of torn brown paper bag from the local grocery store.

Fortunately for the bridge's toll taker, my father was a better lawyer than he was a big money man, and a piece of brown paper bag, with a check for ten cents written to Eads Bridge and signed and dated by my father, later came through with the rest of the bank statements, and Mother duly noted it as she brushed away her tears of laughter.

Daddy came by this somewhat disengaged attitude toward money honestly. The Internal Revenue Service (IRS) came once to audit the *Herald*. J. O. welcomed them, ushering them into a large room with bookcases filled with law books—a definite interest of J. O.'s and, indeed, the entire family—and a huge library table with a couple of side chairs. The table was piled high with brown paper bags, the kind one still occasionally gets at some grocery stores and on which my father had written his 10-cent check. Each bag was filled with receipts.

> "What is all this?" the IRS men demanded, somewhat confused.
>
> "Those are my receipts. My tax records for the newspaper. Help yourself. I have nothing to hide," and with that, J. O. returned to the far more interesting task of caring for the country.

Supposedly the IRS men stayed for three days trying to make sense of the putative records for the *Herald*. They finally left, claiming they never wanted to see my grandfather again and grumbling that anyone so disorganized could not possibly be able to successfully rip off anyone, let alone the government of the United States.

Lest you think J. O. was too casual as a manager, he actually did fire someone once. He got mad at Elmer Hazzard, the local sports editor, a man genuinely informed about sports but notoriously a little too laid back when it came to journalistic deadlines. One day, J. O. had simply had enough. J. O. yelled at Hazzy that he was fired.

"Just get your hat and leave!" J. O. angrily ordered Hazzy out of the office. Everyone was amazed, and poor Hazzy muttered something unintelligible as he edged out of the room.

When J. O. left for lunch an hour later, he bumped into Hazzy, sitting on the front step of the *Herald*. "What the hell are you still doing here?" J. O. demanded.

"I don't have a hat," the man replied, quite honestly.

"What?"

"You told me to get my hat and leave. But I don't have a hat."

J. O. stared, incredulous at the poor fellow, a man obviously both confused and upset. Then J. O. started to laugh. "Oh, for god's sake. Just go back inside. You've got your old job back."

Other insights into J. O.'s managerial style come from a woman who worked for the *Herald* for many years. Marilyn may vaguely have been related to someone at the *Herald* through marriage; the *Herald* always seemed to hire lots of friends and family, something I attribute less to nepotism and more to charity and disinterest on the part of the managers in having to engage in a formal process of hiring, the Monroes being notoriously lousy at business. Whatever the origin of her job, Marilyn had worked for years at the *Herald*. Once, she told me, she was working late, reading type with J. O. far into the night. At one point she felt him reach down and ruffle her hair. She had heard stories about J. O.'s womanizing and looked up, shocked and a bit trepidatious. "Your hair was on fire," J. O. replied matter-of-factly. "My cigarette ash fell into your hair and it was on fire, so I put it out. Not to worry. Now can we get back to reading type?"

As Marilyn told me this story years later, laughing, she recounted that she was not sure if she were more amused or relieved. She didn't have to spell it out for a college girl who listened a lot. I had heard the stories of my grandfather's womanizing. Rumor had it that he was personally responsible for bringing into the Democratic Party many of the local ladies of the night, and that he frequently cheated on my grandmother. I'm not sure how I picked up this information. Children are far more adept than we realize at getting the nuances of adult conversation and sizing up adults in general. Probably the information came from Mother.

Fiercely loyal to those she loved, Mother instinctively recognized the threat J. O. posed to her husband and to Daddy's independence. (J. O. was the man, after all, who needed to get re-elected to the Illinois Senate, and hence asked three of his sons to come back to Collinsville and enlist in World War II in order to appear in uniform at one of J. O.'s political rallies. Raised a child of the Vietnam war era, I always wondered what kind of sicko would risk his children's lives just to get re-elected to political office, and always wished I had asked my father why in the world he gave up a good job in the U.S. Treasury Department—along with its draft deferment—so he could help satisfy his father's ego.)

Whatever the cause, Mother fought J. O. with a fierce strength that must have surprised everyone, especially J. O., a man long accustomed to walking all over women.

"He wasn't really warm toward your grandmother," Mother once told me. "I've seen him sit at the breakfast table, ignoring her as she asked him for grocery money. She'd continue to beg and finally he reached into his pocket and pulled out his pocket change and threw it on the table as he got up to leave the room."

"The house belonged to Frieda, you know. It had been left to her by her mother, Elizabeth Koch. I think J. O. respected Grandma Koch but she was the only woman J. O. ever felt that way about. Every time J. O. had another election campaign he'd bring in the papers and Frieda would dutifully acquiesce, and they'd mortgage the house to pay for his re-election campaign. Every damn time! Frieda always signed the mortgage papers! I don't think it ever entered her mind to say no."

"He tried the same thing when your dad was starting out. Jimmy was hungry for political office and J. O. cut a deal with the local political machine so that Jimmy could get a judgeship if he'd agree to resign after one term and let one of their stooges have the seat. J. O. wanted your dad to do it."

"Your father and I discussed it. I knew he wanted it. Even more, he wanted to please your grandfather. But I told him his personal integrity was too high a price to pay. We drove down to the *Herald* and your father went in to tell J. O. what he'd decided."

"I waited in the car with you. I think you were asleep in the back seat." She stopped and smiled, "You always fell asleep in cars."

"Anyway, your dad was in there for a long time. Then J. O. came out. He stormed over to the car and stuck his head in the window, wagging his finger in my face."

"You just keep your god-damned nose out of that boy's business," he said. "He can make up his own mind without any interference from some god-damned female!"

"I just shoved my finger right back in his face and said I'd be glad to keep my god-damned nose out of Jim's business as long as he did the same thing."

"He glared at me, turned on his heels and stalked back into the office. A few minutes later your daddy came out and that was the last we heard of the machine appointment. Your daddy didn't run then and when he did run later, he was his own man."

"But I went to Irving Dillard. [Irving was a family friend and editorial editor of the *St. Louis Post-Dispatch*.[3]] I told Irving, "Jim wants to run. Bill Burton [head of the local political party machine] says he can guarantee it." There was never any guarantee of a payoff later. But if you get elected to be county judge, they didn't do anything that amounted to much. They just played golf all the time. So, the people who had that county judgeship, that was an easy job. The whole idea was that if you got to be county judge—and that involved cases with kids, and as time went on that became a big problem but, in those days, there wasn't a lot of juvenile crime—but the idea was that if you got "judge" before your name it was easier to run for circuit judge later. Being a circuit judge was a serious job. When your dad was elected, he was elected circuit judge. And he got it on his own merits."

"I asked Irving. 'Jim has a lot of respect for you. I don't think it's wise, this deal his dad proposes. I don't know how you consider it. But if he does ask you for your advice, I hope you will remember that I feel it's a mistake to owe something to Bill Burton.'"

"Jim never told me if he talked to Irving. Irving never talked to me about any followup, never told me if he had talked to Jim. But there was no more talk about the county judge job."

Mother didn't always fare so well, however, but then neither did J. O. Both J. O. and Mother were bested when J. O. married his second wife, Lil, who went down in the family lore as a rather disagreeable little gold digger who left town with too much of J. O.'s money and their brand-new Thunderbird convertible, a hot new car just off the assembly line.

I don't remember Lil well; I think I met her only once in a rather dimly lit Italian restaurant and she made no impression on an 11-year-old. But her fights with my parents, and with my aunts and uncles, became the stuff of family legend and she worked her way so deeply into my mother's subconscious that Mom told she used to dream Lil was mopping up the floor with her.

"It was 2 a.m. and I had had a busy day. You remember how hot and miserable it could be in August in St. Louis? I think you hated the heat worse than anyone else. Your brother would be sick. Nothing serious, just a child's summer cold. You know what it's like now that you have children, I suspect. A slight fever that peaks at night and makes them restless all day."

Mom smiled, remembering. "He'd wanted to go outside and play anyway, despite the little fever. Well, I finally got him settled and I staggered off to bed. I don't think my head had hit the pillow more than an hour when the phone rang. It shook my whole head with its shrillness. I groped across your father—nothing ever woke that man—hoping I could get to the phone before it woke one of you kids. When I got it, it was that goddamned Lil!"

"'How do you like being wakened at 3 o'clock in the morning?' she asked in this voice dripping with saccharine and sweetness, and then hung up. I was so mad." Mother laughed, rocking back in the chair, her greying hair contrasted against the silk cream of the upholstered cushions, remembering a time when she was young, and life was full.

"I guess I was too damned mad to go back to sleep because I lay there and fumed for an hour, cursing her, feeling sorry for myself, feeling angry at everybody and anybody. Then I thought to myself, 'Well, she asked you a question. Why not answer it?' So, I got out of bed, padded down the hall to the study and picked up the phone and called her back. 'I don't like it one bit,' I said. 'How do you like being wakened at 4 a.m.?' Then I hung up the phone and went right back to sleep. Slept like a log, too."

"Oh, Mom. You didn't!"

"I sure did." She smiled. The young wife, overworked and tired but free, filled with the joy of life. Then she grinned. *"The only problem was, you see, I'd been pretty tired and by mistake I hadn't called Lil. I'd called Karl and Mary's number instead. I'd realized it almost immediately. But I figured they'd get back to sleep and best not to call and explain at that hour and risk waking them again."*

"The next morning around 10 o'clock Mary called, just spitting nails. She was so mad."
"Do you know what that Lil did to us last night?" she demanded.
"Well, Mary. Let me take a guess," I ventured cautiously.
"She called us at 4 a.m., asked us how we liked being wakened at 4 a.m. and then she hung up!" Mary was clearly outraged, Mother continued.
"Mary," I tried to interrupt Mary, but she just kept right on going."
"I told Karl, 'I've had enough. I'm calling the police.'"
"Oh, Mary. No!"

"I sure did. We told them all about the calls and they said they'd go down and speak with her. Karl insisted they go immediately so they sent a squad car at 5 o'clock. Got them both out of bed and gave them a warning."

"Oh, Mary. You didn't, I kept saying." Mother was laughing by then.

"That was when I told her all about it. She understood." Mother leaned forward to take another sip from her coffee. The smoke from her cigarette curled upward, dispersing around her steel-gray curls and her dark eyes, crinkled by laughter and smudged darker by life.

"She wasn't mad at you?"

"No, of course not. She knew what it was like. We had a good laugh on ourselves."

The light filtered through the large, tinted window above us, and the sound of my young son floated in from the garden, as we sat there, remembering.

It's just me remembering now. They're all gone, these grown-up people who looked so big and who controlled the world, at least to the eyes of a child.

I seldom think about J. O. He constitutes no place in my emotional panoply. Yet even though I was not conscious of the part he played in my life, J. O. did manage to fix my constellation, for the entire family was, in some way, warped by his ego. I don't think any of his children truly broke loose from his orbit. Most of them admired the old man, even when they realized what a taker he was.[4]

His legacy for me was complicated. I knew he was arrogant, and I avoid such people like the plague. I remember driving J. O. somewhere one night, shortly after getting my driver's license. It was 10 p.m. and we stopped at the red light onto Vandalia Street, even though no cars were in sight. "Why are you stopping?" the old man quizzed me.

"It's a red light, Grandpa," I replied, quite truthfully.

He scoffed! "Young lady. I wrote that law. You can go through the light now. There's no one here."

This kind of personal exchange, set next to the backdrop of the other J. O. stories I heard, helped set the indelible imprint of what a politician is like up close and personal. I've always distrusted political figures, always thought them people who have good ideas and good intentions but eventually become seduced by their own press releases, by their own conviction that 'you have to get power to do the good things.' I see them as people who succumb to their own need for fame, adulation and even, in too many instances, money and power. I've admired some politicians briefly but seldom find one to whom I truly want to give my heart. I neither need nor want larger than life heroes. I don't trust them and think it's better to just have—and be—a normal, mildly neurotic, flawed human being, like everyone else.

I used to think my weakness would be that I might sell out for fame and glory. Perhaps that is my natural bent. But academia is such small potatoes that one can't but wonder why otherwise good people become so vicious when such little bits of power or glory are at stake. I think I fear what feels like a slippery slope to me, a deep-seated dread that I might be done in by my own ego and my need to feel important. So far, I've successfully resisted. (When the Dean told me, I was the choice to be next chair of the department, I just laughed. "I'm giving you a Sherman, Willie," I said, invoking William Tecumseh Sherman's famous reply when asked to run for president after the Civil War. "If nominated, I will not run. If elected, I will not serve.") Even a little bit of power scares me.

I think Grandfather J. O. had something to do with this reaction. Whenever I am dazzled by the prospect of doing something big, leaving a legacy that will last beyond me, or become too comfortable with praise from others, I stop. It's like riding along on a train and seeing someone far in the distance, a haunted harbinger of what your life could become. There stands J. O., a slight man with a white head of hair and piercing, translucent blue eyes, smiling as he smokes, his cigarette dangling precariously between his lips. A man who squandered his talents, betrayed his own values by failing to develop the best parts of himself, a stark reminder of how deadly a seductress fame and power can be. J. O. reminds me always to resist the itch for power, to remember how fleeting fame and glory are, to be more comfortable under the radar, behind the scenes, trying to do what little good things I can to help others, but quietly and without fanfare or notice.

It's peaceful being no one of significance. Money, beauty, power, fame, all the things too many of us want, these tend to distance you from other people. They can be used to do good, I know; but they often can act as barriers, separating you from the important things in life, which for me all center on that wonderful sense of closeness that comes with human connection. They get in the way of that astonishing sense of communion when you get to know someone who likes you for who you are, not because of what you can do for them or the reflected glory you might provide. The kind of moment when it's just two human beings sharing something real and trusting each other.

I'm not sure J. O. ever grasped this concept. His loss, but a great gift for one of the many grandchildren he never bothered to get to know.

REFERENCES AND FUTURE READINGS

Foot, Philippa. 1978. *Virtues and Vices and Other Essays in Moral Philosophy*. Berkeley: University of California Press/Oxford: Blackwell.
————. 2001. *Natural Goodness*. Oxford: Clarendon Press.

————. 2002. *Moral Dilemmas: And Other Topics in Moral Philosophy*. Oxford: Clarendon Press.

Nussbaum, Martha C. 1999. "Virtue Ethics: A Misleading Category?" *The Journal of Ethics*, vol. 3, no. 3: 163–201.

————. [1986]/2001. *The Fragility of Goodness: Luck and Ethics in Greek Tragedy and Philosophy* (second edn.). New York: Cambridge University Press.

————. 2000. *Women and Human Development: The Capabilities Approach*. New York: Cambridge University Press.

————. 2001. *Upheavals of Thought: The Intelligence of Emotions*. New York: Cambridge University Press.

————. 2018. *The Monarchy of Fear: A Philosopher Looks at Our Political Crisis*. New York: Simon & Schuster.

————. 2019. *The Cosmopolitan Tradition: A Noble but Flawed Ideal*. Philadelphia: Harvard University Press.

Williams, Bernard. 1972. *Morality: An Introduction to Ethics*. Cambridge: Cambridge University Press.

————. 1973. *Problems of the Self*. Cambridge: Cambridge University Press.

————. 1981. *Moral Luck: Philosophical Papers*, 1973–1980. Cambridge: Cambridge University Press.

————. 1985. *Ethics and the Limits of Philosophy*. Cambridge: Harvard University Press.

————. 1995. *Making Sense of Humanity*. Cambridge: Cambridge University Press.

Readings

Listen to Stephen Sondheim's "Children will listen" for a great reminder to be careful what we "teach" children, through our acts as much as, or even more than, our words.

For those interested in philosophical works on this approach, consult any text discussing virtue ethics. One of my favorites is Martha Nussbaum's *The Fragility of Goodness* (Cambridge University Press 2001. See also Nussbaum 2000 and 2001. Bernard Williams (1972, 1985 and 1995) and Philippa Foot (2001, 2002) also have excellent texts in this area.

Virtue ethics is one of the main approaches to normative ethics. It grew out of the ancient Greek approach to ethics which emphasizes the importance of character and the virtues that are found in our character. Its major concepts concern *arête* (or excellence or virtue), *phronesis* (the concept of moral wisdom or practical wisdom) and *Eudaimonia* (human flourishing). The goal of life is to flourish; the best way to do this is to acquire the kind of practical wisdom that will enable you to judge what best will foster such flourishing and the route to that is through developing a certain type of character.

Virtue ethics was an important ethical system in the West, indeed perhaps the prevailing approach to ethical thinking in both the ancient Greek and Roman periods and up through the Middle Ages. It lost popularity in the modern period with the growth of both deontological ethics, with its emphasis on duty to rules, and consequentialism, which judges the right/wrongness of an act from the consequences or outcome of the act itself. In a short but intriguing article, Nussbaum takes some issue with this juxtaposition of virtue ethics from other schools of philosophy, arguing that virtue ethics has much in common with both Utilitarianism and Kant's philosophy. See Nussbaum (1999). Virtue ethics effectively argues that it is the process of developing morally desirable virtues that then will produce the character or identity that naturally leads us to take good moral actions when such decisions do need to be made. Virtue ethics thus places an emphasis on "being" a good person rather than "doing" a particular act. Its key focus is on developing character or a certain identity.

Aesop's Fables and *Bible* stories illustrate the ways in which virtues are taught to children. Many young children's books also discuss moral character. See *The Butter Battle Book*, *The Sneeches* by Dr. Zeuss or some of the Bernstein Bear books. And then there are all those Disney movies, where virtue triumphs.

Class discussion/ writing assignment. Consider Harper Lee's two novels, both autobiographical though fictionalized. I wondered if some of what happened between the time when Harper Lee wrote her first draft of it and the publication of *To Kill a Mockingbird* (Grand Central Publishing (October 11, 1988)) might have reflected a different view of her father. Students might want to write on how things change and how we think differently about our parents at different times in our lives. Consider one of the following prompts.

(1) Why do you think Harper Lee changed the depiction of her father in the first draft (*Go Set a Watchman*) and the second (*To Kill a Mockingbird*)? Was it merely a literary shift or did it represent something in her own attitude toward her father? (2) Dealing with our families. How do our views of them shift over time? What lessons can we learn from their mistakes, their good points? Who was important in your life in shaping your character, in what ways and why? Can you learn important lessons from people you dislike? From people you hardly know?

CHAPTER 3

FORGIVENESS AND
THE THIN RED LINE

I like to think of myself as a forgiving person. Only twice in my life have I ever drawn a line through someone's name in my emotional address book, and doing so did not make me feel good about myself. After all, it's better to forgive, isn't it? Holding onto an angry grudge will only trap you back there in the pain; isn't that what everyone says?

Thinking about two incidents when I did not forgive someone, however, made me revisit the whole concept of forgiveness, and now I'm not so sure it is always the right thing to do. Mostly I find forgiveness more complicated than I had thought before. We too easily confuse the essence of forgiveness—absolving the offending party for having done harm—with the act of relinquishing our own anger and resentment against the one who hurt us and then finding a way to craft an ongoing relationship with them.

The first story involves my friend Josie (not her real name). I'd been very close to Josie in college. I had been the one who introduced her to her husband while I was in grad school. And even though we lost track for much of the post-grad school years, we did keep in touch. So, when I moved to New York City, I reconnected with Josie, along with other mutual friends from Smith.

This was not the best time in my life. My only brother, Jamie, had been diagnosed with leukemia shortly before I began teaching at New York University (NYU). My second year there, Jamie's illness worsened and he died in December 1978. My father had died three years before Jamie got sick. Grandpa Bob died in July 1978, and my then boyfriend dumped me in January 1979, a month after Jamie's death.

The Christmas after Jamie died was bleak. I had no emotional energy to deal with anything except my mother's pain and grief from a wound so deep it went beyond anything words can capture. Losing a child must be the cruelest blow of all in life. When I returned to New York City after Christmas break, however, I called Josie to tell her about Jamie. Her husband answered the phone. I told him why I was calling, and he told me Josie was busy feeding their baby. "I'm so sorry about your brother," he said. "I'll tell Josie and she'll be sure to call you."

I thanked him and hung up.

In May, after what turned out to be the worst four months of my entire life, I returned home to my apartment and opened the mail to find a note from Josie.

"Dear Kristi," it began. "I tried several times to call you at the office but never got through the switchboard and I didn't want to bother you at home." (Josie always called at home. There was no one else there to bother in the pre-answering phone/pre-cell phone days, and the office staff at NYU always took messages if faculty were not in, so Josie's explanation reeked of mendacity.) Nonetheless Josie continued, briefly expressing her sympathy and concluding with these words: "You mean so much to me. Please let me know if there is anything I can do for you."

I stood there, looking at the letter, not knowing whether to laugh or cry. The thought that flashed through my mind was harsh and nasty, reflecting all my hurt at my own loss and incredible sense of vulnerability. "Dear Josie. Thank you so much for your letter of May 12th in response to my phone call of January 14th, expressing your sympathy over my brother's death and telling me how much you care. There IS something you can do for me. Write me again in four months and tell me once more how much I mean to you."

The quickly—and bitterly—composed mental letter was never sent, of course, just thrown in the emotional trash heap where it belonged. But for the first time in my life, I figuratively drew a big red line through someone's name in my emotional address book.

At our next Smith reunion, Josie was there and came up and threw her arms around me. I stiffened and said nothing other than the polite hello, then walked away as quickly as I could without making a scene and sat down to talk with other friends. One of them asked why I was so cold to Josie. "Josie knows why," was all I replied.

I rarely see Josie—I seldom attend Smith reunions now that I live in California—and on the few occasions when we were in the same place, I was civil but not really friendly. When I recently received a request to friend her on Facebook, I just clicked *delete* and moved on.

The second story involves another dear friend, someone who was bright and funny and sensitive, the first friend I had whom I loved like a sister. We went through several of life's traumas together: professional insecurities, my romances, her divorce, remarriage and second divorce, her new life as a politician, my life as a new wife and mother, all peppered with lots of great late night phone calls and occasional visits. Probably because she so excelled in politics and because I had three children and a high maintenance husband plus a career, our lives did not converge until she moved to Los Angeles. I was delighted to have her nearby and we spent some lovely times together and with my family.

I soon realized, however, that she wasn't too crazy about my children and, more particularly, the somewhat loose disciplinary style in which they were being raised. I also recognized that she had a rich, busy, grown-up life, with soirees, opera, travel and social and cultural events I simply did not have time for anymore. Still, now that she was living so nearby, we saw each other more frequently. I invited her for Thanksgiving dinner and introduced her to my California friends, some of whom then became her friends. I was hurt, therefore, when I learned she had thrown herself a huge 50th birthday party and had not invited me.

Unlike Josie—who I never gave a chance to explain—I did call this friend. I told her I heard she had thrown herself a big birthday bash and wondered why I was not invited. "I'm not sure," she replied. "I realized afterwards that you weren't there and I remember wondering why I had not invited you. I guess I just figured it was too far for you to come."

"Come on," I chided her gently. "You invited Judy and she lives farther than I do."

"Well, why don't we get together and talk about it. Maybe you could come up for lunch."

"Okay," I agreed. "I'll be out of town for two weeks, but I could do it any time after that. Why don't you check your schedule since you probably have more constraints than I do, and call me back, to suggest a time and place?"

She agreed and we left it at that and rang off. I walked into the kitchen and told my husband, "I called her."

"What did she say?"

"It was interesting," I replied, reflecting on our conversation. "I'm going to make a prediction. First, she'll never call me back. Second, she didn't say the one thing I would have said without thinking: 'I'm so sorry. I never meant to hurt you.'"

I was right. I never heard from her again.

It wasn't pleasant but I made myself think deeply about my part in both of these exchanges since I had never before deleted someone from my life. Even now, doing so feels mean, punitive, cruel. It doesn't feel like me. I like to think of myself as a compassionate, loving person, someone who understands the other person and who can see things from their point of view and, as a result, find the understanding and empathic insight that is said to precede forgiveness.

It was painful and uncomfortable to have to evaluate my role in the series of interactions that led to the act that wounded and hurt me and left me feeling wronged and in need of an apology. Self-examination is not always fun to do and doing so reminded me how much I was at fault in both instances. I recognize that I can be remarkably insensitive to little slights and hurts that I might impose on others, usually without noticing. I am not big on ceremony at the best of times and the 1960s and 1970s constituted a historical period, in my life, anyway, when such ceremonies were viewed as trivial, insignificant, superficial. (Fly across the country for someone's wedding? No way. It was expensive—I was on a graduate student budget, after all—and frivolous, not the kind of thing a hippie-scholar did.) The fact that—as I now remember it—I wasn't invited to Josie's wedding is some kind of indicator that many other people at that time did not engage in such cross-country symbolic visits of affection.

Yet even if I were not the only person during this time period who was devoid of great concern for ceremony, I was surely at fault for ignoring the importance of building a sense of community. I forgot how coming to another person's wedding or sending their child a gift can underline how important that person is to you. So I am certainly not free from blame in the first vignette. Still, it felt to me, at least at the time, that Josie's acts fell beyond the pale. When someone is *in extremis*, in the kind of distress precipitated by multiple deaths, some forms of human compassion are *de rigeur*. And yet, I now remind myself, Josie did not know how I felt or what I was experiencing. Perhaps I am being unduly unfair.

Maybe. But then I compare Josie's behavior with that of my friend Nancy Moss from high school, another friend to whom I had once been close but someone—like Josie—I had not seen for many years before Jamie got ill. Nancy too was someone with whom I retained the same kind of emotional closeness I felt for Josie, despite our divergent lives. When Nancy heard—not from me; presumably from a mutual friend—of my brother's illness, I received a handwritten note. "Dear Kristi, Some things do not change. If there is anything I can do for you, I am here. Love, Nancy."

That's the kind of person you want in your life. That's the kind of human being who really is a friend. If this woman ever wants a favor, I am there for her.[1]

I went through similar soul searching after the break with my second friend. Again, I had been far from the perfect buddy. Once I had left the educational institution in which we both taught, I made a new life for myself. I did keep in touch, but both our lives essentially moved on. At some conscious level, I realized, too, that politics changes people, makes them think differently about who they are friendly with, introduces an element of considering what friendship can do to help careers. I was not on that wavelength, however, and probably never would be. I don't naturally think instrumentally or strategically and on the few occasions I do move into that turf, I am terrible at it. I am not comfortable putting something as precious as friendship on the same scale as status, prestige, or professional or social advantage.

A few years ago, I supervised a thesis on forgiveness, written by Adam Martin.[2] The thesis is an extraordinarily fine one, analyzing forgiveness after 9/11 and asking how families or survivors dealt with forgiveness after such a loss. What struck me was the literature review. My student summarized the scholarly work on forgiveness, prominent in fields ranging from religion and philosophy to sociology and political science. What Adam found surprised me. Essentially, what I think of as a Christian view toward forgiveness as a highly desired ethical stance is not judged by the psychologists to necessarily be good for people. Forgiveness, the psychologists tell us, can trap you in relationships with people who hurt you and treat you poorly. Better for us to dump them and move on.

This conclusion is reinforced by scholars from evolutionary biology and psychology, who take a long perspective, arguing that revenge once was in our interest evolutionarily speaking. (Evolutionary biologists talk a lot about acts that are "evolutionarily adaptive," which basically means an action will help us survive as a species.) I'm not keen on evolutionary perspectives when it comes to thinking about our own actions. Too long a time period is involved. My mind doesn't think in terms of eons.

Nor am I into revenge. But thinking about these literatures, and returning to my own personal stories, makes me wonder what purpose forgiveness plays in our lives, and whether sometime the refusal to forgive can be a useful thing, functional in the sense of helping us arrive at a better understanding of what situational factors can lead us to more civilized behavior.

I've learned over the years that I am always better at taking care of my children than I am at caring for myself, so I have one last story to throw into the intellectual hopper. This anecdote concerns Chloe and what my failure to forgive someone when Chloe was involved taught me about forgiveness. The story is not so much about forgiveness, perhaps—since the injury was so slight—but I found it instructive in thinking about the dynamic relation between people after an injury occurs.

When Chloe was in first or second grade, we had a mother's helper named Marilyn (again, not her real name). Marilyn wasn't the sharpest tack in the box but she was reliable. She picked up Chloe after school and brought her home. One day, however, a very upset little girl came racing up the stairs to my bedroom where I was working. Marilyn was close behind her. "She disrespected me," Marilyn charged, with anger in her voice, pointing at Chloe. "You need to make her apologize."

I looked at the anguish and fear on my daughter's face and said to Marilyn, "Can you please wait outside while I talk with Chloe alone?"

Marilyn left the room as I leaned down, put my arms around Chloe and whispered in her ear. "I want you to know that I will believe absolutely whatever you tell me."

I could feel Chloe's little body relax. She told me that when Marilyn picked her up after school, she had put Chloe into the car and then stood there, insisting Chloe put on her seatbelt BEFORE Marilyn closed the door. Chloe had always been pretty bright, and she asked Marilyn—quite logically, to my way of thinking—why the seatbelt buckle needed to be snapped into place before Marilyn closed the door and walked around the car to get inside and start the engine. "Wasn't it enough to just fasten the belt before the car was started?" Chloe wondered.

Marilyn brooked no such questions, viewing them as reflecting insubordination rather than curiosity. Marilyn insisted that Chloe obey her and buckle her seatbelt immediately. Chloe needed to do as she was told, to abide by what the adult told her to do, Marilyn threatened her. When Chloe persisted in wanting to know why that was the case, Marilyn told Chloe she was disrespecting Marilyn and that she would "tell her mother" on her.

I called Marilyn back into the room, asked her to tell me her side of the story, listened and then said I thought Chloe had been right.

"Well," Marilyn replied in a huff, raising the ante in what was probably a subconscious ploy designed to get me to capitulate, "I can't work in a house where I am not respected. She needs to apologize, and you need to back me up!"

"OK," I said, and walked downstairs. I got the check book and wrote her a check.

"What's this?" Marilyn demanded.

"That's your pay, plus two weeks' severance," I replied. "I don't want you to have to work anywhere you are not fully comfortable. We'll make other arrangements. Thank you for your time."

And so we did. I don't remember what happened after that. I imagine we found someone else, someone more attuned to what Marilyn surely considered overly indulgent parenting. But I trusted my daughter. I knew she was a reasonable person, even at an early age. I thought she needed to be treated with the respect and dignity any human being should be accorded. The adult was in the wrong here. The kid was right.

Should I have forgiven Marilyn? Certainly, the injury was minor. Should I have given her another chance? That possibility never even entered my mind. Vulnerable human beings—and that is surely what children are—need to be protected and nurtured, not subjected to some idiotic adult concepts of order and discipline and respect. Treating children badly is a cardinal sin in my book. It is something unforgiveable. I think my unwillingness to excuse Marilyn and to give her a second chance was the right decision. Failing to do so would have sent the wrong signal to the child involved.

So forgiveness is a tricky thing. Having already rejected the general evolutionary approach[3] and having the impression that most psychiatrists and psychologists emphasize the impact of forgiveness on the person who is asked to forgive, I wondered about the various insights from scholars and religious authorities on ethics. As one would expect, forgiveness is a big theme in most religions. In general, Eastern religions adopt a more psychological view of forgiveness, one that asks what the act of forgiving does for the party who forgives. In contrast, the Abrahamic religions speak with more distinctly moral overtones.[4]

The Abrahamic religions—Judaism, Christianity and Islam—all partake of, indeed contributed to, the creation of what I find the general cultural attitude in the West: the idea that forgiveness is a noble deed, an act that pleases God. In contrast, the Eastern religions—Buddhism and Sikhism, for example—move toward an emphasis not on the value of forgiveness in pleasing God but rather on the impact forgiveness—or the failure to forgive—has on the wronged person, the person who does or does not forgive.[5] In general, all religions argue that forgiving will free us from the anger and bitterness that results from a failure to forgive, keeping us "back there," trapped in the role of aggrieved party.

On first blush, this view of forgiveness makes sense. But ultimately, this view creates conceptual confusion. It combines several closely related but distinct acts and lumps them all together as "forgiveness." For me, the core of forgiveness is genuinely granting pardon for an offense; the essence of forgiveness lies in absolving the offending party for having done harm. What often sneaks into the core definition of forgiveness, however, is the *logic* or *encouragement* to forgive because of its impact on those who do the forgiving. This conceptual confusion probably grew out of the Christian view of forgiveness, as an act that ennobles us and frees us of our bitterness.[6]

But we should not confuse these by-products of forgiveness with the essence of forgiveness itself. We can fail to absolve people of the harm they did and still let go of our own anger, relinquishing our bitter feelings and ceasing to feel resentment against the ones who hurt us. Abandoning or giving up our own anger and bitter feelings, in other words, can occur without forgiveness. We can maintain our belief that the other people have wounded us. We can fail—or refuse—to absolve or pardon them for their offending act and yet still move on and not be crippled by our own feelings or anger or victimization. Similarly, we may forgive people without necessarily feeling ennobled by that act.[7]

So letting go of our anger, relinquishing our bitter feelings and releasing us from the hurt, does not necessarily entail forgiving those who hurt us.

Considering what I believe is a by-product of forgiveness focuses us on the impact of holding onto a hurt, letting it fester and trapping you in the past. Anything that condemns us to relive the hurtful act and feel helpless and aggrieved is not something we should do. If you must forgive the person who hurt you in order to free yourself, then forgiveness becomes a tool of your own well-being. It creates what I would call instrumental forgiveness: an attempt to forgive in order to achieve the by-product of what everyone says is involved in forgiveness: not tying yourself down by the anger, resentment and the negativity that come with such loathing and hurt.[8]

True forgiveness—in the sense of absolving the person who hurt you, of granting them pardon for their offense—entails four key components, all equally critical.

First, the wrong must be recognized as an offense by the person who committed it. Second, the offender must acknowledge that he or she did, in fact, commit the offense. Third, there must be a sincere apology. Finally, there must be an authentic, genuine, good-faith effort to change the behavior that led to the initial injury. Only then can true forgiveness—as opposed to instrumental forgiveness—come.[9] Only then should it come.

When forgiveness involves papering over the reality of how we are made to feel about ourselves by this instrumental forgiving, then I think exonerating or absolving those who hurt us actually is harmful. It puts us on the wrong side of a thin, red line between forgiveness and tolerating ongoing abuse. When that happens, then forgiveness can keep us in friendships—or marriages or jobs or babysitters – that result in our being treated like a second-class citizen.

Friends, lovers, spouses, babysitters, colleagues, parents, all those we hold dear should make us feel better about ourselves. They should see the potential in us that we ourselves may not recognize. They should nurture that potential, laughing with us in the good times and being there—like my friend Nancy—in the tough times. If you don't get that in your relationship, if after you genuinely examine your role in this process and you conclude that your part was *not* a major contributor to the wrong, then drawing a thin red line in your emotional address book might not be a bad idea. *Au contraire*, it might be good for you. Not forgiving someone may be part of saying that you deserve better treatment than the treatment you received from your erstwhile friend, spouse, caregiver or parent.

Refusing to forgive someone who hurt you that deeply might actually be a step forward toward finding new people who actually *will* treat you well. Ironically, then, retaining anger—often a protective mask for hurt—may propel you to make the changes you need to move into a better situation. It can help you find friends who are more worthy of you, or a babysitter who will care better for your child. If that's the case, then forgiveness can only be a bad thing and I'm with the elephants—those magnificent creatures said never to forget— rather than all those religious leaders who preach forgiveness.

The little elephant, the one in the parlor who gave the title to the last chapter in this book, refers to our identity, our self, the person we are. That self should be protected, cherished and nurtured above all, by us and by those we love. When it is not, then we suffer.

It's one of the hardest things in the world to feel you have been let down by those you love, to feel they have not done what they should do to appreciate, esteem and protect you. Being hurt by those we trust makes us feel betrayed and wounded, confused and questioning of our own judgment, sad about ourselves, alone and embarrassed in some odd way for the loved ones whose behavior suggests they either do not understand how their actions have wounded us or they simply don't care.[10] When that occurs, that precious little elephant that represents our most vulnerable self should walk right over and sit down on the big sofa with that older elephant, the one who never forgets, and ponder the situation. Whether we decide to forgive and stay friends with the people who have hurt us, whether we keep those people in our lives, on their terms—terms that suggest the hurtful behavior may well occur again—is a thorny, complex yet delicate question. It gets mixed up with magnanimity, reconciliation, rapprochement, peaceful coexistence, or other forms of establishing some kind of ongoing ties with the person who hurt you.[11] It involves our own self-esteem, our own ability to judge reality, to make sure we are not being overly sensitive, that we have not done something to invoke the behavior we find hurtful. It partakes of fairness. It reminds us that even if someone wronged us, that wrong does not make it okay for us to be unethical to them. Nor should our hurt blind us to the fundamental responsibilities of social communication; we must remind ourselves that we are all imperfect communicators and cannot expect someone else to read our minds and know when we are vulnerable or feeling especially sensitive. The act of forgiving, then, should be set in the context of the possibility that we may have misunderstood, misinterpreted, or misappropriated the cause of our suffering.

Whether we trust the other person enough to tell them they have hurt us and give them the chance to apologize, explain and perhaps "fix" it in future is a tough judgment call to make, especially when one is upset and emotionally bruised. But at the very least, it's not at all clear that forgiveness is always the best way to rise above our hurts, be free of the pain, or the way to a more noble character. Sometimes forgiveness can just mean subjecting yourself to more of the same abuse, and that's certainly not a good thing.[12]

When that's the case, I'd move beyond "forgive and forget" and try out another well-known adage: "Living well is the best revenge."

REFERENCES AND FUTURE READINGS

Bstan-'dzin-rgya-mtsho, Dalai Lama XIV, Thupten Jinpa and Śāntideva. 1997. *Healing Anger: The Power of Patience from a Buddhist Perspective.* Ithaca, NY: Snow Lion Publications.

Digeser, Peter. 2001. *Political Forgiveness.* Ithaca, NY: Cornell University Press.

Duggal, Kartar Singh. 2004. *The Holy Granth Sri Guru Granth Sahib.* New Delhi: Hemkunt Publishers.

Gardner Feldman, Lily. 2012. *Germany's Foreign Policy of Reconciliation: From Enmity to Amity.* Lanham, MD: Rowman & Littlefield Publishers.

Holy Bible. 1968. New York: American Bible Society.

Maimonides, Moses. 1997. *Mishneh Torah.* Translated by Eliyahu Touger. New York: Moznaim.

Martin, Adam Bryant. 2012. "Forgiveness in an Age of Terror: The Political Psychology of Forgiving the Perpetrators of the 9/11 Attacks." Diss., University of California, Irvine.

McCullough, Michael E. 2008. *Beyond Revenge: The Evolution of the Forgiveness Instinct.* San Francisco, CA: Jossey-Bass.

Nussbaum, Martha C. 2016. *Anger and Forgiveness; Resentment, Generosity, Justice.* Oxford: Oxford University Press.

Shantideva. 2006. *The Way of the Bodhisattva: A Translation of the Bodhicharyāvatāra.* Translated by Padmakara Translation Group. Boston: Shambhala.

The Jerusalem Talmud. Talmud Yerushalmi. Seder Nezikin. Masekhtot Shevi'it Ve-'avodah Zarah. 2011. Translated by Heinrich W. Guggenheimer. Berlin: De Gruyter.

The Qur'an: A Modern English Version. 1998. Translated by Majid Fakhry. London: Garnet Publishing.

CHAPTER 4

"I GOT NOTHING!"

One of my mother's favorite stories was based on that old children's verse, "Twinkle, Twinkle Little Star." Mother's version begins with a little boy who loves the stars and wants more than anything else in the world to become an astronomer. Each night the young boy ventures out into the dark to gaze longingly at the heavens, saying, with awe and reverence, "Twinkle, twinkle, little star. How I wonder what you are."

As the boy grows older, he studies the stars in school, goes off to college and majors in astronomy. He studies for a PhD at one of the top universities and writes a pathbreaking dissertation about the stars, one that puts him at the forefront of the profession and brings him great acclaim. The boy—now a young man—feels good about himself. He has done what he started out to do. So now each evening he strides proudly into the night and looks up confidently at the stars, pronouncing with great satisfaction and a sense of fulfillment, "Twinkle, twinkle, little star. Now I know just what you are."

The young man accepts a position in a top astronomy department and continues to teach and write about the stars, advancing the field with great brilliance. He becomes an accomplished teacher, nurturing many young scholars, and achieves great fame and many honors in the process of writing his award-winning books and articles. He increasingly wears his celebrity lightly, however, driven always by his love for the stars and his desire to understand them better.

Just as the little boy grew into a young man, so the young man matures and ages. As the now distinguished but elderly gentleman nears the end of his life, he continues his nightly pilgrimages into the starry night, gazing up at the heavens and declaring, with great reverence and quiet respect, "Twinkle, twinkle, little star. How I wonder what you are!"

Mother meant this, of course, as a folksy homily on the fact that we all think we know things only to learn later that perhaps we didn't know quite as much as we thought. Humility, Mother was telling me, comes with age.

The message hit home hard, as I received comments on the essay on forgiveness from Jennifer Hochschild and Lily Gardner Feldman, both dear friends and formidable intellects, with huge hearts and the kind of sensitivity and insight into human nature that is rare. Jennifer raised the question of how our acts—in this case forgiveness—affect other people, especially the innocent bystanders who nonetheless will be directly affected by our response toward the third party who hurt us. What about children in a divorce, Jennifer wanted to know. Would they not be impacted by a husband's decision to forgive—or not to forgive—his wife for infidelity or physical abuse? What about a brother who sexually abused his sister? If the sister breaks with the brother, refusing to forgive him or to ever see him again, would this refusal not affect their parents and other siblings, each of whom would also be impacted by this decision? Do we have an obligation to consider such people—potential collateral damage, as it were—as we ponder whether to forgive someone who harmed us?

Lily took a slightly different tack, couching her comments in the context of her own extensive studies of reconciliation among states after wars (Gardner Feldman 1984, 2012). Her work analyzes German–Israeli and German–Polish relations after World War II, so her concerns, although also focused on what we do *after* an injury occurs, were directed more at the state level than between individuals. Lily's question differed slightly from Jennifer's but also touched on the aftermath of an injury: What are the alternatives to forgiveness? If one cannot—and should not—forgive, what are the other emotional pathways one might pursue if you wish to or must have some kind of an ongoing relationship?

In puzzling about the questions Lily and Jenny posed, I realized there are many dimensions to the issues posed by my dear friends. My conversations with Lily were easier to answer, but only because of Lily's generosity in sharing her wisdom gained over many years of work in the field.[1] In particular Lily helped me realize that forgiveness exists on a kind of continuum with revenge. As outlined in Lily's work, we might think of this continuum as follows:

Forgiveness–Reconciliation–Magnanimity–Rapprochement–Peaceful coexistence–Exit–Revenge.

True forgiveness—absolving the person who hurt you and granting them pardon and absolving them for their offense—lies at one extreme. Close to it is reconciliation, which occurs when two people or groups become friendly again after an argument or disagreement. (Reconciliation also can be used to describe the process by which this coming together again occurs, or even to the process by which we find a way to make two different ideas, facts, etc. coexist or be true at the same time.) With reconciliation, we need not forgive the person, but we must feel some genuine friendship and establish good ties with them again, for whatever reason. Thus, I think of reconciliation as involving some kind of active friendship and trust, which forgiveness need not include.

Coming next on the continuum is magnanimity. Magnanimity is the kind of high-minded benevolence that reveals a nobility of character and a generosity of spirit; essentially, magnanimity could be defined as being big-hearted in ignoring an injury or an insult, with no pettiness, resentfulness or vindictiveness. It implies a willingness to refrain from the enforcement of something—a debt, an obligation—that is owed one—such as the genuine apology that I suggested earlier (Chapter 3) must precede forgiveness. Magnanimity suggests someone who is patient and able to deal with a difficult person or situation without becoming angry.

Moving more toward the middle of the continuum we find *rapprochement*, a concept frequently used to discuss post-injury behavior among states or governmental actors. It is not usually applied to individual human beings. But its general conceptualization—as an establishment or reestablishment of harmonious relations—could equally well be applied to two individuals. Consider two ex-spouses who must work out *a modus vivendi* that does not harm their children, children who love both parents and who will be hurt by parents who continue to fight with each other. I think of *rapprochement* as warmer and friendlier than peaceful coexistence, but these two phenomena seem so closely related that we might think of them as going hand in hand.

Exiting a relationship—what I effectively did with my two friends and with Chloe's babysitter (Chapter 3)—means a breaking of ties between you and the person you believe hurt you.

At the extreme end of this conceptual continuum lies revenge, which involves inflicting harm on someone for the injury or wrong you—or someone you loved or value—incurred at their hands. Vengeance, reprisals, retaliation and even recriminations would fall into this general category of behavior, all designed as payback or punishment for the initial harm. I note it only for conceptual balance not for further discussion or advocacy, since none of these forms of revengeful behavior would seem to follow forgiveness, although they are, in fact, often options we find exercised in a world where forgiveness is not possible.

My conversations with Lily were extremely helpful in letting me disentangle the various aspects of potential behavior that can come after forgiveness.

But then I reflected further on the general comments from both of my friends. Their immediate concern was with forgiveness and how we interact later with the person who hurt us, especially when others are affected by our future interaction. I found this question actually part of a broader question, one that lies near the heart of ethics? That question is: *How do we relate to other people in general when there is a potential conflict between doing what is good for us and what is good for others?* Framing things this way then led to a range of related questions. How do we parse the difference between caring for ourselves and caring for others? Taking care of ourselves versus taking care of others? What do we owe ourselves? What do we owe those we love? What happens when one cannot care for one's self without harming others, and vice versa? What about people we scarcely know but whose lives can be dramatically altered by our actions? What do we want to give them, and how does this differ from what we feel or believe we owe them? What others might think we owe them? How far does their happiness influence our own? What principle can we derive—if any—that guides us as we thread the moral needle between our own needs and what we want to do to care for others?

In one sense, a subject close to and intersecting with this intellectual topic has preoccupied much of my professional existence: altruism. I started thinking about altruism in 1988, wrote my first article on it shortly thereafter, and soon found it preoccupied the next twenty some years of my academic life. Indeed, my first book on the topic—*The Heart of Altruism*—was sent out for review the month before Chloe was born; it appeared in print, shortly after Chloe came into my life, in 1996.

Chloe knew little of this, of course. But when Chloe was in fourth grade, she entered a special program called APAAS, short for Alternative Program for Academically Advanced Students. According to the website of the Irvine Unified School District:

> *APAAS students are taught in a self-contained classroom and are given opportunities to make choices about how to personally engage with the material and demonstrate their depth of understanding of the core academic content. Students successful in the Program are individuals who have an innately high level of curiosity, think outside the parameters of conventional ideas and are motivated by complex, open-ended options. The Program is constructed for students who independently handle high-level assignments, collaborate with others who are like-minded, and have a strong foundation with expressing ideas in writing.*

In practice, this meant Chloe had extra homework, was introduced to Shakespeare in fourth grade—something her parents found a mixed blessing— and got through a lot of math quite early. (An eventual history major in college, my daughter had completed AP Calculus AB by her junior year in high school.) She also learned to write beautifully at an early age, and still writes far better than do I.

As part of their instruction in writing, the spelling words for fourth grade APAAS students fell into three categories: (1) ordinary words (the ones all other students were expected to master at this grade level) (2) slightly more advanced spelling words and (3) what were called, "wonderful words" chosen from the list of words taken from the SAT exams. Chloe liked the wonderful words and came home with the first list. She proudly described the list to me and asked if she could test me on them. Quietly competitive at that age, Chloe's game was to catch up Mom by seeing if I knew what the wonderful words meant and how to spell them.

Chloe pulled the list out of her backpack. "Here's the first word on the list of wonderful words, Mom. It's altruism. Do you know what altruism is and how to spell it?"

By chance, I had just finished writing an encyclopedia entry for altruism that week. I had already published several articles and two books on altruism. People at conferences would see my badge and say, "Oh. You're the altruism lady." I would receive emails and phone calls inviting me to conferences as an expert on altruism.

I looked at my daughter's beautiful, shining face, so pleased with herself for finding a new word. Was she hoping to know more than I did here? Or would she be proud of me if I knew the word?

I decided to be honest. "I think so."

Chloe smiled. "It's a good word."

Indeed. It is a great word, one I can spell and which I have frequently defined although, in my case, I fear I have always borne a closer resemblance to the little boy or the old man than to the confident young professional in Mother's story about the astronomer.

I can tell you what I think altruism is. It is behavior designed to help another even when that behavior might entail a risk of potential harm to yourself.[2] I am more comfortable telling you what I think altruism looks like. It looks like Otto Springer, a German Czech who rescued some 100 Jews during the Holocaust before he was sent to concentration camps, where he continued to bribe guards and engage in altruistic activities whenever he could, fueled only by his compassion for others and his psychological ingenuity.[3]

It looks like Isabel B___, a woman I have never met but who is—according to the person who gave me Isabel's name—an incredibly beautiful woman. Isabel was Catholic and married someone who was Jewish back in the days when those kinds of differences still mattered.[4] Her husband's family initially disowned him because of the religious differences, and Isabel worked as a model to put her husband through college. The family eventually reconciled, and Isabel and her husband enjoyed great success in a family business that put them in touch with the rich and famous. Isabel could easily have spent her time hanging out with interesting celebrities and rich, attractive people. Instead, she started Camp Isabel to help children who were physically and emotionally abused. She was inspired in her life of charitable giving by taking what she described as a "wrong turn that turned out to be a right turn." This occurred when Isabel went to her son's school to take the party treats for a holiday. Instead of turning right into the hall leading to her son's classroom, Isabel turned left and ended up entering a classroom for what were then called the special education kids. As Isabel told me later, "When I entered the classroom, there were no decorations on the wall. No food for the kids. Nothing special for them." Isabel decided to give the special education kids the food and party favors for her son's class. Her spontaneous and kind gesture might not seem like much. Certainly, staying and giving her son's treats to other children who had nothing is hardly comparable to Otto's risking his life and enduring concentration camp. But every time I think of this story my mother's heart is touched, and I fight back tears as I imagine how difficult that must have been for Isabel to take food prepared for her own child and give it to strangers, knowing her son's class would then lack their party treats as a result.

So, when people ask me what altruism looks like, I tell them it looks like Otto Springer or Isabel B___, a woman I never met but who was kind enough to share her story with me over the telephone in a series of interviews conducted for my first book on altruism (1996).

As a good social scientist, I also can tell you what my studies suggest causes altruism. They suggest that all the critical factors we so often think of as causing altruism—education, socialization, religion— actually serve more as trigger mechanisms for what seems the central influence: a perception of a shared humanity. How we see ourselves in relation to others determines how we treat them. Where the rest of us see a stranger, an altruist sees a fellow human being. This perception of being bound together by a common humanity is the unifying theme among the different types of altruists I interviewed: philanthropists, Carnegie Hero Commission recipient winners, and the Yad Vashem medalists who risked their lives and those of their families to save Jewish strangers during World War II. This altruistic perspective is what separated them from the rational actors I interviewed, and what made them altruists.

But what do I really know about altruism after a professional lifetime of studying it, of listening for hours to life stories told to me by altruists like Otto and Isabel? I'm still not sure about so many of the basic questions that initially drove me to study altruism. I know that altruism is important because it can inspire feats of moral courage, such as Otto's rescue of Jews during the Holocaust. Altruism can move us to everyday acts of kindness that can change a child's life, as Isabel's did when she established a summer camp for physically and mentally- abused children.

I can tell you that altruism matters as well because it challenges the basic assumptions of so much political and social theory that is based on the self-interest assumption. In this sense, altruism is a powerful reminder that we need to modify our basic theories of political life. A politics based only on benefit/cost analyses that assume everyone wants more—wants more prestige, money, fame, or the material goods that, indeed, most of us do want more of—this kind of politics forgets that we also want to be happy, and that happiness partakes of more than just the material. Happiness is about our material and professional well-being, yes. But it also is about others and about how we treat others and are treated by them in turn. In this regard, altruism signifies because it reminds us that we should think about what we want and need to flourish as human beings, and how a great part of that is living in a community with others whom we help flourish and prosper as human beings. If we think only of ourselves, and ignore others, we lose much of the richness in life that comes from human relations.

But despite all this knowledge, accumulated so carefully over the years, the most important things about altruism continue to elude me. Why do we do it? Why do I do it? What do I owe to other people? What do I genuinely *want* to do, want to do not because I feel obligated to do it but simply *because*?

Sometime after *The Heart of Altruism* received some small notoriety, I was being interviewed on a show on National Public Radio. As any academic worth her salt can tell you, after giving a fair number of talks and thinking about your subject matter for a long time, a good scholar gets to the point where she can anticipate most of the questions that will be posed. We even develop standard answers to some of these basic questions in order to succinctly make the main point. But this day the interviewer asked me a question that surprised me. "Have you ever saved anyone's life?" she asked.

I was totally taken aback and had to think a minute. I genuinely had never even thought of this question. "Actually, I guess I have. Twice." I pondered further, then continued. "Once during graduate school, I was visiting my parents during the summer. Mom and Dad live on a lake and I was sitting on the little dock that extended out into the water. I was busy talking with Mother, the next-door neighbor, and the neighbor's daughter and grandson. I don't remember much of what happened, it was all so quick. But I do remember that the neighbor's daughter had a grandson who was a baby, probably about nine months old, lying on a blanket. I remember seeing the baby rolling toward the edge of the dock and then I don't remember anything except my being in the water with the baby and the mother screaming. But I cannot remember anything that happened in between. No thought process, no calculation of action, nothing. I can't even remember jumping in the water or how I got the baby in my arms."

"So," my NPR host asked, pressing the point, as would any good interviewer. "What caused you to move so quickly?"

"I really don't recall. It was totally spontaneous, I suppose." I had to smile. "I guess it did happen as I described it in my book." Then truthfulness and frankness kicked in. "But I have to add that it really wasn't a big deal. I didn't think I did anything heroic or especially good. Truly. I'm a good swimmer. The lake is not very deep there, not more than nine or ten feet perhaps. There was not any danger for me. But I wear contact lenses and never open my eyes under water, especially not in a lake. If you asked me now, I'd say that because of that I would not be the right person to jump in a dark lake to make the rescue because I'm pretty much blind as a bat without my lenses in, so I wouldn't have even been able to see a child in opaque lake water. But none of that went through my head. I just did it."

The interviewer asked me about the second incident. I had the same response.

"The same thing occurred. It was during grad school when I was visiting a friend in NYC. I was standing on a street corner near the Plaza Hotel and realized the lady next to me was starting to walk out into the traffic just as I saw a car coming around the corner. I instinctively reached out and grabbed her back. She gave me a dirty look and said something like, "What the hell?!" in surprised anger. But she calmed down after I explained that a car had been about to hit her had she walked into the street. This, too, was not a big deal. As witness by the fact that I have never even thought of either of these events till you mentioned them just now."

My answer partook of much that I had found in studying other people's altruism. In neither instance could I remember thinking at all before I acted. There was no conscious thought. It was totally spontaneous. As Otto had said to me in explaining his many acts of altruism—far more interesting and significant than my two little, tiny acts of nothing, except perhaps for the people saved— "The hand of compassion was faster than the calculus of reason."

Nor did I think my acts were at all significant. Just as all my altruists had insisted their acts were "no big deal, nothing special", so did I define my little acts of altruism as insignificant trifles, so paltry that I had never even thought of them as altruism until an interviewer whose name I have now forgotten embarrassed me on national public radio show by asking about my own acts of altruism.

So, what made me do it? Why then and not some other time? It certainly wasn't duty. It wasn't driven by religion since I am not a religious person. I didn't know the people involved; indeed, I cannot now even remember their names. I never knew the name of the woman in New York, never saw her again. I didn't expect any praise; even retelling the story here seems immodest, and that embarrasses and disconcerts me for I do not want praise for something I do not deserve. And so on.

Even my two little personal excursions into the land of altruism left me clueless as to why then and not other times and what caused me to do it. I am similarly at a loss concerning virtually all the other important acts of kindness performed toward others. Why do I go the distance with some people and not others? Why am I sometimes moved to give money, and not at other times?

All this went through my head as I thought of the questions raised by my friends Jennifer and Lily, and reflected on the more basic question they raised: "How do we deal with people who will be hurt by our actions, even actions that may be good for us and good from a general ethical point of view?"

I had only one response. "I've studied this for thirty-plus years now and I got nothing!"

I have no answer to Jennifer's questions about how to behave after a divorce, when your desire to avoid your former spouse may hurt your children. No counsel for a friend who has been sexually or even verbally abused by a parent and wants to know whether she should break with the parent, refuse to help the parent in the parent's old age or cut ties entirely, knowing that doing so probably will hurt her siblings because of that rupture. No advice for a divorcee who was beaten by her spouse and wonders how to handle future interactions involving their children. I have no answer to statesmen who ask, after a brutal war has ended, whether it is "better" to forgive and move on or to have trials that will bring the guilty to justice, or attempt to do so.

After 30-plus years of studying altruism, I end by having no way at all to tell you how to figure out what to do when taking an action that is good for you—an action that is otherwise ethical and moral—yet will hurt others. No advice for any of the complicated acts that involve others, not just those immediately involved in the primary interaction.

In my own life I've erred in both directions. Sometimes I did what was right for me, and then felt guilty for hurting someone else, especially when it was someone innocent. (Collateral damage, as it were, is a concept that may work well in statecraft but which leaves me personally unsatisfied.) Sometimes I put my own needs aside, failing to take proper care of myself in order to help someone else, only to learn later that my sacrifice was not necessary, that the other person actually didn't care that much, would not have been harmed at all, or harmed so minimally that their harm became virtually irrelevant. That situation left me feeling foolish, like some crazy, misguided martyr.At other times, I've made a sacrifice and it was appreciated. In this last case, my feelings were more mixed.

After a lifetime of studying altruism, a lifetime of trying to figure out how best to deal with those who may or will be hurt by our acts, I still don't understand the essentials. The heart of altruism eludes me. I remain as humbled by the little knowledge I have gained as the old astronomer in Mother's story, as intrigued as the young child who wanted to understand the stars.

The best I can do is tell you to talk with friends, with people you know and love and respect. This is probably appropriate advice for a book on ethics since ethics is, after all, something each of us must figure out for ourselves. Talking and thinking about difficult ethical issues with those we trust is a good way to gain that self-knowledge. (It is also advice that partakes of that timeless cop-out, used by faculty and parents everywhere, when faced with a question for which they have no answer: we tell our class or our children that it is a question only the student or child can answer.) The examining life, again, must be examined by the person who lives the life, not by some outside observer.

So, with apologies, let me end with one of my favorite stories, from "*The West Wing*."[5]

"This guy's walkin' down a street when he falls in a hole. The walls are so steep he can't get out. A doctor passes by and the guy shouts up, "Hey doc! Can you help me out?" The doctor writes a prescription, throws it down in the hole, and moves on.

Then a priest comes along, and the guy shouts up, "Father, I'm down in this hole; can you help me out?" The priest writes out a prayer, throws it down in the hole and moves on.

Then a friend walks by. "Hey, Joe, it's me. Can ya' help me out?" And the friend jumps in the hole. Our guy says, "Are ya' stupid? Now we're both down here."

The friend says, "Yeah, but I've been down here before and I know the way out."

If ethics is about self-examination, then being puzzled—even troubled—by ethical dilemmas is not surprising. Talking about these difficult issues with those you respect and trust may be a good idea. Be grateful you have friends.

Other than that, I got nothing!

REFERENCES AND FUTURE READINGS

Gardner Feldman, Lily. 1984. *The Special Relationship between West Germany and Israel.* Winchester, MA: Allen & Unwin.

———— 2012. *Germany's Foreign Policy of Reconciliation: From Enmity to Amity.* Lanham, MD: Rowman & Littlefield Publishers.

Monroe, Kristen Renwick. 1996. *The Heart of Altruism: Perceptions of a Common Humanity.* Princeton, NJ: Princeton University Press.

————. 2004. *The Hand of Compassion.* Princeton, NJ: Princeton University Press.

Sandel, Michael. 2012. *What Money Can't Buy: The Moral Limits of Markets.* New York: Farrar, Straus and Giroux.

CHAPTER 5

"IT'S AN IMPORTANT POLITICAL PROBLEM. I SHOULD KNOW ABOUT IT." AGENCY

Like most offsprings of academics, my children have grown up frequenting scholarly conferences. A 3-month-old Alexander nursed in Rio de Janeiro and slept through a band playing the Brazilian national anthem at his first meeting of the International Political Science Association. As he neared his first birthday, Alex practiced walking up and down the steps of the Palmer House in Chicago during meetings of the Midwest Political Science Association; he attended later meetings while he was in high school, and was thrilled when two attractive, young, female graduate students from Oxford asked if he were writing his dissertation yet. .

Nik went on several job interviews with me. He freaked out an elderly faculty member who wasn't quite sure he was ready for a breast-feeding colleague, and was dragged to Lund, Sweden, as a teenager, not quite sure he still wanted to travel with his parents.

But it was Chloe who took in the most travel, happily logging the miles with her parents as she became an academic conference baby. In Chloe's case, the acronym was ISPP-baby, for the International Society of Political Psychology.[1]

During this time, I should note, it was never clear who was really in charge. My academic conferences may have set the venue, but it was Chloe who defined the vacations. There was the ice cream and aquarium tour of Northern Europe. This was the year the ISPP met in Berlin, but we remember it as time structured around Chloe's love of sea urchins, dolphins, porpoises and whales. We saw every fish in every aquarium in Northern Europe, and Chloe suckered her parents into ice cream every chance she got. The ice-cream part of the tour climaxed in Norway when, after taking the night train from Oslo to Bergen, we were so exhausted we took turns sleeping and touring with Chloe during that first day. At dinner that night, as Chloe asked for ice cream for dessert,

I said, "This will make twice today. You had ice cream this afternoon after the aquarium, remember?"

"Ice cream with Mom?" my husband demanded. "You had ice cream with me this morning!"

Chloe just smiled; she got her third ice cream for dessert at dinner.

In 2009, Chloe accompanied me to Dublin for the ISPP meetings, where we stayed at Trinity College. For those not familiar with it, Trinity College is lovely. It was founded in 1592 by the first Queen Elizabeth to educate the Irish Protestants who—the bitter joke ran—graduated from Trinity College and simply walked across the street to the Parliament, taking their place as rulers of their country, keeping the Catholics oppressed and out of government and power. Trinity College thus was quite old; fortunately, it had been renovated and hence sported quite modern interiors. We had a brand-new shower in the bathroom of the student apartment we shared. Both Chloe and I had individual bedrooms, always useful when travelers are jet lagged and on slightly different schedules. There was one large living–dining–kitchen area, which was open concept and lovely, with views of the original quad.

We spent most of our time in that light-filled room on the fourth floor, and Chloe and I had a great time, curled up on the sofa (Chloe) and a rollaway bed (me) placed in the living room. The view from our window faced the other seventeenth-century buildings in the college and Chloe was fascinated by the figures carved on the building across from ours.[2] We noticed that one of the stone adornments—gargoyle or Greek vase with flowers in it; we were never sure but opted for the former—on the building opposite us was wrapped, whether as part of repairs or to keep it from disintegrating, we never learned.

I had meetings that Chloe attended, or she stayed in the room and read a history book in preparation for her AP history course that fall. But I also had signed us up for some of the side trips that the ISPP coordinated as part of its program and we walked and walked—and walked!—throughout the city, often in the rain, on excellent tours conducted by guides who were professional historians who presented impressively thorough and thoughtful historical analyses of the Irish political situation. Chloe soaked it up and was hungry for more, as was I. We were hoping for a Thursday arrival of Chloe's elder brother, so I had not signed us up for the Saturday tour of Belfast. I had visited Belfast in the early 1980s during one of the recent spikes in the ongoing political troubles in Northern Ireland. The city remained etched in my memory as bleak and foreboding, filled with too many checkpoints and guns pointed at unwary tourists.

As the conference was winding down on Friday, my daughter asked if we were going on the tour to visit Belfast. "No," I replied. I explained that I had thought Alex might be joining us that day and had thought we would be more interested in each other's company than in tourism.

Chloe nodded. She understood. But then she looked me right in the eye and my ever so shy, gentle daughter raised the question of visiting Belfast. "It's an important political problem. I should know about it."

Shy and quietly gentle, yes. But her words suggested to me a tremendous sense of agency. Was what I thought of as "agency" simply the sense that she mattered? Certainly that. It might also have been that she felt she possessed some slight ability to have an impact on events in the world. Or perhaps just that she was a person of worth, of value, someone who counted and thus who should be informed about what was happening in a critical part of the world, irrespective of whether she would ever be called upon to act on that particular problem.

Whatever it was, I was very proud of her and we went to Belfast the next day.

We did not go on the ISPP-arranged tour but on our own, taking the day train. The train was filled with well-dressed women, many of them middle aged and quietly talking or reading. As we gazed out at the beautiful countryside, I leaned over and asked one of the women if she would tell me as we approached the border.

"We crossed the border a long time ago, love," she replied.

No guns. No check points. Nothing. Just green.

We spent the rest of the day roaming around Belfast, took a tour of the area where "the troubles" had occurred and noted that the tour guides were decidedly different from the ones in the South. Instead of offering detailed description of what had happened, who the players were, the right and wrongs analyzed in some way, the only comment was "Here's the Peace Wall" and "Everything's fine now. Used to be we had troubles but that's all over now." The phrase suggested to me that the troubles were still so raw that no one dared scratch the wound, lest it open or fester. We stayed for the day, and then I noticed the area downtown was feeling a bit dodgy—seedy, an American would say—and we judged it prudent to head back to the train station, grabbing fish and chips wrapped in brown paper, to eat on the return to Dublin.

Chloe's request to visit Belfast stuck with me, however, and made me think about agency and what it involves. Agency is a concept, used frequently by both philosophers and social scientists, to indicate the capacity of an agent to act in a world. The actor may be a fictitious character (Elizabeth Bennett in *Pride and Prejudice*) or an institution (The League of Nations in pre-World War II) and not need be "real." (Alas, for all of us Austen lovers, Elizabeth and Mr. Darcy do not exist). Having the capacity to act need not necessarily imply a specific moral dimension related to the ability to make a choice to act, moral agency being a separate concept. But the concept of human agency implies the capacity for human beings to make choices and to impose those choices on the world. Human agency thus is frequently contrasted to natural forces (such as gravity or the pull of a tide) which are causes involving only unthinking, deterministic processes. In this regard, agency would be subtly but distinctly different from the concept of free will, which philosophers and theologians will debate over but which I—an untutored novice—think of as a philosophical doctrine holding that our choices are not the result of causal chains but are significantly free or undetermined.

In contrast to this view, human agency makes the uncontroversial and weaker claim that humans actually do make decisions and act them out in the world. The process of *how* human beings come to make decisions—whether by free choice or some other process—remains another issue, one I do not address here.

It is significant that the capacity of a human being to act as an agent is highly personal to that particular individual. Hence Chloe's assertion that the Northern Irish political situation was a political problem that was important *for her* to know about was structured in a deeply personal sense. Chloe was not claiming that everyone must know about it; merely that it was important *for her* to know about it. As the illustration of Chloe and the trip to Belfast demonstrates, considerations of the outcomes that result from particular acts of human agency—for Chloe and for others—can invest a moral component in a given situation where an agent has acted; doing so brings in moral considerations and involves us in the concept of moral agency.

Whenever a situation is the consequence of human decision-making, people such as Chloe may have the duty to apply value judgments to the consequences of their decisions. They thus become responsible for those decisions. Human agency entitles—perhaps even obligates—observers such as Chloe to ask, if only to themselves, *"Should this have occurred?"* in a manner that would be ridiculous to ask in circumstances that lack human decisions makers, such as whether it should rain every day in Belfast, as it does in Dublin.

I first was struck by the importance of agency when I did work on bystanders, rescuers and perpetrators during World War II and the Holocaust (Monroe 1996, 2004, 2012). Bystanders saw themselves as weak individuals who could not make a difference in the world. When asked what they did during World War II and whether they helped save anyone—such as Jews or allied airmen— they would look at me in amazement, and say: "But what could I do? I was one person, alone against the Nazis."

Rescuers told a quite different story. In explaining their acts to save Jews— usually at great risk to themselves and to their families—they would also look at me in some bewilderment, and say: "But what else could I do? They were human beings like you and me."

The same puzzlement. The same lack of choice. But quite different conceptualizations of themselves in relation to others and tremendously different views of themselves in terms of their own assessments of their ability to make a difference in the world. One rescuer—whose cousin was a bystander—had been condemned to death by the Nazis and was living in hiding. He thus has precious few resources. No job, no home even. Yet he insisted that there is *always* something you can do to help others. In contrast, his bystander cousin, who lived in a large house, with economic affluence and the resultant material resources, nonetheless insisted there was nothing she could do to help anyone. Her sense of agency, her estimation of her own ability to affect the world and its happenings, or even to shape her own life, was so low that she saw no options for herself, no possibility to help anyone. She was simply someone to whom events happened. She had no control over them or their outcomes. She was what philosophers would call low on agency.[3]

The Nazi supporters also differed in terms of agency. Unlike the rescuers, however, the Nazis I talked with viewed themselves not as free agents or even as individuals who mattered but rather as individuals pushed along on the winds of history, by forces beyond their comprehension let alone control. To count, they had to be "in harmony" with the *zeitgeist*, the defining spirit of the times as captured by the critical ideas and beliefs of that time. They thought of their acts not as acts by individual agents who could make a difference. No. Even as individuals, they mattered only to the extent to which they were in tune with the greater forces: Greater Germany, the Fatherland, the Fuhrer.[4]

I found that a sense of agency and how we think about it can carry great moral implications. It plays an important role in our perceptions of who we are and what we can do in this world. I think it relates closely to self-esteem, hence my pleasure in seeing my shy girl have such a quiet determination to take action—even if so trivial a one as visiting a formerly troubled area—to ensure she would receive what she needed to be who she was, the person she felt that she wanted to grow into, the human being she wanted to become. Feeling that one matters in the world, that it is imperative for one to be informed about what Chloe acknowledged were "important political problems" surely has something to do with one's own sense of self-worth. How can I help if I am not a creature of worth, a being of some consequence myself?

I again saw how critical this sense of self was when Chloe attended another vacation organized around yet another ISPP meeting, this one in Barcelona circa 2006. As part of that trip, we visited the Dordogne Valley, a place I had never visited before but one that was a favorite of my father's. (One of the few times Daddy even attempted to bribe me—and then I'm sure it was mostly in jest—was in college, when he offered to pay for a wedding and honeymoon trip to the Dordogne Valley for me and the lucky husband-to-be if we would forego the expense of what my father rejected as the American tradition of large, bourgeois weddings.)

The husband of one of my favorite students—now deceased—was living in the Dordogne Valley and we visited her widower and his new wife for a few days after the ISPP's Barcelona conference. The scenery in the Dordogne was lovely—lots of sunflowers, as I recall—but hot and muggy. Very muggy. On one of our excursions, we ended up in an open-air café with wonderful food and overlooking a beautiful, scenic countryside, highlighted by a bucolic, picturesque sheep meadow. Unfortunately, after we had found a table at the charmingly rustic restaurant and placed our orders, we realized the lovely meadow was filled not just with the picture-perfect sheep but also with the sheep dung and the flies that soon follow thereafter. Most of the restaurant customers were simply ignoring the flies, putting up with what felt to me and my husband like an incredible and unhealthy invasion of vermin, hovering suspiciously close to their food.

Both of the spoiled Americans complained bitterly, wondering out loud, if discreetly, how people could put up with so many flies. Chloe did not complain a bit. She simply got up, carried her plate with her and walked slowly around the table as she ate, her movement just enough to deter the flies and hence allow Chloe to eat in comfort but without the irritation, frustration and the grumbling in which her parents were engaging.

Only 12 at the time, Chloe already had more sense and good grace than her parents, and a tremendous awareness that she could take charge of her destiny and shape it in a way that was acceptable to her. It was not consciously thought out. It probably was not even something she was aware of at the time. But there it was. Agency.

REFERENCES AND FUTURE READINGS

Conrad, Joseph. 1899. *The Heart of Darkness*. London: Blackwood's Magazine (3 installments).

Kernis, Michael H. (ed.). 1995. *Efficacy, Agency, and Self-Esteem*. New York: Springer.

Koestler, Arthur. 1943. *Arrival and Departure*. New York: MacMillan.

Monroe, Kristen Renwick. 1994. *The Heart of Altruism: Perceptions of a Common Humanity*. Princeton, NJ: Princeton University Press.

———.2004. *The Hand of Compassion*. Princeton, NJ. Princeton University Press.

———. 2012. *Ethics in an Age of Terror and Genocide*. Princeton, NJ: Princeton University Press.

CHAPTER 6

NICOLE'S FATHER IS NOT GERMAN! THE MORAL SALIENCE OF DIFFERENCE[1]

My daughter Chloe and her friend Nicole were playing one afternoon when the subject of ethnic background arose. Both girls went to Turtle Rock School but Nicole was in a different classroom than Chloe, so her class had not yet done the ancestry study where students trace their family trees. Nicole was interested in the topic, nonetheless.

"Chloe's a mutt," I told Nicole.

"What's a mutt?" Nicole demanded, her 11-year-old mind not familiar with the concept.

"It means she's got a lot of different nationalities roaming around her background. Part Greek from her daddy's father. English and Scots from his mother. And just about everything from Northern Europe plus a teeny bit of Cherokee on my side."

Nicole thought about this a moment.

"You're a mutt, too," I continued.

Now Nicole was paying close attention. "How do you know that?" she quickly demanded.

"Because I know your mother's mother is French and your dad is part English and part German."

Nicole's face froze, her retort sharp and indignant.

"My father is NOT German! He's art history! He's chair of the department!"

Raised in an academic ghetto, by a father who indeed was chair of the art history department and a mother who was both an art history professor and associate dean of humanities, Nicole's outraged protest reflected her particular worldview, her knowledge of what was important for academics' kids: academic disciplines. Nicole did not care a hoot about ethnic, racial, religious, or national backgrounds. But little Nicole, so seldom party to the

69

social science dinner table conversations that too often bored Chloe, as a child of a political scientist and a lawyer, illustrates several important concepts that all academics and, indeed the populace as a whole, should incorporate into their discussions of race, ethnicity and group politics more generally: the concept of moral salience, which I define as the psychological process by which differences between people and groups become deemed ethically and politically relevant.[2] Doing so will have profound effects on our discussions of differences. It will heighten our awareness of the social construction of the political and moral significance of differences, and reveal how the framing of our discussions of such differences will shape prejudice, discrimination and the treatment of such different groups.

Let me expand on this, beginning with my experience with Chloe and Nicole.

For an academic's child, disciplines matter. Disciplines are what allocate resources. They are the divisions around which passions cleave. Few in American academia notice, let alone care, if their colleagues are French, Brazilian or Chinese.

Nor do academics care much about religion now that anti-Semitism has (thankfully) become largely a thing of the past.[3] A religious colleague tells us she is reluctant to talk about her Roman Catholic faith, however, and Islam has now become controversial on many campuses, as in the country at large. So the bad old days are not behind us. But overall, what is relevant in academia is field, your area of specialization and perhaps your methodological approach. Faculty brats thus are not raised to think in terms of racial, ethnic, religious or national prejudice. These differences are simply not relevant for them. They carry no moral salience.

My elder son, Alex, went off to a summer program at the University of Chicago the summer before his senior year in high school. During the orientation period, Alex was approached by a young, rather attractive fellow student, who told him her name and introduced herself as being from New York City and "just your ordinary JAP."

Alex was taken aback. Although Alex had been born in Manhattan, he had been raised in California and had no idea what JAP meant. "Ah, you don't look Japanese," he stammered, "and why would you call yourself that?" the sweet young man asked, not realizing how naïve he sounded.

"Jewish American Princess!" the young woman threw back at him. "What planet are you from?"

Like all my children, Alex had essentially been raised in a university ghetto. A bubble, Chloe calls it, a bubble populated by children from all parts of the globe and comprising most of the ethnicities, languages, religions, gender preferences, and skin tones known to man. So, the view of the world—what is "natural"—to a child from University Hills may look quite different than it does to most of the rest of the world.

Indeed, Alex phoned home his first year at college to tell us that there were "none of my people" at Chicago when he first arrived.

"What do you mean?" we asked, confused.

"There are no Asians here," Alex explained.

We assured Alex that there probably were, in fact, a fair number of Asian students at the University of Chicago; there just weren't as high a proportion as there were in his honors or AP classes at University High school, or on UCI's campus itself, with its 54 percent Asian population. And, then we gently reminded Alex, "You're not Asian."

His rejoinder was quick and to the point. "I know. But they're my people." And so they were, with Alex eventually majoring in East Asian History.

Alex was able to choose his *people*, select the group with which he wanted to affiliate, the people with whom he wished to associate, to spend time with. That's as it should be. We all should be able to determine how we define ourselves; we should not be restricted in this self-definition, as long as how we do that does not hurt ourselves or others. (John Stuart Mill again.)

When Chloe visited colleges, she was impressed by the girls at Bryn Mawr because they told her that the most important thing Bryn Mawr wanted you to do there was to figure out who you were. The college encouraged that individual questioning, growth and self-definition, in a wide range of areas. Chloe liked that and, even though she told me she initially sometimes felt like the straight, blond-haired girl from California, she mainly felt free to develop her own sense of who she is, find her own way, whatever that way may be, and shift and carve out her own identity, with the support of those around her.

I wish our political discussions of identity in American politics could reflect such concern for individual freedom and self-definition. Even in American political science as a discipline, I find an odd confusion between group politics and what is known as identity politics. There is a surprising tone in our discussions of differences, one that implies that the group distinctions that currently dominate American politics exist because they reflect some immutable dissimilarity between groups in our society.

I accept that variations among people exist, and that some of these distinctions indeed may even be immutable. But this is not the critical factor in ethics or in politics. What matters is the political and moral salience we accord these differences.

The salience—the ethical or political relevance of a difference—is what is central in how we treat others. Why do certain societies sometimes judge religion to be relevant for how we treat people? Why not make it mathematical ability? Why does the color of my skin matter politically, but not my ability to speak a language or manage money? Why are linguistic differences sometimes politically significant, while athletic abilities are not?[4] There are so many ways in which people differ; why do we as a group decide some of these differences carry political or ethical importance, but not others? The designation of one characteristic as politically pertinent is totally and artificially constructed by society; in reality, the treatment of a difference is often constructed by a small group within that society or culture.

To be clear, social constructions are not necessarily easy to break. We speak of countries—such as France or Germany—as if they had always existed. Yet when we consult any historical atlas, it is immediately evident that countries come and go. Even the very concept of a nation is socially constructed, a concept created by human beings.[5] States do not exist in the same way mosquitoes exist.

Nor does race. We speak of race as if it existed, with skin color denoting some kind of difference that is permanent, immutable. Yet from a biological point of view, we are all members of the same race: the human race.[6]

Kids get this. Both Nik and Chloe at some point in their early years came in and asked if they were black. They simply had no clue what it meant to speak of a "black person." Try explaining to a 5-year-old why some people got to designate some physical differences as ones that justified oppression and inequality.[7] When you attempt that, it is immediately clear how foolish it is to accept as a given that the differences we grow up assuming are ethically relevant are cast in stone and must condemn us as a society to ongoing prejudice.

Is prejudice inevitable? Does it have to exist? Must we have an in-group and an out-group? One of the best social science theories that speaks to the important question of prejudice against other groups—reflected so concisely by Nicole in her rejection of her father as German—is social identity theory.

Social identity theory was formulated by Henri Tajfel, a Polish Jew born in 1919. Interested in studying chemistry, Tajfel was Jewish and thus prohibited from studying chemistry in Poland, so he went to France and studied at the Sorbonne. When World War II broke out, Tajfel enlisted in the French army and was captured by the Germans. Miraculously, Tajfel survived but after the war he returned to Poland to find all his family and most of his friends had perished in the Holocaust. Deeply affected by this loss, Tajfel initially worked for the United Nations, mostly helping resettle Jewish orphans. After Tajfel married Anna-Sophie Eber—herself a German Jew who had moved to Britain before the war—he, too, relocated to Britain. In 1951 Tajfel enrolled at Birkbeck College, University of London, where he studied psychology. He was graduated and worked as a lecturer, first at that university and then at Oxford. It was at Oxford where Tajfel examined several different areas of social psychology, including nationalism, social judgment and the cognitive aspects of prejudice.

So Tajfel comes of age during the Holocaust. His entire life, both personally and professionally, is changed by it. Because most of his family and friends perished in the Holocaust, Tajfel had deeply personal reasons for wanting to understand what had allowed the Holocaust to happen, especially in Germany. Other postwar scholars joined Tajfel in their response to the war. They were—quite naturally—aghast at what had happened and attempted to determine why and how such an event could happen in Germany, previously considered a wonderfully civilized, advanced nation, with a great tradition of learning and culture.[8]

Much of the first work on this question—"Why did the Holocaust happen in Germany?"—came from psychologists—such as Theodor Adorno—who stressed personality factors.[9] The Germans, so one theory ran, were more authoritarian than were other nationals, and hence would be more inclined to follow orders.

Tajfel disagreed, and rejected this explanation. His personal experience had shown him how large numbers of Germans—not just Germans with personalities of a particular type—happily gave their support to Nazism. To Tajfel, the Nazis would not have been successful were it not for the support of "ordinary" Germans. Tajfel's work on social judgment led him to ask whether the roots of prejudice might originate not in extreme personality types but rather in the "ordinary" processes of thinking. Thus, began thousands of studies, by Tajfel and his students, such as John Turner, designed to try to decipher the psychological basis of the kind of prejudice and discrimination at the heart of the Holocaust.[10] The first step, for Tajfel and his students, was the belief that people naturally categorize.

Tajfel noted what he called an inherent psychological need to eventually identify and associate with certain groups. These Tajfel called in-groups. Associating with a particular group plays an important psychological function in bolstering our sense of who we are and how we feel about ourselves. We have complex identities, Tajfel reasoned, and sort ourselves and others into categories. We label people as members of diverse groups. These groups then are juxtaposed in pairs. We classify people as men or women, young or old, rich or poor, friend or foe, or, in the instance that initially motivated Tajfel's work, the Nazi classification of Jew or Aryan.

As part of this process by which we think about ourselves, we compare our in-groups with other so-called out-groups, and demonstrate a favorable bias toward the group to which we belong. This phenomenon is evident in Nicole's outrage stemming from the fact that her father was being recategorized out of what she had been taught to think of as a desired group: art historians.

Tajfel's social identity theory thus roots prejudice, discrimination and the violence that can result from it in an innate psychological need for distinctiveness, self-esteem and belonging. We naturally form groups and then we desire our group identity to be both distinct from and compared positively with that of other groups. The critical intellectual traction of social identity theory lies in establishing a clear link between the psychological and sociological aspects of group behavior, in effectively linking the micro-level psychological need to distinguish, categorize and compare ourselves with the broader social phenomenon of group behavior.[11]

The theoretical claims of social identity theory have been substantiated in thousands of experiments conducted by Tajfel and his students in what became known as the Bristol School of Social Psychology.[12] The classic experiment takes a group of previously unconnected individuals and randomly assigns them to group A, B or C. Everyone in group A is then offered option 1 or 2. Option 1 will give all members of group A $5, all members of group B $10 and all members of group C $15. Under option 2, all members of group A will lose $5, all members of group B will lose $10 and all members of group C will lose $15. As we might expect, most members of group A (roughly two-thirds) will take option 1, which gives money to the members of their group and to the other groups as well. Everyone gains in Option 1. But with a surprising consistency, roughly one-third of the members of group A will choose option 2, the option that costs them money. Tajfel's explanation? Under option 2, members of group A indeed lose money but so does everyone else. The critical factor in their decision-making is that members of Group A do better than all the other groups. Their need to do better than others, to feel superior in some way, trumps their need to actually do better in objective terms.[13]

I've conducted this experiment informally in several classes, and it almost always comes out as Tajfel would have predicted. I was invited to speak at Nik's fifth grade class in one of those school visitations where children's parents are invited into class to describe what work they do. I decided to use the Tajfel experiments to convey what a political scientist/political psychologist does. I asked the fifth graders to line up around the room and I randomly designated them as an A, a B or a C. Then I offered them the two options Tajfel developed. The students in the fifth grade AAPAS class at Turtle Rock School followed the same general experiment outlined by Tafjel and his colleagues. Roughly one-third of the little fifth graders cared less about getting money and more about doing better than their friends.

The key here is the random, arbitrary assigning of people to groups. The groups themselves are not "real" or inherent or immutable. Once you are put into a group, however, you find shared interests and identity. There is nothing inherently in common that you share; the collective sense of identity is totally and artificially created by the external experimenter, in this case Nicholas's mother. But in the "real world" these categories are often just as artificial. (Who was a Tutsi and who a Hutu in Rwanda-Burundi during their ethnic cleaning? Who was a Jew and who an Aryan in the Third Reich? This distinction was often quite artificial, with much intermarriage and many people classified as Jewish who were totally secular, and for whom being Jewish was a minor part of their identities before the Nazi period.) It is important to remember here that groups do not automatically flow from preexisting differences; often group identity can be artificially created. The artificially created group precedes the discovery of a common difference and the creation of its political and ethical salience.

I think the Tajfel framework provides a valuable beginning point for understanding how important both real and perceived differences can become when encounters between individuals are conceptualized as encounters between group members. For Nicole and for Chloe, the relevant out-group would be those greedy people in the biological or hard sciences, as they hear their academic parents grumble about resources going to the biological or the physical science end of the campus. (Worse, the Medical School!)

Fortunately, most members of the Schools of Humanities or the Social Sciences do not rise up and slay all the hard scientists on campus. So why do others kill, or at least engage in prejudicial treatment of some "different" groups, as opposed to others? Why did the Nazis pick the Jews? The homosexuals? The gypsies to exterminate? Why not choose the munitions makers? The Lutherans? Why do these—but not other—differences get selected as politically relevant?

Beyond this, what makes neighbors—people who are members of different religious or ethnic groups but who have lived together in peace, often for centuries—suddenly find these differences politically and ethically germane?[14] This was the case with many Jews and their Aryan neighbors during World War II. It occurred in the former Yugoslavia, where Muslims, Orthodox Christians and Roman Catholic Christians suddenly found these differences mattered, in this case because of events that had occurred over 600 years in the past.[15]

The interesting point for us is the extent to which many of the most frequently discussed political cleavages in America—race, religion, ethnicity—assume immutability about the in-group/out-group distinctions and the hostilities associated with them. Yet we all know that there is one human race and that—as the news media repeatedly reminded us during the 2008 presidential campaign— a man from Africa can wed a woman from Kansas to produce a child who can become president of the United States of America, just as a Catholic and a Jew can marry, or a German and a Japanese, a Serbian Orthodox wed a Roman Catholic, a Hutu and a Tutsi and so on.[16] There can be friendship, affection and love across these "differences." Hostilities across the divides are not necessary.

It's interesting, biologically speaking, of course, to consider the concept of "hybrid vigor." This concept means that what is called "out-group breeding" offers reproductive advantages in the form of minimizing shared genetic inheritance or proclivity toward certain diseases. (When I had amniocentesis with my first child, my husband and I were told, with great pride by the lab technician, that we were good "maters" since we shared some, but not too many genetic similarities. It is our ethnic differences, ironically, that produce healthier offspring, from a biological point of view.) In this sense, then, what the Nazis condemned as cross-racial breeding is actually the superior genetic choice and should be encouraged by any governments engaged in any genetic manipulation to produce strong populations. (Not that I am advocating this!)

The critical question, then, is why a particular in-group/out-group combination becomes politically and ethically salient. The 2008 election year encouraged many of us to hope America could move beyond the traditional discussions of race to more substantive discussions of the meaning of such differences for all members of society. As the Trump and now the Biden–Harris years unfold, with the reemergence of white nationalist groups and events like the Black Lives Matter movement and the Derek Chauvin conviction, we would do well to ponder both the theoretical foundation and the experimental support for social identity theory. We can remind ourselves that while group differences do exist independently of politics, the political and moral salience or these groups is totally socially constructed.[17] Political leadership becomes key, with political leaders such as Donald Trump exploiting fears of differences while others such as Bernie Sanders reminding us that religious differences are personal and not a question for political discussion.[18]

This returns us to the initial question on which little Nicole picked up: the political relevance of categorization. The central nature of racial encoding as a marker for in-group versus out-group status results from particular theoretical models of categorization and learning. The social scientist in me would tell my graduate students that a classical model of behavioral conditioning, or learning, means any conditioned stimulus—like race—can be associated with any unconditioned stimulus—like fear—simply through repeated associations between the two. Such linkages can be learned vicariously, by watching the reactions of others, such as one's parents, or leaders who wish to exploit our fear of those who are "different" for the leader's own political gain.

In this way, for example, Chloe and Nicole can learn to react with outrage to out-groups who are faculty members in the biological, medical or hard sciences by witnessing their parents' reactions to them as "others" who are selfishly hogging scarce university resources. Similarly, white men can be told by politicians that this country is no longer theirs, that their political power and economic well-being are being threatened by "the others" who are coming to take over our country. This kind of model not only assumes the equipotentiality that suggests that any two stimuli are equally likely to be associated, but also assumes that fear acquisition becomes easily linked to certain categories—race, ethnicity, religion or academic disciplines—in the encoding of out-group status.[19]

Rodgers and Hammerstein said it more succinctly, and with less jargon in *South Pacific*, their award-winning play and movie about war and prejudice.[20] South Pacific features two love stories. The first is between a nurse from Arkansas, who falls in love with a dashing Frenchman. Unfortunately for Nellie the nurse, she discovers the two charming little Polynesian children that she considers "half-breeds" are children from the Frenchman's previous marriage to a Polynesian woman with dark skin.

The second love story occurs between Joe Cable—a Princeton grad from Philadelphia—who falls in love with Liat, a beautiful Polynesian girl whose Polynesian mother repels Joe. Each of the Americans is troubled by their own prejudice, and they try to explain it to others—and to themselves—in "You've got to be taught," which captures the idea that prejudice is not born into us; it happens via a slow, insidious process of socialization in which we are taught to be afraid of people who are "different." That difference can be skin tone or, the shape of one's eyes, but the end result is that we get told, at a very early age, to hate the people our relatives hate, just as Nicole reflected solidarity with the humanists because they numbered her art historian parents. This approach clearly locates the blame for prejudice on socialization. It suggests prejudice is not naturally a part of our DNA.

But doesn't the work of scholars like Tajfel, and the continuing prejudice that clouds all societies, suggest that hate and prejudice are inherent parts of our human nature? Do we just shift the group around, sometimes disliking the Jews or the blacks, other times hating Muslims or Hispanics, or being angry at the humanists or the hard scientists in physical or biological science?

No. Absolutely not. The interaction of social and endogenous factors in developing racial stereotyping and discrimination does not render such processes any more immutable than locating its origins in the processes of socialization alone. Rather, as with any complex phenomenon, the intersection of endogenous features with particular environmental cues introduces the possibility of intervention and amelioration along a wider variety of avenues.[21]

Susan Fiske's work on prejudice, social cognition, discrimination and stereotyping provides an interesting case to consider in this regard. Like Tajfel, Fiske accepts it as natural that people categorize and feel more comfortable with groups of people with whom they identify. She notes, however, that in our social interactions we are drawn to people whom we view as warm and competent, and that our perceptions here are strongly swayed by factors such as age, gender, disability and race, etc. The quick snap judgments that we make about people result in widespread stereotyping and discrimination.

One of the many fascinating aspects of Fiske's work is the extent to which views of out-groups can shift dramatically according to how the discussion about these groups is framed. So, for example, consider views on immigrants. If the discussion about an immigrant group focuses on the immigrants' taking away American jobs, then the views of immigrants will be negative. But if the discussion of the same immigrant group is framed to emphasize (1) the extent to which immigrants are performing jobs nobody who is a US citizen wants to do and (2) that the immigrant's help will increase economic growth for us, or introduce us to interesting food and cultural innovations, then attitudes toward immigrants swing noticeably favorably. The same immigrants just denigrated, are now described as cooperative, as people who share American values and goals. People feel well-disposed toward them. So, the priming of a discussion is critical. The prejudice is not necessarily destined to take a particular form.

If prejudice, stereotyping, discrimination are all malleable—and that is the view from serious scientists, such as Fiske, who study these phenomena carefully—then this makes the role of political leadership key.

The good news is that because the moral and political salience of a "difference" is totally an artifact, essentially a social construction, then we are not locked into patterns of prejudice. It is far easier to intervene to change the moral salience attached to differences than it is to change the immutable characteristics themselves, such as skin color or biological sex.[22] It is not difference that is key; it is the moral salience we attach to that difference. The prejudice, stereotyping and discrimination against any group is malleable, highly susceptible to the way in which the difference is presented to us, by the press, by our political leaders, by those we respect in our private lives.

For those of us who care about ending prejudice—be it based on race, ethnicity, gender, disability, or religious difference—and believe we can best see the common humanity in others by broadening the boundaries of those included in the community of concern, the scientific evidence provides reason for hope.[23]

REFERENCES

Cunningham, William, Marcia Johnson, Carol Raye, Chris Gatenby, John Gore and Mahzarin Banaji. 2004. "Separable Neural Components in the Processing of Black and White Faces". *Psychological Science*, vol.15, no. 12: 806–13.

Fiske, Susan T., Amy J. C. Cuddy, Peter Glick and Jun Xu. 1999. "A Model of (Often Mixed) Stereotype Content: Competence and Warmth Respectively Follow from Perceived Status and Competition". *Journal of Personality and Social Psychology*. Copyright 2002 by the American Psychological Association, Inc. 2002, vol. 82, no. 6: 878–902.

Hart, Allen J., Paul J. Whalen, Lisa M. Shin, Sean C. McInerney, Hakan Fischer, Scott L. Rauch. 2000. "Differential response in the human amygdala to racial outgroup vs ingroup face stimuli". *NeuroReport*, vol. 11, no. 11:2351–54.

Johnson, Kareem and Barbara Fredrickson. 2005. "We All Look the Same to Me: Positive Emotions Eliminate the Own Race Bias in Face Recognition". *Psychological Science*, vol. 16, no. 11:875–81.

Kurzban, Robert, John Tooby and Leda Cosmdies. 2001. "Can Race Be Erased? Coalitional Computation and Social Categorization". *Proceedings of the National Academy of Sciences*, vol. 98, no. 26: 15387–92.

Lijphart, Arend. 1977. *Democracy in Plural Societies: A Comparative Exploration.* New Haven: Yale University Press.

Michener, James. [1947]/1984. *Tales of the South Pacific.* New York: Fawcett.

Monroe, Kristen R. 2004. *The Hand of Compassion.* Princeton: Princeton University Press.

———. 2008. "Cracking the Code: The Moral Psychology of Genocide". *Political Psychology*.

Ohman, Arne and Susan Mineka. 2001. "Fears, Phobias and Preparedness: Toward an Evolved Module of Fear and Fear Learning". *Psychological Review*, vol. 108, no. 3: 483–522.

Oxley, Douglas R., Kevin B. Smith, Matthew V. Hibbing, Jennifer L. Miller, John R. Alford, Peter K. Hatemi, and John R. Hibbing. 2008. "Political Attitudes Are Predicted by Physiological Traits". *Science*.

Phelps, Elizabeth A., Kevin J. O'Connor, J. Christopher Gatenby, John C. Gore, Christian Grillon and Michael Davis. 2001. "Activation of the Left Amygdala to a Cognitive Representation of Fear". *Nature Neuroscience*, vol. 4: 437–41.

Smiley, Marion. 1992. *Moral Responsibility and the Boundaries of Community: Power and Accountability from a Pragmatic Point of View.* Chicago: University of Chicago Press.

Staub, Ervin. 1992. *The Roots of Evil: The Origins of Genocide and Other Group Violence.* New York: Cambridge University Press.

Tajfel, Henri. 1970. "Experiments in Intergroup Discrimination". *Scientific American*, vol. 223: 96–102.

―――――. 1981. "Human Groups and Social Categories". *Studies in Social Psychology*. New York: Cambridge University Press.

van den Bos, Wouter, Samuel M. McClure, Lasana T. Harris, Susan T. Fiske, Jonathan D. Cohen. 2007. "Dissociating Affective Evaluation and Social Cognitive Processes in the Ventral Medial Prefrontal Cortex". *Cognitive, Affective, & Behavioral Neuroscience*, vol. 7, no. 4: 337–46.

CHAPTER 7

SCIENCE FICTION FANTASY, MORAL IMAGINATION AND THE ABILITY TO CONCEPTUALIZE YOUR WAY OUT OF A PROBLEM

At one point my younger son, Nicholas, wanted to be a writer. He is just graduating from law school as I write this—two weeks in fact till his graduation—specializing in intellectual property law, so possibly he will end up being a writer well versed in the legal issues surrounding publishing his own books and stories. Nik does love science fiction, especially what he tells me is science fiction fantasy. Mothers try to be close to their children by understanding what their children love and I would occasionally ask Nik—who majored in creative writing at UCLA (the University of California, Los Angeles)—to suggest books he thought I might enjoy. I got some great suggestions that way, in fact, so this is a general policy I can recommend.

One night while Nik was still living at home, he found a book for me to read and placed it on the floor outside my bedroom door. I picked it up as I staggered into bed around 1:00 a.m., thinking I would read a bit before drifting off to sleep. I started the story, which was well written and engaging. I was already exhausted by a busy day and hence perhaps exhibited even less than my usual level of alertness to detail, so I perhaps missed a few of the telltale signs. But when I got to the part where the grandfather's tentacles stretched out, I thought, "What? This is odd." As I read on, I realized Nik had given me a science fiction story. I was not amused!

Nik was then a high school water polo player who had to be up, fed and in the chilly water of the outdoor pool at University High School by 6:00 a.m., even in the middle of December. The next morning, after he had gone to school and I had time I read more in the book, I changed my mind. The book turned out to be a compilation of science fiction stories; one by Octavia Butler I found especially intriguing.[1] More autobiography than science fiction, Butler's work posed a question that resonated for me when she told how she is frequently asked why a Black woman would write science fiction fantasy. Her reply was that science fiction allows us to consider the possibilities and that doing so is especially important in letting us find solutions to problems that trouble us today—such as the unequal place of Black Americans and women—by reconceptualizing these problems, rethinking the possibilities. That made sense to me, and I was grateful to Nik for sharing Butler's story with me.

From my feet-on-the-ground political scientist perspective, what I think Butler is talking about is the moral imagination, something even someone not trained in the intricacies of modern literature can understand and appreciate. If imagination is the human ability to consider that which is not, to discover and understand—to think ourselves into other people's lives—without having actually experienced it ourselves, then moral imagination is the ability to view moral issues in a different light, to imagine new possibilities, to consider not just the traditional options for acting in any given situation but also the capability, talent and the sheer gift of envisioning alternative possibilities, visualizing new and nontraditional potentialities that might help.[2] The ability to imagine new worlds, new realities resonates in Robert Kennedy's oft-quoted campaign quip: "Most men see things as they are and ask why. I see things as they might be and ask why not."[3] Minus the moral imagination, we would be captives of our own experience. We could act only against wrongs with which we ourselves have personal involvement.

This is not to say that any of us can ever fully put ourselves into the place of others. Nor can we fully grasp the agonies of people who have endured famine, war, insidious poverty, or slavery and genocide. Empathy can take us only so far. But it is unfeeling, and neglectful of our responsibility as human beings to simply accept that the suffering of people we do not know lies beyond our comprehension, closed off to us, or that a sense of fellow feeling is impossible and that the resultant acts of human kindness and rescue are not required by our common humanity.

This is where the moral imagination enters. Why—my son's attraction to science fiction fantasy thus says to me—do some people remain so rooted in this reality that they can see only the world as it is, whereas others have the ability, indeed sometimes possess the need, to perceive things differently? Isn't it the case that stories, not just science fiction fantasy stories, play the important role of encouraging us to think more creatively than we had before? Don't they design characters who feel real enough to us to help us take that imaginary leap between our reality and other newer realities, to worlds in which these characters reside?[4]

One important part of the moral imagination is the ability to conceptualize your way out of a problem, to see what you want to do and then figure out a way to get from A to E. Not to just recognize that you are at point A and would like to be at point E. But to employ your imagination to grasp how you can essentially construct a point B and a point C and how these intermediate points then can lead to points D and E, if you will.

This process probably has something to do with self-esteem, with the feeling that you deserve the happiness, that you are worthy of being at point E. You have earned the right to live in the better world that most of the rest of us can only imagine. To jump off the path chosen for us by tradition and family, and find the bravery to shake off this traditional paradigm, the conventional way of seeing the world, the worldview that everyone else shares and which was inherited from our particular family, culture or society. This in turn probably relates to thinking for yourself and to the ability to take dispassionate assessment of your own values, determine where they are holding you back, where they are lacking or where they no longer serve you well at all.

It doesn't always happen. Life sometimes in fact does equate to a zero-sum game. Not all situations are tractable. But I am always amazed at how many times in life we can conceptualize our way out of problems. One trivial example leaps to mind. A friend was in the mail room at the office one day, bemoaning the fact that her teenage daughter had broken her leg and would need someone in the house to help her get around, fetch her food, get her to the bathroom, etc. Trivial aid, unless and until the help is not there. How, my friend wondered, would she handle her classes and still care for her daughter?

"Are you teaching a small class this term?" I asked.

"Yes. It's a grad course."

"Why don't you ask them to come to your home? You live on campus so it's an easy walk and students usually enjoy being invited into professors' homes. You could give them pizza and make it a very relaxed class. Then when your daughter needs help, you could excuse yourself for the few minutes and still take care of your professorial obligations."

Probably I was able to conceptualize my way around this problem because it wasn't my conundrum. I was not the one feeling trapped between honoring duties to two groups, both loved and valued: daughter versus students. But I later utilized the same advice I'd given my friend when my own daughter was too young to be left alone during the summers and I was running a summer internship program for students. I would ask the interns to come to my house for meetings, often providing food. They liked it. The garden was lovely, and we'd sit outside and talk—I think—more freely than in a formal structure. I liked it because Chloe was close at hand and I did not need to leave her alone.

Sometimes if I did need to be at the university, I would ask Chloe to come with me, arranging for her to sit in an office next to mine while I met with students. Chloe was an amenable, easy child and she had her own little space in my dingy research office, with an antiquated computer and some books. I think she enjoyed her time there. I hope it got her used to the pleasures of being a scholar in a dusty room filled with books and the glorious freedom to do whatever you wanted with those lovely books. I hope it helped her see that a woman could be a mother and a scholar at the same time, that it provided a template for how to balance different parts of life. But whatever it did for Chloe, this strategy did at least allow me to combine my roles and my duties as a mother with those as a scholar.

Other times I was not so good at this reconceptualization. My first year in graduate school was a tough one for me. I was living alone, in a city I did not like, unclear what in the world I was doing with my life, with no plan, just a strong and striking realization that I loved the books I was now reading and did not want to leave the library. The problem? I was in love. (I'll call him Ben, though that is not his real name.) But in love with someone on the East Coast, and someone putting a lot of pressure on me to transfer to his school and get married. We bumbled along for a time, broke it off the end of my first year then patched it back together that summer when Ben asked if he could come out to Chicago to see whether we shouldn't rethink our decision to break up.

Things came to a head at Christmas my second year, however, when I had to either take my now completed MA and move to Boston where Ben was studying economics, or stay at Chicago and enter the PhD program. I chose to do the latter.

Being young, it didn't take either of us long before we both found other people. By that summer, Ben was living with the woman he eventually married— ironically enough, also named Kristen—and I was in love with another economics student who took a summer job in New York City. (Ben had a great sense of humor and his joke was that at least I had settled on a profession, if not a particular man.) I was going to visit my new beau in Manhattan and wrote Ben, whose parents lived in New Jersey, to ask if he might be in the NYC area during the time I was visiting New York. Ben wrote back that he would come down from Boston for the day and suggested we meet for lunch.

It was a bittersweet lunch, tinged with the kind of poignant nostalgia that accompanies the loss of young love. Each of us was quite happy in our new lives and there was no regret, no acrimony or hard feelings. As I walked Ben to the car, to tell him goodbye, however, he turned to me. "You know, the entire time we were trying to figure out how to get together and get married neither one of us ever suggested I transfer from Harvard to the University of Chicago."

"I know."

"It's a better Economics Department," Ben noted.

I smiled. "I know."

I often think of this as illustrating how strong the norms were circa 1970 that the woman follows the man. In that time period and my particular world, it was part of the *zeitgeist* that every young woman wants to marry a bright young man on his way up. (A man from Harvard was perhaps the ultimate score.) Maybe my lack of creative vision was the result of such social cues. Perhaps I just didn't want to marry Ben. In retrospect, I think it's more likely that I wasn't ready to marry *anyone*. Still unsure of who I was and what I wanted in life, I needed time to figure out these things before I could make such an important decision, before I got into such an intimate relationship that my own identity might be overwhelmed by someone else's or crushed by the unexamined and unquestioned norms of the society in which I lived, a society in which women still followed bright young men. (Think Hillary Rodham, before she became Clinton, if you like, and how she gave up great job possibilities to follow Bill to Arkansas. I knew enough to know I did not want *that* particular route to happiness.)

I like to think this is why I couldn't conceptualize myself out of what I later realized was not at all an intractable problem. But this was after I had grown up a lot more and had found a partner who I trusted would let me develop fully as my own person and as a scholar.[5]

Whatever the reasons for my being able to conceptualize my way out of some problems yet remain stumped by others, I think this ability to think creatively, with vision and originality, to find a way to conceptualize your way out of what looks like a dilemma—and indeed which may be a dilemma for many other people—is a large part of what goes on as we try to compose a life. I am not saying that there are not actual dilemmas or that we are failures if we cannot find a conceptualization that allows us to have our cake and eat it too. I'm just suggesting that philosophers have not focused enough on this particular problem. I find the moral imagination a critical part of my own thinking about what is important in life, what matters as I think about who I am, what I want and the purpose behind my life.

One of the poems my brother, Jamie, asked to have read at his funeral captures an important aspect of the mind's ability to find solutions to our dilemmas.

'pity this busy monster, manunkind'

pity this busy monster, manunkind,

not. Progress is a comfortable disease:
your victim (death and life safely beyond)

plays with the bigness of his littleness
... electrons deify one razorblade
into a mountainrange; lenses extend
unwish through curving wherewhen till unwish
returns on its unself.

　　　　　　　... A world of made
is not a world of born ... pity poor flesh

and trees, poor stars and stones, but never this
fine specimen of hypermagical

ultraomnipotence. We doctors know

a hopeless case if ... listen: there's a hell
of a good universe next door; let's go

e. e. Cummings.

Every time I read this poem, I always catch at the word: "listen." Cummings captures so well the intricacies of the world in which we live, a world where leukemia still kills, as it did my brother in 1978. A world where doctors are so highly educated, and science and medicine are so specialized. A world so well known. The real world.

I am not one of those fortunate people born religious. Faith in an afterlife offers no solace in the face of death for me. When I try to imagine what must be a large part of the attraction of religion, however, it seems to me that it must lie in religion's ability to provide an alternate universe, a place where life is better than it is here. This I can understand. This I can relate to. I could not live without the belief that there just might possibly be some kind of a "hell of a good universe next door." I'd like to think that world is one in which pain in the face of intractable problems need not overwhelm us, a world where we can find a way to make cancer chronic, not a killer. A world where moral imagination can help us dream things that others have never seen, and find a way to make them come true. Where dreamers and idealists envision a world where man can fly, and invent the airplane. Where scientists like Louis Pasteur or Joseph Lister can devote their lives to research that does not fit into the immediate existing scientific paradigms. Many of these scientists may be wrong; but some will be right and, regardless of their success or failure, I admire their ability to have faith and pursue the unknown.

I think the key word here is "listen." Listen to people who deviate from the mold, to people who think outside the box. To people who don't even know a box exists! Listen to those who take chances and put themselves out there, knowing full well they may make fools of themselves or may crash and burn. At least they are trying.

I like a world in which a Black woman can write science fiction fantasy and speak to a tired mother, a white political scientist, with little creative literary imagination, and no understanding or *a priori* appreciation of science fiction fantasy. A mother who has no inkling at all of what her son sees in that genre, until late one night she hears the voice of a woman she will never meet but who opens her eyes to a small part of what her son is all about.

I like to think there is "a hell of a good universe next door" and that it's not just for religious folks. That even we poor old agnostics can partake in some of that hope. I want to believe that moral imagination can help get us there, that moral imagination can help us conceptualize our way out of all kinds of problems, big and little, personal and societal.[6] It's a small leap in the dark but one I couldn't live without taking, and one that makes me thankful for all those crazy visionaries who defy conventional wisdom, even if they fail.

I'm very grateful to Nik for showing me his story about why it makes sense for a Black woman to write science fiction fantasy.

REECOMMENDED MOVIE

See the 2011 movie, *The Adjustment Bureau*, based on a short story by Philip K. Dick entitled the *Adjustment Team*. In the movie, Matt Damon plays a politician destined to become president of the United States, until he meets and falls for a dancer, played by Emily Blount. It turns out that the group of men who run the world need to keep Damon unhappy enough so he will pursue political fame and popularity; if he marries Blount, he will be satisfied in his personal life and hence not need the public acclaim that comes with high office. At the end of the movie, after a surreal chase scene and a harrowing escape through mysterious doors, Damon and Blount are allowed to be together. The movie ends as the lovers walk down the street together, while the narrator says: *Most people live life on the path we set for them, too afraid to explore any others. But once in a while people like you come along who knock down all the obstacles we put in your way. People who realize free will is a gift you'll never know how to use until you fight for it. (The Adjustment Bureau)*. The movie and Dick's story are not identical but I love that this profound thought about finding one's own path comes from a science fiction writer. Dick's story was first published in *Orbit Science Fiction*

(September–October 1954, no. 4) in 1954, not a period in the United States especially noted for its emphasis on individuality.

REFERENCES AND FUTURE READINGS

There are many excellent books by Octavia E. Butler. I recommend *Unexpected Stories*, published by Subterranean (2020) after Butler's death. It features two works originally written in the 1970s. "Childfinder" follows a Black woman in the 1970s who imagines the future of the human race.

Butler, Octavia E. 2020. *Unexpected Stories*. Burton, MI: Subterranean Press.

Carpenter, Charli. 2016. "Rethinking the Political Science Fiction Nexus: Global Policy Making and the Campaign to Stop Killer Robots". *Perspectives on Politics*, vol. 14, no. 01, 53–69. Published online by Cambridge University Press, March 21, 2016.

Dick, Philip K. 1954. *Orbit Science Fiction* (September–October 1954, no. 4).

I love the poems of e. e. cummings, who had a different way of viewing the world—as witness by his eccentric spellings—and recommend in particular "the Cambridge Ladies who live in furnished souls" in addition to the poem cited here.

CHAPTER 8

PASSION

Autograph books hit Lanham School when I was in 5th grade. All the girls had them. Mine was small enough to hold in one hand and had pastel-colored pages: green, yellow, blue and pink, if memory serves. Mostly the inscriptions were eminently forgettable and sappy. "Roses are red, violets are blue; no one loves you like I love you. Judy, your best friend forever." Or else they were annoyingly uninspired and distinctly puerile, not funny except in the warped way of the young preteen mind. "Roses are red and violets are blue. You have a big head but I still like you. Ha ha ha," the equivalent of today's LOL.

In a rash moment, I asked my mother to sign my book. (Just on the off chance that I might forget her??) Mother took the book, kept it overnight and then returned it to me with what seemed at the time an extremely odd poem. A real poem, not the "roses are red" variety I'd come to expect, and one I had never read before.

"Barter"
Sara Teasdale

Life has loveliness to sell,
All beautiful and splendid things,
Blue waves whitened on a cliff,
Soaring fire that sways and sings,
And children's faces looking up,
Holding wonder like a cup.

Life has loveliness to sell,
Music like the curve of gold,
Scent of pine trees in the rain,
Eyes that love you, arms that hold,

And for your spirit's still delight,
Holy thoughts that star the night.

Spend all you have for loveliness,
Buy it and never count the cost;
For one white singing hour of peace
Count many a year of strife well lost,
And for a breath of ecstasy
Give all you have been, or could be.

I didn't appreciate it, or even fully understand the poem at the time. But Mother's message stuck, as much a curse as a blessing.

I know now that passion is important in life. Loving someone or something more than reason dictates is a great gift. Just having that moment, in whatever form that fleeting instant takes, is transfigurative. It carries us out of ourselves and connects us with something akin to the divine.

When I got married, I asked a family friend to read Mother's Teasdale poem at the wedding. My then fiancé and I wanted a personal service, and both of us spent hours searching for *le mot juste*, precisely the right words to tell each other and the world how we felt about each other on this special day.

Neither of us was religious but my fiancé was more adamantly opposed to any mention of god than was I so we chose a judge to be officiant, partly to honor my father, who had died several years before I met my husband-to-be, and partly to avoid the religiosity accompanying most ministers. Unfortunately, the weekend we chose for our ceremony also happened to be the weekend of a legal convention and most of the judges we knew were going to be out of town. But Mother had met a minister at a dinner party and told us how the man had taken on another guest who was a member of the moral majority, a somewhat right-wing and ideologically narrow, puritanical group during the 1970s and 1980s, not unlike the Tea Party or QAnon movements of today. We met the minister, told him we had the service written already and just needed him to officiate. My fiancé insisted, "No mention of god."

"Not a problem," the minister replied. We agreed and all was well. We thought.

The day of the wedding, however, as we stood before family and friends in the beautiful, non-denominational Graham Chapel at Washington University in St. Louis, the minister slipped in the word god. Knowing my fiancé, I thought it was entirely possible he would interrupt the ceremony in protest, and we would stand at the altar, engaged in a long philosophical discussion about the use of the term and our agreement. To my surprise, my fiancé offered no protest, and the ceremony continued as planned. Until Irving Dilliard, friend of the family and special comrade-in-arms to my father, stood up to read *Barter*.

Irving's deep, rich voice boomed out throughout the chapel, intoning what to Irving's eyes must have looked like the first lines of Sara Teasdale's lovely poem.

"Life has loneliness to sell ..."

I started to giggle. Perhaps it was nerves. More likely it was simply a quirky sense of humor, filled with visions of the fates screaming at me via the great Teasdale: "Marry this man and you will be forever lonely." My almost-husband, not sure if I were laughing or crying, squeezed my hand, to comfort me. Unfortunately, I had put my engagement ring on my right hand, in order to receive the wedding band on my left hand during the ceremony, and the diamonds were twisted toward the little finger. With each loving squeeze, the ring was digging more deeply into my finger, a fact that merely added to the humor in my mind and caused me to laugh even harder.

Finally, once I was able to catch my breath, I corrected Irving. "Loveliness," I stage-whispered. "Life has *loveliness* to sell, not loneliness." Irvine was unflustered and began again, providing me with Teasdale's—and my mother's—true wish for me: loveliness in life.

But, as Teasdale knew and I was to learn, loveliness must be purchased and the cost life demands is often high. That's only part of the rub. For me, the kicker is not the purchase price itself but rather what you do with it once you have it, this brief, "white singing" hour of joy beyond compare? By definition, that kind of passion cannot last, can it? And then where are you?

Little children in Collinsville—the town in which I was raised—like little children throughout the country and elsewhere, I suspect, were fond of taking a daisy and tearing off the petals to learn whether the person they adored at the moment truly loved them, as if demolishing a poor daisy would actually determine whether the object of our affection is similarly inclined. "Loves me, loves me not," we would say, as we ripped away the defenseless daisy petals.

The French have a slightly different version called *effeuiller la marguerite* (pluck the daisy). Like the American game, *effeuiller la margueritte* consists in pulling off the petals or leaves of a plant—traditionally a daisy, hence the name *margueritte*—to determine whether someone loves you. The French version, however, is more complex, perhaps reflective of a more nuanced attitude toward love among the French. The French version of the daisy-pull says: "*Il/elle m'aime ... un peu ... beaucoup ... passionément ... à la folie ... pas du tout.*" When I first heard the expression in French, I had no difficulty grasping most of the concepts. "He loves me a little, a lot, passionately, *a la folie*, not at all."

It was the phrase: "*a la folie*" that gave me pause. What does it mean to love someone "*a la folie*"? The literal translation would be "at the folly." Does that mean he loves me too much, at his folly and peril, with the poor lad destined for heartache? Does it mean head over heels in love, the kind of crazy love where you fly down the street with your head in the clouds, blissfully happy? Or does the phrase conjure up the concept of loving someone more than life itself, the kind of selfless love that makes us do extraordinary things, growing as people, taking us outside ourselves to a place where we simply want the best for the other person, want them to be happy at all costs?

Loving someone at your folly in the first sense seems something to be avoided, a bad thing that brings unhappiness and pain. Loving someone so much you fly down the street smacks of a rather light, airy and ultimately slightly vacuous love. Reminiscent of the callow, young Freddy Eynsford-Hill in *My Fair Lady*, a man so enamored and wrapped up in the image of an Eliza he doesn't really even know but nonetheless is happy to be near, "On the Street where [she] you live[s]." Freddy is not in love with Eliza the person but rather is in love with the romanticized idea of being in love itself. This seems a pleasant sensation but one that lacks a bit of good old-fashioned reality testing or what Mother would call Middle Western common sense.

So then we come to the concept of loving someone more than life itself. Surely this is the kind of love religious texts speak of, where we give our all to someone or something and are ennobled in doing so, no? It certainly hints at the kind of thing Mother showed me in the poem *Barter* where you give all you have for loveliness, buying it and never counting the cost. I am not a literary person and may have it all wrong here but it seemed pretty clear to the young Kristabelle that Mother was showing me something akin to passion, the kind of love that takes you out of yourself and focuses you on the beloved.

Here's my problem. I've had those moments, not frequently but more than once. I remember experiencing it the summer after my son Nicholas was born. We'd all had dinner and his father and I were putting both Nicholas and Alex to sleep, Nicholas then still a baby; his big brother Alexander was four. It was early nightfall on the soft summer night and we'd been swimming together before dinner. We all were in the master bedroom, my husband to my left, our baby in between us on the big, king-sized bed and Alex on a mattress on the floor, just to the right of the bed on my side, placed there so we could all be in the same room. So Alex would not feel left out. I had nursed the baby and as Nik lay sleeping in my arms, I chose a record to play on my old-fashioned record player, a gift from my college days. I chose the Chopin *Piano Concerto #1, Opus 11, in E minor*, the lovely Romance (Larghetto) movement, so beautiful that it tears at your heart and makes you appreciate that a mere mortal can experience loveliness in its purest form. As we all lay quietly in the bedroom, listening to this exquisite music, I realized Alex was crying. I asked him if he were OK and he assured me he was not sad. He just was crying because the Chopin was so beautiful.

I thought, as I realized how sensitive my beautiful boy was, and how happy I was at that moment: "It doesn't get any better than this. This is what life is all about."[1]

I think about that moment now, now that the children are grown and on their own, as they must be. Not needing to be tucked in at night, or soothed into sleep by lullabies or Chopin. Fighting their own little battles, no longer needing their mother to protect them. Again, as it must be, as I want it to be for them. I remember all those other times when life took me to the edge and pulled aside the curtain, just a moment, and let me catch sight of the infinite. Moments when I knew what it was all about. No complex philosophical discussions about the meaning of life or our purpose here on earth. I just *knew*. *This* was it. *This* was real. *This* is what it means to be alive.

I've had these moments, and I understand that such ecstasy cannot, almost by definition, last. I know I'm a lucky woman, and I feel selfish on the nights when I feel empty, focusing too much on the loss of those loving little arms. I remind myself that the trick is to feel happiness and then remember it later.

But sometimes when I sleep alone at night, I have a recurring dream. In the dream I am back in the house where the children were young and we were so happy, wrapped up in the daily comings and goings, the busy time of rushed breakfasts before school, of the snack before homework, or the warmth of bedtime stories and lullabies as one of them fell asleep in my arms. I force myself to remember that I often was so tired that it was I who feel asleep first, waking up after 20 minutes to stagger down the hall and work for an hour or two before collapsing in bed at night.[2]

It's not the fatigue I remember though. That remains only a mental memory. The *feel* of that time is gone. What I remember as the texture and sensation of life then is the warmth and the laughter and the security of being at the center of a loving family. My memory recalls the ecstasy of that love. The joy and the delight of that passion.

I've lost that center now, not because of the tragedy of a death but merely by the healthy progression of time, in which my beautiful little children have grown up and gone out into the world as magnificent human beings, on their own. I know this is good. I want them to go on and have their own lives. I get it, that point about ecstasy and passion being fleeting.

But sometimes, when the ache is especially deep,[3] I want to ask my mother, or perhaps even the great Sara Teasdale, "What is the point of all that passion? You showed it to me. You gave it to me by giving me the strength to fully experience it. You just forgot to tell me what to do with it once it is gone, that fleeting essence of being totally alive, of being happy, of so blissfully loving someone more than your own life itself. Happiness and love *a la folie*. What do you do when it passes?"

"You showed me that passion," I want to ask them. "What do I do now?"

REFERENCES AND FUTURE READINGS

Hellman, Lillian. 1973. *Pentimento*. New York: Little Brown. *Pentimento* is a series of stories about Hellman's imagined life. One story discusses passion, this time passion between a man and a woman and how Hellman first learned of it, and how it, too, can come and go in your life.

Hilton, James. 1934. *Goodbye, Mr. Chips*. London: Hodder & Stoughton. Also made into two very sentimental movies. *Goodbye, Mr. Chips* describes the affection held for his students by an English teacher.

Rosten, Leo. 1937. *The Education of Hyman Kaplan*. New York: Harcourt Brace. A lovely, if dated and probably politically incorrect in its characterization of immigrants and their language, *The Education of Hyman Kaplan* captures the joy of learning. It is written by a former political scientist at the University of Chicago.

Schulman, Tom. 1989. *Dead Poets Society*. A 1989 movie about a 1959-conservative boarding school, written by Tom Schulman, directed by Peter Weir, and starring Robin Williams, *Dear Poets Society* captures both the impact of good teaching and the stuffy, conformist pressures of 1950s White Anglo-Saxon Protestant (WASP) America.

CHAPTER 9

CAT

It's odd, the things that pop into our minds in a crisis. When the doctor called to tell me the biopsy had been positive and that I had breast cancer, the first two thoughts that flashed through my mind were: "I've never had a calico cat!" and "I want to be buried in Walnut." Fortunately for me, my cancer was DCIS, *ducal carcinoma in situ*. Effectively, these little stage-zero cancer cells are precancerous cells, akin to 10-year-old kids who want to be gang members but don't quite know how to do it.

"They'll dress up like what they think gang members look like and will try to mimic their acts but they don't really know how to do it," the doctor told me. "But if you don't get them out, sooner or later a few of them finally will figure out how it works and they'll become real cancer cells and will go on the prowl. That's when we need to worry."

I was lucky and the tissues were clean; there was no cancer in the lymph nodes and the doctor concluded that, in fact, the biopsy had probably gotten out all my little gang members. No need to worry about where I was to be buried, at least not for the immediate future.

Nonetheless, I figured my subconscious was telling me something and, since our cat had died several years before, and our dog had succumbed to leukemia shortly before that, I realized we were petless. So, one fine summer's evening, as my daughter and I took our swim together—one older brother now off at college, the other working in Europe, and her father on a business trip —I responded positively when Chloe raised the subject of our getting a cat.

"Nicole has two cats, you know," she said honestly. "I don't have any."

We discussed as we swam, slow, comforting, companionable side strokes, none of this thrashing and slashing through the water in a fast crawl or free style, as it's now termed. Swimming was relaxing and companionable for me and for Chloe. I told Chloe we would need to speak with Dad, who I suspected would prefer a dog, and reminded her that there was a lot to think about in terms of responsibility with an animal. But I was sympathetic and told her that at the very least, it was a good topic for family discussion. I did go on the record as preferring to have a rescue animal since I thought many of these animals would otherwise not live long. But that was my only constraint.

The next day Chloe got on the web and began what I later learned was a quite extensive research job on pet shelters and animals in the local area. She was excited about the prospect of a new cat and, after her father returned late from a business trip to the East Coast, she got up early with him and told him all about potential cats in the area. I was sleeping in that morning, and never learned much about the conversation from Chloe. But after Chloe left to play with Nicole, it was obvious that my husband was upset about something.

When I asked him what was bothering him, he erupted into a rage, furious that I would decide about getting a cat without consulting him. I tried to explain what had happened but he was too far gone, wound up for unknown reasons of his own, and angry at feeling excluded. There was no dialogue. No conversation. No room for communication or correcting of misinformation.

In retrospect I think it was just one fight too many. It may have been the realization that I really was not a participant in the fight, just someone who happened to be in the room when his temper exploded. Probably the fact that my son—home for the weekend—heard the fight also entered into the calculus. Perhaps viewing the situation through my son's eyes made me realize I could no longer stay with someone who became so verbally abusive for so little cause. Whatever the reasons, my marriage ended that day.

A divorce brings a myriad of feelings, mostly unpleasant and sad, but in my case, at least, it also brought a sense of release, a feeling of freedom that I no longer had to work around someone who had become more irascible than loving.[1]

Parenthetically, I now realized I could get a cat.

That first weekend after her father moved out, Chloe went on the web and found a lovely little calico kitten in the nearby town of Garden Grove. We called the woman who had listed her rescue cat and drove up to bring home our new kitten. We were told to put the cat in a small room at first, not to overwhelm her with a large new house. So, we put the little kitten into the downstairs bathroom, complete with litter box and food, and left the door open to the adjoining bedroom so we could all have cuddle time together.

We had not told anyone about the cat. When Nik arrived home from college that weekend, Chloe and I were out. Our new pet was locked into her two little rooms, with food, drink and kitty litter nearby. Nik always brought his laundry with him when he came home from UCLA for the weekend, and this visit, as with so many others when he arrived to an empty house, he went immediately to the laundry room to begin washing his clothes. Nik opened the washer, only to find it filled with beanie babies. (These are the tiny stuffed animals Chloe loved. She must have had over 400 of them, accumulated each birthday, Christmas and other gift-days. I had decided to wash them, which I did every several years to remove the dust that accumulated on their fur. Hence the full washer.) Undeterred, Nik opened the drier to put the wet beanie babies into the dryer so he could wash his own laundry. He found the dryer too was filled with beanie babies. Placid in the face of all obstacles, Nik is nothing if not persistent, so he removed the beanie babies from the dryer, placed them in the clothes basket, then shifted the beanies in the washing machine to the dryer so he could then begin the washing of his own clothes.

Task completed, Nik turned to the bathroom. In retrospect, Nik says he remembered thinking it odd that the door to the bathroom was closed since it usually was kept open unless occupied. Nik was peacefully utilizing the facilities when he realized he was being watched. He looked down and realized a strange cat was closely regarding his movements.

When Chloe and I returned home, we told Nik the story of how we acquired the cat, named—by Chloe—Casaluna Hathaway Dinwiddie. (Chloe has more imagination than I do. I probably would have called her Callie since she was a calico.) But Cassie she was, and a beautiful cat indeed. A white calico, with beautiful black and reddish tan markings, quite delicate and striking in her graceful movements. When we got her, she was only a few months old, and so tiny she would almost fit in your hand. Cassie was a feral cat, captured with her mother, who escaped once the animal shelter people tried to get the mother out of the trap and into the pound. Only her baby remained, trapped and deserted and alone.

The woman who found Cassie was a tender-hearted human being, in addition to being an animal rescue person in Orange County. Kellyanne realized that if she took Cassie to the shelter, then Cassie would probably be put to sleep since Cassie had mange all over her body. The poor animal was a mess to look at and a horror to try to pet. Not the best recipe for adoption. So Kellyanne took Cassie to her own apartment, kept Cassie in the bathroom (isolated from the other five cats already living there), fed her by hand and with a food dropper and put salve on her mange. Within a few weeks, Cassie's mange was gone, leaving her with a coat so beautiful people now comment that she would make a gorgeous stole. And—probably because of the compassionate Kellyanne and that medicine dropper—Cassie went from being a wild, ferocious feral cat to being the most affectionate of animals.

Chloe was ecstatic, as was I.

I realized quite early on, however, that Chloe wanted two cats. After all, her friend Nicole had two cats, huge, sleek black tomcats who purred and prowled the house in majestic splendor. So, when Chloe suggested we go to Petco to get cat food for Cassie, I knew full well that little Chloe was hoping to see another cat there and perhaps coax me into adopting another cat. No worries. I'd already mentally approved the as of yet unspoken request. I said sure, and we headed off to Petco, only to be greeted by Kellyanne, the woman who had rescued and then given us Cassie.

"Chloe! Kristi!" Kellyanne called out to us across the store. "Come see my other cats."

The cat Chloe fell in love with was a grey Himalayan or Ragdoll; neither we nor the vet ever totally ascertained Zosia's provenance. But she had seal point markings and big, beautiful turquoise eyes. She was soft and fluffy, with incredibly thick fur over a somewhat stocky body. She left Petco and came home with us that very afternoon. We stopped *en route* to pick up Nicole and her little sister, Pauline. We engaged in the same routine as before, when we had obtained Cassie: Zosia was shut in the little bathroom, adjoining the downstairs bedroom. As Zosia lay on the bed, amidst three adoring young girls and with her body cuddled up next to mine, we admitted Cassie, thinking we would introduce her to her new pal. Cassie was put on the bed, behind me, so she could not yet see what lay on the other side. Cassie was smart, though, and immediately figured out something was going on just beyond the human barrier. She rather gingerly stretched out her little paws, peeking over my body to see what lay on the next side. As she viewed the new cat, Cassie let out the most incredibly human sigh of sorrow, disgust and anguish: "Oooooh." We gathered the two might not be the best of friends.

Nik now reenters our story. We had again forgotten to tell Nik that we were henceforth the proud owners of yet *another* cat, and when Nik came home that next weekend, he found it was deja-vu all over again, as they say. Nik walked in the front door of a quiet home. Realizing Chloe and I were out, he went to deposit his laundry in the washer. (No beanie babies this week!) But when he went into the same downstairs bathroom, he had the same feeling that someone was watching him. He realized it was yet *another* cat, and later told us no way was he coming home again the next weekend. Nik was *not* tempting fate. Two cats were quite enough.

Other than that little bit of humor, however, the week went on peacefully. Cassie slept with me and Zosia seemed to favor Chloe. I made sure Chloe fed the cats and we later realized that Cassie was fine with the dry food but that Zosia loved the wet stuff, little Friskies Tuscan Feasts being her favorite.

Alas, as beautiful as she was, it soon became evident that Zosia had a major character flaw: she was timid in the extreme. Indeed, Zosia would give a panicked look and scurry quickly out of sight whenever a human approached. We realized Zosia's tail was shorter than usual and wondered if her tail might have been cut off before we met her. Could this trauma explain her current isolationistic behavior? The vet confirmed the shortened tail theory but could offer only conjecture as to the extreme nervous shyness.

The feral cat, in contrast, had been fed with an eyedropper as a baby and, perhaps because of that, Cassie was amazingly affectionate. She loves Chloe but she is *my* cat, for she follows me around like the proverbial puppy dog. She comes to my computer table as I work, and butts her head against my leg, purring loudly, to inform me that I may pet her if I wish. She hops up on my chair while I type, and graciously allows me to rub her tummy or under her chin as I read emails. She even sits on the arm of my computer chair, no small feat given the size of the arms and the need for precarious balance. All the while purring loudly. If I move to the sofa to read or go to another room, Cassie accompanies me, butting her head against the door if it is closed, demanding entrance and, once admitted, sleekly winding her body around my feet, waiting for me to pet her.

Cassie's not perfect. Oh, no. She coughs up hairballs, despite being fed dry food designed to prevent this annoying trait. The favored spot is the white rug on the stairs and the hall right outside my bedroom door. I have tried to suggest Cassie spit up hairballs downstairs, where the floors are hardwood and therefore clean more easily than carpet. So far, no luck.

So Cassie is not easy. But she does seem to love me with a love that borders on the unconditional. At least for a cat. Chloe reminds me that cats were once worshipped as divine and have never forgotten it. Another aphorism holds that dogs have masters and cats have minions. Articles in the few scientific journals I consulted describe cats as inscrutable enigmas, even to their owners. Frustratingly independent, cats are depicted as cool and aloof.

Cassie never got the memo. Cassie found a human she loves, and that love involves following around that human and purring a lot, watching carefully to make sure I am doing what I should. She is there when I wake in the middle of those bad nights we all have occasionally, when I find myself missing the children, wondering what I am doing alone at this point in my life. At those moments, it's wonderfully comforting to have something warm and furry jump on your bed, curl up next to you and purr loudly at your touch. Knowing some living thing responds so favorably just to your mere presence is strangely reassuring in the dark of a bad night.

I've been lucky enough to have received unconditional love from a few people in my life and I can tell you there's nothing to match it. No strings, offered freely and without regard for what the other person does for you, unconditional love wants nothing more than for the loved one to be happy. If you have the amazing good fortune to stumble across it—even though you have no idea what you did to deserve such luck—grab it. Cherish the person who gives it to you. Always look in *their* eyes when you judge yourself, never the eyes of those who are critical of you. Treat them well, these givers of unqualified, unrestricted and unreserved love. They are precious not only because they love you so entirely, with no reservations, but even more because they are smart enough and sensitive enough to see—even perhaps when you do not see it yourself—*why* you are so special, so worthy of this total and complete love.

Above all, be appreciative of unconditional love. Even if it's only from a cat.

REFERENCES AND FUTURE READINGS

Munsch, Robert. Illustrated by Sheila McGraw. 1986/1995. *Love You Forever*. Firefly Books. This children's story describes a mother and the lullaby she sings to her son, throughout the different stages of his life, no matter how difficult the boy becomes. Eventually, of course, the mother grows too old to finish the song so the son continues it for her, and then ends by singing the lullaby to his new baby daughter. When Alex's first grade teacher read the class this story, Alex realized where it was going and began to cry. The teacher saw Alex and she then broke down in tears, and had to have the aid complete the story.

CHAPTER 10

BEST FRIENDS FOREVER

Chloe has a child's painting in her bedroom, hanging on the wall where Chloe can see it as she lies in bed and falls asleep at night. The painting is of a large red heart, with big turquoise letters saying: "I love my BFF." It was painted by her best friend, Nicole and the letters BFF stand for Best Friends Forever. Nicole gave it to Chloe when the girls were quite young. I don't remember the precise date.

Chloe first met Nicole at the red park, so named because of the large red jungle gym in the play area. The girls were six, and life was simple and easy. Uncomplicated. Irvine is a pediocracy, organized around children, and life on the campus of the University of California at Irvine provided us with that mythic 1950s neighborhood, where youngsters could play unsupervised without fear of danger.

Over the years, Chloe and Nicole were in and out of each other's homes. They alternated dinners as they grew older, one Friday night with Nicole's family, one with ours. We had a series of "little girl Thanksgivings" with Nicole's family, one year at their home, one *chez nous*. (Nicole's mother made the best flourless chocolate cake ever.) The girls always were together in the mornings at Turtle Rock School, their closeness and rapport so strong even the teachers noted it. To this day, I am occasionally asked by one of Chloe's former teachers, when we happen to meet, how Chloe and her little friend Nicole are doing.

The girls took dancing lessons together at the local dance academy. Each spring, I had the pleasure of putting on their makeup for their recitals and practices, when beautiful little girls were transformed into miniature streetwalkers, with painted faces and rouged cheeks. Nicole has thick red lips and pale eyebrows with profuse platinum hair, to *dye* for, Chloe's father used to quip. Chloe is also blonde, but her hair is more honey blonde and not so thick. She has long, dark eye lashes that make me jealous.

They loved their dance classes—tap, modern, ballet; I think they must have taken everything except possibly hip-hop—and there was a period of several years when the girls would get together and draw up elaborate schedules for what they called their beanie baby dancing school. These classes involved the girls choreographing intricate dance sequences. They would dutifully line up the beanie babies, check role, give demonstrations of the various routines, and play music for the dancers, all blissfully unmindful of the fact that the beanie babies could not move, let alone dance. It didn't matter. They girls were having fun.

There were picnics in the parks, phone calls and the occasional overnights. Every morning before school the girls could be found on the schoolyard swings, mostly talking. But always together. At 10, Nicole began attending a different school so she had a two-week vacation, with only one week of overlap with Chloe's spring break. In an impulsive moment I asked Nicole if she would like to accompany Chloe and me to Illinois to visit my mother at Pine Lake. We were delighted when Nicole's parents said yes. I had meetings in Chicago that year and so we—Chloe, Nicole and I—flew to Chicago and checked into the Palmer House, the venue for my political science meetings.

The girls were great. We had a tight schedule but after a cab ride from the airport I told them we could take a swim if they would agree to exit the pool without any fussing after one hour. On the dot. They agreed and honored the pledge to the minute. We then dressed and went to Trader Vic's, an ersatz touristy restaurant in the basement of the Palmer House, heavily decorated in somewhat kitschy Polynesian décor. The girls loved it! They ordered and the food came, in plenty of time for us but apparently somewhat slowly for the staff's taste since the waiter apologized and treated the girls to a free dessert. (The dessert delighted the girls, as much for the fact that it was *gratis* as for its taste.) We played cards then went to bed, only to be awakened at 1:00 a.m. when the tired businessman next door returned to his hotel room and blasted his TV. No matter. The girls were together, and having fun.

The next day, Nicole's grandmother came down from Evanston. (Nicole's grandfather taught French at Northwestern.) Mimi took the girls to the Art Institute while I had my meetings. We then took a train to Alton, Illinois, where Mother met us in the snazzy, white convertible she had purchased on her 75th birthday. I had been unsure about the train seating so, fearing an overcrowded train, with no seats to spare, splurged and spent $5 extra for business class tickets. As part of this business ticket, the girls were each given a $5 coupon to buy anything they wanted in the club car. Such freedom, and they discussed the various options like stockbrokers plotting a billion-dollar takeover. (I think they went for hot chocolate and chips, plus one hot dog they shared. It was the autonomy and choice involved that signified, not the food itself.)

When we arrived at Pine Lake, Mother gave the girls her bedroom, with two twin beds and a private dressing room and bath. She and I shared bedrooms adjoining the Jack and Jill bathroom between my brother's old room and mine. That first trip set the norm for later spring visits to Pine Lake: one dinner at Red Lobster, where Chloe and Nicole ordered huge bowls of clam chowder, snarfed down enough cheesy biscuits to choke a horse and walked home with their third *huge* glass of pink lemonade, courtesy of a friendly waitress whose generosity was inspired by the girls' ability to swig down as much lemonade as they had. Ice cream one night at the local Dairy Queen (sundaes for the girls, a banana split for Mother, a chocolate dip bar for me), and a trip to the K-Mart (now closed) for a small purchase for the girls. (The first year it was matching swimsuits. Two piece and hence a bit racy.) They raked leaves in Mother's large yard, explored the lake and rode in Mother's convertible with the top down, where I was the odd woman out, the lone red-head with two blondes and a silver-white haired older woman driving. We all hung out in the park up the road from Pine Lake, where the girls again played on the swings.

The girls had a habit of walking slowly, always ahead of Mother and me. (I suppose we wanted to keep them in our line of vision.) The young ladies, however, often would suddenly stop in their steps, so engrossed in conversation that neither they nor we realized they were no longer perambulating. Deep in our own conversation, Mother and I often didn't notice the halting either and would sometimes plow into them. It was a time of laughter and joyful peace, doing nothing and yet doing everything. Together.

Mother always got annoyed at me for buying groceries, as if my trying to provide her with food somehow insulted her ability to be independent. I just wanted to care for her. But the annoyance was minor grousing, never real anger. One day Mother was complaining that she had too many bananas. It was my fault, of course, since I had purchased too many and we had not eaten enough.

"Oh, well," I countered, blithely, "just make banana cream pie for dinner tonight. The girls will love that." Mother is a master pie-maker, and she took this challenge as an opportunity to teach her granddaughter the art of making an excellent pie crust. (Each Christmas, Mother made the holiday pies for our family. She and my then husband always engaged in what I think of as the great Crisco-lard debate, with Mother insisting Crisco made the best pies and my husband insisting on lard. Each side lobbied me furiously but to no avail. I have no knowledge, let alone preference on how to make a good pie-crust; I buy ready-made pie crusts in the grocery store, to the despair of both my mother and husband.) The girls, however, were inducted into the Crisco school of pie-making and greatly enjoyed being asked to help make the banana cream pie, spreading flour all over the kitchen, which looked as if a white tornado had attacked it.

As we were eating the pie that night after dinner, Nicole emitting happy sounds as she ate, Chloe engrossed in the gustatory delights as well, Mother raised the delicate issue of the bananas yet again: "I still have four bananas left over. What am I supposed to do with them once you leave?"

Nicole came out of her food-induced haze to utter an "out of the mouths of babes" remark: "The way you carry on about bananas, you ought to have a banana farm," she said. We all broke up laughing, and Nicole's remark became one of those lines repeated and laughed at as an in-joke by members of the family for years.

There were many other wonderful times together for Chloe and Nicole. Walks, dancing, attending the annual Christmas *Nutcracker*, usually at a local dance company, often with my mother or Nicole's grandmother or mom. Mostly hours and hours of the kind of shared confidences when you open your heart and your head to another person, enjoying the wonder of allowing another human being to walk around inside your head. Parents are not privy to such moments but I know these times with Chloe's kindred spirit were crucial to Chloe's happiness and well-being.

Friday nights became a cherished routine, where the girls would attend dance class, then alternate dinner dates, one week with Chloe's family, one with Nicole's. After Chloe's father and I divorced during her freshman year in high school, the Friday evenings became her father's domain, and it was he who alternated the evenings.

All this stopped in late January–early February of Chloe and Nicole's sophomore year in high school when something suddenly went awry with Nicole. For weeks, months, both families were in despair, trying desperately to figure out what was happening to our beautiful little Nicole. No clear answer ever emerged. There were visits to doctors at UCI and UCLA. Conversations with many excellent specialists. Lots of reading in journals and on the web. Eventually, over the next few years, numerous medications were tried. Some medical cocktails worked to varying degrees for short periods of time, but nothing was able to stem the tide and Nicole eventually drew more into her own world, leaving the rest of us behind, bereft, desolate, panicky, desperate for a cure, forlorn, alone.

I watched this mostly through the eyes of my daughter, who remained so steadfastly loyal and loving, always trying to create as much normalcy as possible. Still going to the University marketplace for ice cream with Nicole, even though Nicole could no longer engage in the meaningful, intimate conversation of yore.

Still having the Friday night dinners. Still spending time alone together with her best friend. But the time together became more just physical presence and less communion. More alone, and less together.

Eventually Chloe left for college, seeing Nicole only at vacations, trying to speak with her on the phone, not receiving emails anymore from her friend, who used to be such a whiz on the computer. (Nicole had included Mother on her I-mail list and, since Nicole got up early and there was a two-hour time difference between California and mother's home in Illinois, Nicole would often send Mother a quick I-mail early in the morning, ending the series of exchanges with: "Got to go now. School!")

I watched my daughter grieve the loss of her kindred spirit over this long time period. I listened as she told me that losing Nicole was the worst thing that ever happened to her, worse even than the divorce. This made a guilty mother feel slightly better, I confess, but it also broke my heart. It made me think about grieving and those special people we come across from time to time, rarely, unbidden and unplannable, and what they mean to us.

Mark Twain supposedly wrote when Tolstoy died, "As long as that man was alive, I was never alone in the world." I knew what he meant as I watched Chloe deal with her heartache, and then later as, precipitated by the death of my mother in 2015, I wrestled with my own grief. The sadness was not just for Mother's passing, as hard as that was; Mother was 94 when she died, old and in physical pain and desperately lonely, having lost most of the people she cared for in life except me and my children, a few family members and friends. The desolation and the anguish were also for the loss of the shared past. The past with my family of origin: all the fun with my brother and father and mother, trips together, dinner table conversations, Sundays by the lake and barbecuing after lying in the hammock and reading while drinking lemonade, waiting for life to begin for me as a young girl, still looking on at life from the wings. Loss of my own family, the one I had created with a man I thought would be the love of my life but turned increasingly to be the one who hurt me, and mostly the loss of children I had loved more than life itself, and now realized I must let go, watch—indeed encourage—them as they flew away on their own, as they say. I grieved for the used to be.

There are moments of realization in life, when you must step outside yourself, look carefully and without passion, sorrow or anger but simply with objective eyes and assess where you are, what you want and who you are. Grief often takes us to those moments, usually without our intention or design, certainly without our choice. No one wants to feel such pain. Each of us must go there unaccompanied, although with the knowledge—as Twain's remark notes—that there do, indeed, exist in this world a few such individuals who, as long as they are alive, can help us feel we are not alone. Others we admire have been there before us. We can take consolation in knowing that such fine individuals also walked in desolation, and endured.

Watching my daughter wrestle with her losses—of her nuclear family, of her friend, the beloved Nicole—so young made me think about grief and about what it means to have a kindred spirit.

Kindred spirits matter. They are people who share the way we see the world. They understand what we mean when we speak. They see who we are, and like that person. They then reflect back the sense that who we are is a good thing, that the kind of person we are is a good one, that it is the right way to live, even when it is painful.

In *Black Lamb and Grey Falcon*, Rebecca West describes a fictionalized train trip in the 1930s through Europe to the Balkans, a land the heroine romanticizes.[1] The heroine and her husband have purchased first-class train tickets; they enter their compartment in Germany to find someone sitting in their seats. The interlopers have to leave; while the heroine and her husband are embarrassed by displacing the people who were sitting in their seats, the other passengers in the compartment seem unfazed. Indeed, they babble on about how wrong it was for the interlopers to have taken seats to which they were not entitled, ooh-ing and aah-ing about the inappropriateness of such gauche behavior.

As the train crosses the border from Germany, and the conductor comes to check tickets and passports, however, it turns out that *none* of the other passengers in this first-class compartment has first class tickets. *None* of them has paid the full fare. Indeed, it apparently is the norm for people to purchase cheaper tickets and then take a first-class seat, hoping no one will rightfully claim the particular first-class seat in which they are sitting. The other passengers in the compartment merely were luckier than were the interlopers. The other passengers simply were not caught.

The heroine muses about this strange behavior on the part of her fellow passengers as the train pulls into a station, a suburb of the larger city which they will be visiting in the Balkans. It is raining slightly and the heroine watches as an elderly gentleman runs through the evening mist. An umbrella held in hand, the old gentleman is crying out for a woman as he runs: "Anna! Anna!" he cries, oblivious—the heroine notices—to the fact that the beloved Anna is not there. The umbrella is not covering her. Yet the cherished Anna feels so real to the old man that he is holding the umbrella out in front of him, as if to shield Anna from the rain. His doing so means the rain is falling on him, of course, but he seems to neither notice nor care.

To West, the old man is not ridiculous. He loves someone and that person is more important to him than is his own physical comfort. He neither is aware of nor minds the rain. "I was back among people I could understand," West says.

I know this feeling. A good social scientist would have a term for it. To me it's simply coming home, being back among people I can comprehend. It doesn't matter at some level if I know these people personally, although that would be wonderful. It means community, in all the good senses of that word, finding another person who is a sanctuary, someone with whom I am comfortable opening my heart and my mind, the way Chloe did with Nicole. The way Mark Twain said Tolstoy made him feel, even though they had never met.

I have experienced this sense of connection many times in my life. I found it with Susanne and Lloyd Rudolph and with Joe Cropsey in grad school, magnificent teachers who introduced me to things I had not known existed and yet realized, once I knew what these things were, that I could not live without them. I found a kindred spirit when I came across Andrea Nevins on day three at college. I experienced it the first time I fell in love, with my college beau, talking for an hour or two after the date had officially ended and we should have said goodnight. Saying things we could not say to others but could now say to each other.

Kindred spirits let us spend hours talking about ourselves, our families, our hopes and dreams, our fears and insecurities exposed to someone who recognizes and appreciates what we are revealing about ourselves. Someone who shares in turn.

Susanne and Lloyd and Joe have all died. I rarely see Andy anymore; I don't see my old boyfriend at all. We parted and went our separate ways and, as is often the case with young loves, our lives no longer intertwine. On the rare occasions when we do interact, we are no longer in a position to speak of such things. Too much water under the bridge.

I've been lucky to find this same feeling of kinship during my interviews with people who are kind enough to speak with a stranger about their lives. Sometimes these people tell me their wartime stories, of how they survived with their humanity intact during one of the many recent ugly wars.[2] Sometimes they explain how they came to rescue Jews during the Holocaust, or why they are philanthropists or risked their lives for strangers.[3] Currently, I listen as people tell of moral courage and resilience in the face of political trauma. I know the narrative analysis is an accepted and respected form of social science research but at its core, it's also just one human being demonstrating the consideration, thoughtfulness, and trust necessary to open their hearts to a total stranger, sharing their life stories, and allowing me to walk around inside their heads for a while.

I'm an outsider, an unfamiliar person to them, and yet they trust me. Why? I've wondered sometimes if perhaps a sympathetic stranger can feel safer, much as a writer of a novel written long ago often can speak to us and share our lives with a surprising insight and closeness. Sometimes this flash of understanding, a recognition of shared values, of a common way of viewing the world, can originate from someone we do not know personally. Maybe outsiders are safer.

I listened one night as a well-known writer spoke about his divorce on television. I felt a sense of comradeship, of shared understanding of the world. The writer said he didn't want to deal in specifics but that going through a divorce had made him a different person, that the grief he experienced forced him to look deeper into himself and grow.

I understood that. After my divorce people were always saying what I'm sure they meant as comforting remarks. Usually this would be along the lines of: "You're a beautiful woman. You'll meet someone else." As if it mattered for my unhappiness and suffering what I looked like. As if the most immediate thing on my mind was finding a new man. I never really got it. What I needed to do was to go deep inside myself, figure out what had gone wrong, work out what part I had played in creating the mess, discover what I had done to get myself into such a muddle in the first place, make sure it did not happen again, and to think about what kind of person I was in the world.

Kindred spirits don't grow on trees, and losing a kindred spirit is a hurt like none other. That's why—I suspect—divorce for most of us is so painful. Marriage, more than any other relationship we have, is one we create ourselves. Our spouse is the one person we consciously choose to trust with our thoughts and dreams, with our very lives. I don't object to people living together but I do find something very brave and wonderful about standing up and saying, with pride and truthfulness, "I shall love you forever. I take you for better or for worse," and trying so hard to make it work.

Most of us still marry for love, not for the money or fame or beauty or position or all those other things some economists or evolutionary biologists say determine who we marry.[4] Love trumps those considerations for most of us in the modern Western world. So when it falls apart, it hurts. It creates an incredible sense of being alone in a hostile world, filled with tourists who buy second-class tickets while sitting in first-class seats, and then criticize others for doing the same. Phonies. Not real. Inauthentic. Worse, the failure of love introduces us to the fearful thought that if we got it wrong once, we could get it wrong again.

That's where grief comes in. Grief comes with loss. It arrives with failure. Failure is not always a bad thing, though most of us dread it. It might just be failure and disappointment that force us to look at the big questions, to step outside ourselves and ask not whether we are on the right career path but whether we are living our lives so we are becoming the people we want to be.

I didn't want to go through a divorce. I didn't want dear Nicole to suffer. I certainly would do anything I could to have shielded my beautiful, young daughter from such loss, loss of her friend, loss of her world when her parents' failure ripped that world apart. I wish I could have spared her all of this. But I could not.

It's tough to tell a child that out of loss and failure can come strength of moral character. To tell them, at such an early age, that the world is not always fair, that there is often little that can be done about this unfairness . Is it enough to hold them as they cry? To offer comfort during those black nights of the soul?

I don't know.

If there's a kindred spirit out there who can answer this question for me, please, get in touch.

REFERENCES AND FUTURE READINGS

Becker, Gary. 1974. "A Theory of Marriage". *Economics of the Family: Marriage, Children, and Human Capital Volume.* Edited by Theodore W. Schultz. Chicago: University of Chicago Press.

Brooks, David. 2015. *The Road to Character.* New York: Random House.

Nussbaum, Martha. 1986. *The Fragility of Goodness.* New York: Cambridge University Press.

West, Rebecca. 1941. *Black Lamb and Grey Falcon.* London: MacMillan.

CHAPTER 11

WRETCHED, SLACKER DISNEY CHILD

Memo
To: Wretched, Slacker Disney Child
From: Stealth Bomber Mom
Re: Advice to parents
Date: Fall 2013

I first encountered the feeling of failure as a mother when my oldest son hit kindergarten. Alex was a bright and independent little boy. When we were living in faculty housing at Princeton, a 2-year-old Alex went to the communal Halloween party wearing the sweater Nani had knitted him out of Icelandic wool.[1] In the midst of ghosts, goblins and pumpkins, Alex stood out. One mother asked with puzzlement about my son's costume.

"He's dressed as an Icelandic eccentric," I replied, recognizing even then that this young man was going—*always*—to be his own person. The trait held and Alex remains bright, lovable and totally his own man, partly unmindful of the extent to which he deviates from norms and expectations, partly exalting in his difference, and enjoying the slight flaunting of authority. It is a trait he inherited from his maternal grandfather in spades, and one encouraged by both his doting parents. (On his college essay Alex took the opportunity to inform the admissions office at the University of Chicago that he found their questions "stupid and boring" and that he would write the question they *should* have asked and answer that one instead. Thank you very much!)

For the most part, I was quite comfortable with this behavior. I had a far different reaction one day when I picked up Alex from kindergarten, however, and realized all the children had drawn caterpillars and placed them around the room. Each caterpillar's face was extensively decorated and featured the child's name in big, bold, colorful letters. A segment was added to the child's caterpillar for every book the child read. The school was one for gifted children—though once it moved through its scruffy start-up stage it became more a school for children with financially-gifted parents—and many of the children were quite busily reading at home, usually under the supervision of adoring mothers. The links on some of the caterpillars were impressive. As was Alex's caterpillar. Impressive for its one teeny segment: one book and *only* one book.

I felt a cold chill cut across my body, heard the siren of the mother police in the distance, approaching, fast, to take me away. "My child does not read! I am a failure as a mother!" It took me a minute to exhale, to remember that how my child performed in life was only indirectly a reflection of me. That I could not live through my child's achievements any more than he could coast on mine. Children are independent. Separate. Their own people. It took a further bit of conscious effort but I did finally loosen up enough to breathe again. Eventually, of course, Alex learned to read just fine. Too well, in fact, for once he left the financially-gifted school, and was in classes with other mere mortals, Alex proved to be a whiz-bang reader. In fourth grade his class would be assigned a book to be read over two weeks; Alex would read it in one sitting, and then move on to other books. When the class had an exam on a book, then, Alex had long since forgotten it, having by then absorbed nearly a hundred additional books. When I went for the parent–teacher conference at this school, I was told by the counselor that Alex would be taking special classes the next year. "What kind of special classes?" I asked, naturally intrigued and pleased to learn that my child was "special."

"Well, just special," the counselor continued. I slowly comprehended.

"Ah, *special.*" Fortunately, by that time I also had learned not to argue uselessly, so I just thanked the counselor, told her how pleased I was to know Alex was doing so well and went out and found him another school. Alex's next year thus was spent at a very warm and fuzzy Waldorf School, where he learned German but otherwise took what we referred to as Alex's sabbatical year.

But let us return to the mystery of Alex's lack of interest in reading in kindergarten. It turned out that Alex loved having bedtime stories read to him and was carefully hiding the fact that he was a terrific reader. This did not come to light until first grade, however, when we had our parent–teacher conference with the sweet, soft-spoken Miss Jones. (So soft-spoken I wonder how she ever controlled a class of rowdy 6-year-olds.) We finished the conference, with Miss Jones saying only good things about our child, a fact that confirmed our belief in her superior intelligence. There was a somewhat awkward silence, and then my husband asked what we in my generation referred to as the $64,000 question: "But what about the reading?"

Miss Jones looked confused. "What do you mean?" she asked.

"Well, Alex doesn't read yet." We were nothing if not honest about our failure as parents.

Now it was Miss Jones's turn to be taken aback. "Alex is one of the best readers in the class. He always volunteers to read first, and he comprehends concepts far beyond his age level. When I was reading *Love You Forever* to the class, I had to stop and ask the aid to finish it because Alex realized where the story was going and began to cry, and it broke me up, too."

We were non plussed. Alex had an extensive bedtime story routine, being notorious as a champion resister of sleep. Only six, Alex stayed up well past 10:00 p.m. most nights, withstanding all our best efforts to be lulled to sleep by hours of bedtime stories or lullabies. Fortunately, I loved watching *Sesame Street* with Alex and remembered the day the show featured a story about Grover. In this particular episode, Grover would not confess to knowing how to read for fear he would lose his nightly bedtime stories. The next evening, as we began the bedtime ritual, I reminded Alex of this story and gently asked Alex if he were a little like Grover. Alex eyed me suspiciously, then replied with a logic and honesty that would do any serious moral philosopher proud. "Well, I know the answer to that question but I don't want to tell you."

For a while after this I thought of myself not as a failure as a mother but simply as one who eschewed the role of helicopter mother, those mothers who hover, waiting to swoop down and bail you out if there is a hint of trouble. In this regard, I recognized how wildly I deviated from the model proffered by my own mother. One Sunday night, when Alex was in sixth grade, he came in around 10:00 p.m., and told me, "Oh, yeah. I kinda sorta forgot. I'm supposed to have made a model of the Temple of Dendur with sugar cubes for tomorrow."

My mother would have lectured me extensively on my lack of organizational skills and moral fiber. She would have driven to the store to get sugar cubes, helped me get started on the project, then made me go to bed at midnight, while she stayed up half the night to complete the task for me. Not I; all those years of therapy paid off, and I simply laughed. "Well, you got a problem, don't you?"

So, I was not a helicopter mother. (My children might disagree with this.)

It was my husband who identified a more accurate aerial model for me when Alex was in fourth grade. We had moved back to Princeton from California and Alex was in a small, private school in third grade. His second-grade teacher in California had been fabulous, truly someone trained for and interested in teaching gifted children, and Alex already knew multiplication and division and was reading books galore, usually far beyond the second "grade level." Alex's third- and fourth-grade teacher at Princeton was a woman—we'll call her Susie, though that is not her real name—who was going through a rather bitter divorce. I suspect she resented the students she felt had parents with too much money and too much time to indulge their spoiled children.

She also had a child in her class who had been taken from his biological parents due to child abuse. The preferred form of abuse took the form of demanding that their children watch them having sex. I had never heard of such a thing, found it boggled my mind and introduced me to the concept of cognitive stretching, a process wherein our own experiences simply will not let us stretch and expand far enough to truly comprehend another's action. The abused child was angry, hostile and disruptive, and the poor teacher, on top of all her own personal problems and coupled with the rawness and vulnerability that accompanies a divorce, had to deal with this frightened, angry little boy. She did little serious teaching during Alex's time in her third-grade class, and when the standardized exams were distributed at the beginning of fourth grade, to determine how her students were doing, she left the class on its own, to take the exam without supervision. The troubled young boy disrupted the class and most of his fellow students in the class did not finish the test, thus scoring—in Alex's case—lower than he had the year before, something that should be impossible on an exam designed to test cumulative knowledge. That fact alone should have been an immediate trigger that something else was going on.

Parents were told to make appointments to speak with the teacher to get their children's test results. I asked if I could postpone it a week so my husband could be in attendance. I explained to the teacher that he was out of town on business all week but that he was very involved with the children's education and would like to be there to go through the results with the teacher. I was told in no uncertain terms that I could not take test results home and that my time with the teacher would be this week or not at all. With some reluctance, I agreed to take the appointment on my own.

At the appointed time and day, Susie showed me the abysmal—and impossible—test results, which told me my son had lost much of his ability to read, do multiplication and so on, in the time period between second grade and the fall of his fourth-grade year. "What do you think of these results?" Susie demanded.

"Well, they seem a bit puzzling, don't they?" I responded honestly. "I think I'd need to reflect a bit further before giving you any reaction."

Susie pushed me, and I replied again—trying to be diplomatic—that I would like to have a chance to go over the results with my husband.

"Don't you have any opinions of your own?" Susie scoffed. "Do you always say only what your husband wants you to say?"

I was taken aback. "No," I said slowly. I tend to become very quiet when angered. I say little and speak deliberately and carefully. The lowered voice would have been a warning signal to anyone trained in such indicators.

"Well, then, why don't you tell me what you think, without any coaching from your husband? Or do you have to have him think for you, too?"

That did it.

"I'm happy to tell you what I think, Susie. I think I brought you a child who was bright and happy and did well in school. Now I have a child who did poorly on one exam, a comprehensive exam in which it should be impossible to score less well on what are cumulative skills unless there is something odd going on with the test itself. The only difference I can see is that this child has had you for a teacher for a year. So, if the test results indicate anything it's probably that you are a lousy teacher."

A slow reactor, by the time I got to my office at the university I was seething. I called California, to ventilate with my husband about the exchange. As he later shared the conversation with a colleague, the colleague interrupted the story just as Susie pushed me on why I didn't have any independent opinions. "Oooh," Bill intoned cautiously, "I would not say that to *your* wife!"

My husband just laughed, and christened me the Kristen-missile, defined as something that goes into play when absolutely necessary to protect an innocent person from being abused by someone in a position of power.

So, it was well accepted around our house that "Mom" could go into high gear in time of emergency. But the Kristen-missile did not function on a daily basis, and there were many, many situations when I felt behind the curve, not doing what my superego—and my own mother—told me I should be doing as a mother.

When Nik was in kindergarten, I picked him up one day at school. I greeted Nik's kindergarten teacher, the wonderful Mrs. Morton. Mrs. Morton greeted me with her usual hearty welcome, adding: "Oh, did you know Owen has been asked to leave the school?[2] All the mothers are so happy!"

I had no idea who Owen was, let alone why I should be happy that a young child had been asked to leave the school. Somewhat sheepishly I explained that I did not know anything about Owen at all. "Oh, he is very mean to the other children. He hits them, kicks them and generally just makes them all miserable," Mrs. Morton explained. "Everyone is so relieved he's gone."

I was totally clueless but I could feel the guilt and shame descend upon me as I responded, with great embarrassment, the mother who paid no attention to her young son and his apparent situation of danger and distress. "Gosh, I feel awful. I don't think I've even heard Nik mention him."

"Oh, Nik never has any problems with Owen," Mrs. Morton reassured me. "Nik just avoids him."

This ability to take care of himself, so evident in Nik from an early age, again surfaced when he was at UCLA. The mother of one of Nik's friends—also from Irvine, and far better organized than I—called me one morning, to bemoan the time she'd spent on the computer, arranging a room the next year for her son.

"Did you have trouble getting a room for Nik?" she asked me.

The superego remains mighty powerful, and I had a few moments of panic as I explained that I had not even known Nik needed a room. I had done nothing. Totally and selfishly wrapped up in myself, I had failed my motherly duties. Now my dear child would be out on the streets, forced to live as some homeless person, wandering the slums of Westwood. (There are no slums in Westwood but there was some reality testing in my fear for Nik informed us during his senior year, when he was asked to share an apartment with three female students, that he had found a mattress for his bed on the street. Aghast at Nik's sense of cleanliness, if impressed by his resourcefulness, we insisted Nik at least get a dust cover to wrap around what we assumed was a much-used, discarded mattress.)

This event remained two years in the future, however, and all I felt at this point was panic and disgrace at my failure to perform motherly duties. I immediately phoned Nik.

"How's it going?" I asked casually. We seldom called Nik at college, and I never called in the middle of a Tuesday morning.

"Fine," Nik replied succinctly. (The family joke was that Nik played it so close to the vest that if the house were on fire, he would tell you only if he truly felt you needed to know.)

"Everything alright?" Again, I tried to be cool, casual, and nonchalant.

"Yeah." Nik's tone was slightly questioning. Nik never missed much.

"You all set for next year? Have a room and all that stuff?" I ooched up to the ignominious question carefully.

"Sure." Nik took the query in stride. "I took care of it last week."

I started to laugh and confessed all. How I'd been panicked at the thought that I had not even known I was supposed to do something, let alone had I done it! We both thought the whole event was pretty funny.

In fact, Nik always pretty much took care of himself. During high school, he was on the water polo team and did much of his homework with his friends after school, as they waited for practice, so we seldom had any insight into what homework preoccupied Nik. Alex was the eldest and hence cursed by having parents who were first timers. Perhaps in response to the failure of his parental unit to recognize our helicopter parent tendencies, Alex was brutally explicit and forcefully direct about wanting us to "get the hell out" of his life, so we never had much input into his homework either.

By the time Chloe came along, then, I thought of myself as reasonably well house trained. But each child is different and Chloe was such a diligent student, that I found myself fussing at her to study *less*. "Have more fun," I'd nag her. "Take off more time for frivolity." This particular child needed to be more of a slacker and less of a grind. More Disney and less serious student.

Our private joke—well, my private joke—ran something like this. Chloe would arrive at college and hear the other kids babble on about how happy they were to be free of parents who hovered over them, supervising homework and pressuring their kids to do well.

"Yeah, I'm really glad not to have my mom around, too," we jokingly imagined Chloe saying.

"My mom was always yelling at me not to work so hard," we laughingly envisioned the fictional Chloe telling her friends.

"You mean she was yelling at you to work hard, not to NOT work so hard," her friends would correct her, assuming Chloe had misspoken.

"No. Mom was always pushing me to work less, telling me I needed to take off more time, worry less about studying and have more fun," Chloe would honestly reply.

"What does your mom do?" her friends would inquire, confused by the general neglect and indifferent attitude of a parent.

"She's a professor."

We giggled about this, I probably more than Chloe.

The point is that I'd pretty well shifted gears by the time my daughter was a teenager. Or perhaps I just realized Chloe did not fit the usual mold, needed different guidance, less encouragement to work hard, and more admonitions to play.

Whatever the reason, I had certainly read lots of books about how to parent by the time I had Chloe. But I had become largely inured, inoculated against the idea that parenting involved giving great advice. (When I forgot this—as I too frequently did—Chloe christened someone named "Mom-Mom" in our house, as in "Mom! Mom! Don't talk yet!")

So, when I heard about *Battle Hymn of the Tiger Mother* I was taken aback, even slightly stunned. Lest I malign and mischaracterize the book—published by Amy Chua in 2011, when Chloe was still in high school and parental concerns about college run high—let me quote from Chua's website, where Chua describes how she came to write *Battle Hymn of the Tiger Mother* (Chua 2011).

> "I wrote this book in a moment of crisis, when my younger daughter seemed to turn against everything I stood for and it felt like I was losing her and everything was falling apart. After one terrible fight, I sat down at my computer, and even though I usually have writer's block, this time the words just poured out...." (Chua 2011)

Chua continues, telling how her immigrant parents were very strict with her and her sisters. Chua's parents allowed no boyfriends, insisted on straight A's (no A minuses), and piano practices and extensive homework sessions. But Chua believes this tough upbringing, plus her parents' love and high expectations for her, made her the person she is today: "*That's why I tried to raise my own two daughters the same way my parents raised me.*"

Both the book and the website make clear how much Chua loves her children and learned from them. She claims that "*we in America can ask more of children than we typically do, and they will not only respond to the challenge, but thrive.*" Chua's book thus ends by advocating the importance of pushing children, telling them they have great potential and should hold themselves to these high standards. Chua argues that we should assume our children are strong, not fragile, and that pushing them to excel is a form of believing in them and helping them realize their potential.

I'm certainly sympathetic to the idea of helping people realize their full potential, and I agree that we should encourage children to find talents and possibilities in themselves that they might not initially realize are there. But there's a fine line between that and pushing a child, making them feel they always need to do more to get our acceptance. I'm an educator and a mother, after all, and I want both my students and my children to enjoy learning; but they need to discover that pleasure for themselves. Parents—especially high-powered ones—might need to jump back a bit, avoid smothering children with our love and expectations, and think about what we really want for our children. Is it achievement, complete with a piano with teeth marks on it? (Chua describes one of her daughters becoming so angry at being forced to practice that she actually bit the piano.) Or is it to stand aside and give children space to find and develop their own interests, lead their own lives, to be able to take care of themselves when we are gone? For indeed we all shall be gone at some point or another and we should not want to keep our children dependent on us.

Around the time Chloe was preparing for college, I also heard a National Public Radio story about a man who wrote a book of advice for his son as the young man departed for college. The book began as a letter to his child, kind words of wisdom to send the boy on his way into the cold, cruel world. The letter somehow morphed into a short book of advice. What was positive about the book was the fact that the book project grew out of the man's love for his son. But as I thought about it—acutely aware that I would soon be sending Chloe out into the world of higher education—I puzzled, "What would I say to my daughter, as she leaves for college?"

The answer was crystal clear. "Trust yourself. You'll do just fine."

So, I'm not a Tiger mother. Nor am I helicopter mom, though perhaps my children would have a different view of that appraisal. I hope they know I am there if they ever need me in an emergency, at which point I can launch the Kristen-missile, or sweep in like a stealth bomber, with protection plus lots of love and support in whatever form they want it, from a sympathetic ear to a helpful question or two but probably not any advice. Otherwise, I am there—or try to be—but way under the radar.

I had this maternal philosophy all worked out in my head, and as Chloe prepared to leave for college, I thought through—and through and through yet again—the oh-so-wise words I would utter as we parted: "Trust yourself, darling. You'll be just fine."

In fact, we did have a conversation somewhat along these lines, Chloe and I. I think I basically got it all out as we walked from Wyndham House to the lecture hall where we would say goodbye. I'm pretty sure I failed to strike the desired-for appropriately casual tone. But as I stood at the door to Goodhart Auditorium, heart breaking as I bid farewell to my beautiful, young and—I suddenly realized—oh so vulnerable little girl, all conscious thought flew out of my head. As I threw my arms around Chloe and hugged her that last goodbye, struggling to hold back *my* tears, I was appalled to hear myself utter words of advice after all.

And what did I say, gentle reader?

"Have fun!"

Guess I'm not as cool as I thought I was. Oh, well. I can live with that. My kids already knew.

REFERENCES AND FUTURE READINGS

Bettelheim, Bruno. 1976. *The Uses of Enchantment: The Meaning and Importance of Fairy Tales.* NYC: Vintage Books (Random House). Portions of Bettelheim's book originally appeared in *The New Yorker.* Using Freudian psychoanalysis, Bettelheim argues that folktales provide children with a moral education that is both subtler and richer than most other forms children are able to understand at that age, and that these fairy tales help children address important issues in their young lives in a manner that is both productive and emotionally enriching. So, for example, the customary fairytales about evil stepmothers capture a reality common in the past: mothers frequently died in childbirth and fathers frequently remarried quickly, often in order to have a mother for their children. It was not unusual for the new wives to favor their own children—as does the mother in Cinderella—at the expense of the stepchildren. But beyond this, Bettelheim argues, fairytales of a wicked stepmother capture another reality: every child has to make an adjustment to the shifting behavior of its own natural mother, and this can engender anger and betrayal at the feeling of loss when the original kind mother who gave you everything—especially her breast—now demands you be weaned and toilet trained. The concept of an original mother who was wonderful and loving thus can be addressed on many levels via the wicked stepmother story.

The Uses of Enchantment was both controversial and influential. It received the 1976 National Book Critics Circle Award for Criticism and the 1977 National Book Award for Contemporary Thought. It is credited with having inspired later works utilizing fairy tales for adults, such as the 2011 film by Catherine Hardwicke, *Red Riding Hood* and the 1986 musical production by Stephen Sondheim and James Lapine, *Into the Woods.* Its controversy arose in 1991, however, when Alan Dundes, a Berkeley anthropologist, claimed Bettelheim plagiarized various sources, including key passages from Julius Heuscher's *A Psychiatric Study of Myths and Fairy Tales: Their Origin, Meaning, and Usefulness* (1963, 1974 rev. ed.). See Dundes, Alan. Winter, 1991. "Bruno Bettelheim's Uses of Enchantment and Abuses of Scholarship". *The Journal of American Folklore,* vol. 104, no. 411: 74–83.

Chua, Amy. 2011. *Battle Hymn of the Tiger Mother.* New York: Penguin.

Quindlen, Anna. 1994. *One True Thing.* New York: Random House. The story of a young careerwoman who returns home to care for her dying mother, only to realize she has greatly underestimated her mother's strength and over estimated her father. Also made into a movie, starring Meryl Streep, Renee Zellweger and William Hurt.

CHAPTER 12

CHLOE, NICOLE AND THE ELEPHANT IN THE PARLOR: THE LAST LECTURE AND SOME FINAL THOUGHTS ON ETHICS AND CHARACTER

Chloe returns this weekend for college and Thursday is my last class with a wonderful group of students. I shall miss all of them. It's always sad to say goodbye to students, people who were strangers at the beginning of the term but who—in many cases—became friends as the quarter progresses.[1] Saying goodbye to my daughter and to these students makes me think about what I am giving them as they go out into the world and whether I have done for them what I should to equip them against all the things that can—that will—befall them. Have I done my job, as a mother and as a teacher?

As I was pondering this question, I ran across a poem about teaching that I would like to share with you in this last lecture as we say goodbye. One of the reasons I like the poem is that it reminds me of the kind of books I poured over during my summers spent with my grandparents in Walnut. These were not great literature by any means, consisting mostly of stories and poetry out of date even then, school textbooks in many cases, filled with the kind of material my grandparents were required to memorize in school and, in this instance anyway, oozing all the sentimentality and Christian religion that dominated the American educational system at the turn of the nineteenth–twentieth centuries, when my grandparents were young.[2] (In fact, the poem was published by Glennice L. Harmon in 1948.) Despite its slightly sappy overtones, I decided to share it with you, my students in what has been an exceptionally rewarding class for me, since I often find it easier to speak of deep feelings through someone else rather than expressing them directly. So here is the poem, with apologies for the syrupy sentimentality.[3]

They Ask Me Why I Teach
Glennice L. Harmon

They ask me why I teach,
And I reply,
Where could I find more splendid company?
There sits a statesman,
Strong, unbiased, wise,
Another later Webster,
Silver-tongued,
And there a doctor
Whose quick, steady hand
Can mend a bone,
Or stem the lifeblood's flow.
A builder sits beside him—
Upward rise
The arches of a church he builds, wherein
That minister will speak the word of God,
And lead a stumbling soul to touch the Christ.
And all about
A lesser gathering
Of farmer, merchants, teachers,
Laborers, men
Who work and vote and build
And plan and pray
Into a great tomorrow
And I say,
"I may not see the church,
Or hear the word,
Or eat the food their hands will grow."

And yet—I may.
And later I may say,
"I knew the lad,
And he was strong,
Or weak, or kind, or proud,
Or bold, or gay.
I knew him once,

But then he was a boy."
They ask me why I teach, and I reply,
"Where could I find more splendid company?"

Putting aside its Christian, white, male-centric views of life, and noting that gay carries a totally different meaning in the poem than it does to most of us today, the poem captures something critical about teaching. Teaching is always a funny business. My cousin Kay, a retired English teacher, well versed in grammar, tells me *teach* is a transitive verb, which means it passes its action onto an object. I don't think I do that when I teach; I'm not that good. In reality, I don't really believe I *teach* anyone anything. In general, professors can inspire and encourage students but students have to learn things for themselves, and the most we as teachers can do is to give you a good list of books to read, point you in the right direction, and hope something in one of the books we suggest strikes a chord with you. Beyond that, if we're lucky or talented, or both—they say luck likes talent[4]—we can convey some of our enthusiasm for our subject, try to help you understand how wonderfully interesting and exciting we find a topic. (Chloe found a joke on the internet about how you know you're a nerd if you leave a classroom and all the other students are talking about how boring it was and you're thinking, "Wow! Was that the best stuff ever!" Well, we all should be nerds for something.[5]) As teachers, we can encourage you to find your thing, even as we show you how delightfully exciting we find our particular subject matter. But the real excitement and joy of teaching comes from watching students as they grow intellectually and come to appreciate a subject we love.[6] If we also get to observe students as they develop into rich, full human beings, well, that's the icing on the cake.

If teaching is always a bit problematic, in ethics it's even more fraught with complexity. Much of what is entailed in all good teaching is making you think for yourself. But ethics should touch not only your head; ethics should partake of emotional wisdom. An ethics class should help gently push you out of your comfort zone and into new arenas, sharpen your ability for self-reflection and self-examination. It's probably easy for students to recognize when they are being "taught" when we stand in front of the class and lecture about the ethical thought of Kant or the Stoics or Utilitarianism, or tell you how the good citizens of Athens made Socrates drink the hemlock because he made their children question too much.

Summarizing the canon in ethics will take far too long and we've already gone through much of it in class. I hope some of it sticks; what doesn't, well, that is something I leave up to you to discover on your own. I hope you'll be inspired to go read some of these great thinkers for yourself, for they too make excellent company, and one of them anyway might just ring a bell with you, make you see the world in a slightly different way, cause you to reexamine your own life and actions.[7]

In ethics classes we also pose moral dilemmas for students, and we've done some of this during the term, too. We talked about the trolley car that's on a track, hurtling toward a place (Point A) where it will hit and kill four people.[8] There's a fat man standing at the point where two tracks touch and if he gets pushed off onto the track, the trolley will go to Point B, not Point A. The trolley then will kill the fat man but the other four people will be saved. We discussed whether or not it was good for the fat man to be killed in order to save four other people. Most of you responded the way most people do when presented with this dilemma. When your doing nothing will result in the fat man's death, and will save other people, you're OK with it. But when you actually have to think in terms of *your* killing someone, you're appalled and aghast. Further discussion, however, revealed yet another fascinating tidbit about how people think about moral issues. When you approach the problem in a mathematical calculus, comparing four lives to one, then it turns out we all think slightly differently about the trolley car experiment. Social psychological experiments actually suggest different parts of our brains light up when we approach ethical situations this way.[9]

My point here is that how we think about things can determine the outcomes we reach. Moral cognition can influence behavior. Different thought processes, different actions. Further, different ethical systems will lead to vastly different outcomes in terms of action. Remember the discussion we had the first day in class, when we viewed a film depicting a couple who had a child born prematurely? The child required massive amounts of medical assistance just to survive, and then had serious, long-term disabilities that necessitated further medical care and expense. Most of us responded as expected; we cheered on the medical teams trying to help the child, were delighted the baby survived, and marveled at the parents' dedication to the child as it grew. So, at the very end of the film, when the narrator said that a different ethical system—such as Utilitarianism—would have raised the possibility of letting that particular child die and using those financial/medical resources instead to keep alive a far greater number of children, most of you were upset. But that was part of the point. The film highlighted the fact that *how* we approach ethics and the particular ethical stance we begin with can lead to quite different outcomes for us.

In this course we've not stuck with the tried-and-true recitation of the great theories of ethics. Nor have we concentrated discussion exclusively on the posing of moral dilemmas in abstract terms, such as the fat man and the trolley problem. We did a few little empirical investigations into ethics ourselves, such as the examination of social identity theory. This was the classic experiment where you all paired off into arbitrarily and artificially-created groups and ended up acting out of those group identities, even when it was against your own self-interest.[10] This was a more hands on exercise, where you actually become subjects of the test you are conducting; you then got to talk about both what the outcome of the experiment taught you substantively *and* what it felt like to take part in an experiment, to be human guinea pigs, if you will.

I'm sure you recall this experiment. We went around the room and arbitrarily designated each of you an A, a B or a C. Then everyone in Group A congregated in one part of the room, Group B was grouped into a different area of the classroom and Group C in yet another spot. We then offered each of you the following option. In option 1, members of Group A would get one extra point in your grade (from C to B, from B to A, etc.) at the end of the term. Members of Group B would get two extra points and members of Group C would get three extra points. In option 2, members of Group A lost one point; members of Group B lost two points; and members of Group C lost three points. Each of you was given the choice: Option 1 or Option 2. Not surprisingly—and in agreement with the thousands of experiments that Henri Tajfel and his students have conducted over time throughout the world since the original experiments in the 1970s—most of you in Group A choose Option 1, which gave everyone an extra point. Everyone gained. But roughly one-third of you in Group A choose Option 2. You were willing to lose something of value to you in order to do better than the others.

Tajfel—a Polish Jew who lived through the Holocaust but who lost most of his friends and family to the Nazi death camps—initially designed these studies to explain how people were driven by identity, by their membership in a group, even one artificially created. When we think of group politics, we usually assume groups are created and coalesce because they share a common interest. (I like to paint so I find others who like to paint. Or I like to play tennis or watch sports and thus find others with whom I share this common interest.) Interests lead to group identity in the traditional model. But Tajfel showed that merely being designated a member of a group led to finding common ground with others who are similarly-designated members of that same group. Identity precedes interest. Further, we define ourselves in contradistinction to others. (Who am I? I am not my mother or my big sister! I am different from them.) And being different from someone else, Tajfel claimed, often eventually leads to a desire to be better than that person. (Who am I? I am not my mother or my big sister.

They are bossy and obnoxious. I am not!) Tajfel argued that this psychological process of needing to define yourself as different from someone else, and then wanting to make your group—the in-group, if you will—better than those in the out-group, this psychological process accounts for much of the prejudice and bigotry that lies at the root of communal violence, such as the Holocaust.

We followed up on the first experiment by having your groups name themselves and then define what was special about your groups. Then we did the same test again, offering the same options. Once you had a chance to think about what you all had in common and why you were special, the voting became even more sharply in-group specific. (Often, the special thing you shared in common was trivial, as in the group that said, "We are the best because we are the group closest to the wall.") Many of you cared not about doing better objectively so much as you wanted to be better off than the other groups. You were willing to give up something concrete (a better grade) for the better position compared to others in the class. The relativity of your well-being compared to others was key. We discussed this experiment, in which you were the subjects, and then you wrote essays about the experience. I hope this hands-on experiment taught you something in a way that simply reading about the Tajfel experiment would not have done. (Your essays indicated this was the case.)

We also read of the Jane Elliott experiments, conducted by Elliott when she was an elementary school teacher in Iowa during the period when Martin Luther King was shot and killed in April 1968. Elliott was appalled at how the "white" news broadcasters kept talking about how they hoped someone of "his people" would surface to lead "them" to peace. As described in the *Frontline* special on Elliott's work, Elliott went into her third-grade school class in rural Iowa on the day after the assassination and talked with the children, asking them if they would be interested in doing an experiment on prejudice.[11] The kids thought this was cool, so Elliott divided the class into blue-eyed and brown-eyed kids. One day the blue-eyed kids were the in-group; the next day it was the brown-eyed kids. When you were the select group, you got praise, special privileges and good treatment. When you were in the out-group, things went badly quickly. No one liked you. The other kids would not play with you on the playground. You got less food at lunchtime, couldn't use the good water fountain, etc.

Elliott was appalled at how easily the good kids turned on the bad kids, even though all the children knew from the get-go that this was a totally artificial experiment. After several years of conducting this kind of experiment, Elliott noticed another fascinating finding. On the days when students were members of the in-group, they performed better on simple reading and spelling exercises. The impact of being told they were "good" had a profound impact on the children's self-esteem. They actually performed better as judged by objective measures. (Their spelling improved, for example.) Taking part in this experiment helped make the young students acutely aware of the damaging aspect of being in a prejudiced group, findings replicated later by academics in many fields.[12]

Then there's our big project: an attempt to determine whether your empathic involvement with someone our society describes as "different" can help you overcome your prejudice or stereotypes about people in that group. The group we chose was the elderly, partly because asking what it means to be "old" feels less explosive than diving in to ask about all the other discriminators our society chooses to select for ill-treatment. (Make no mistake. We don't usually beat up old people or put them into concentration and extermination camps, as the Nazis did the Jews so I most definitely am not equating these forms of ill-treatment; but we do sometimes leave old people in substandard nursing homes, where they can be physically abused and emotionally abandoned, and this neglect is certainly not negligible.) But I choose the elderly for other reasons as well. First, focusing on age discrimination allows us to quickly grasp how artificial the characteristics on which we discriminate truly are. No one is born old. Most of us fight getting old, yet still we crave it, not wanting to die young. Your interviews and interactions with an elder also helped you realize how artificial a number can be. (Seventy can be ancient for one person, and yet still young for another.) Year after year, classes who did this experiment where they had to interview someone who was elderly came back and told me that "being old" is largely a function of resources. If you have decent health, friends or family nearby, and the financial resources to find good doctors to care for you, you can be young at 80 or old at 55.

Second, I chose age as a discriminator not because it is one of the major ones—which it is in this country—but because it will let you interview someone in your family and this opens up all the ties of affection that are so important for emotional growth. If you care for someone—as many of you do for a grandparent or a favorite teacher —you listen more carefully and can more easily get out of your own head and into theirs. (Remember your classmate—let's call her Beth— whose grandmother called Beth's mother after they had done the interview. The grandmother was crying, saying she had not realized anyone in the family loved her that much to take the time to listen closely about her life.)

Creating the empathic involvement with an elder might have felt a bit contrived. Is a short, one-to-two-hour interview with someone who is old truly enough to open your eyes to what being old feels like? Can we as young people understand what it must feel like to lose most of the people you love? To suffer from constant pain? To not be able to do all the things you once took so for granted, even the simple things like driving a car, opening a jar of spaghetti sauce, putting on a dress that zips up the back, or tying your shoes? To being looked down upon as someone who is "past it"? "Over the hill?" Discarded?

Your papers aren't in yet so I don't know whether or not this process had any effect on you. But I have done a lot of what I hope was subtle pushing to get you to think about these issues in your own life, to get you out of your comfort zone by looking at your behavior and those of the people around you. Now that the course is ending, I can tell you that I wanted you to move beyond merely reading the great works of ethical thinkers like Kant. To venture beyond the titillating effect of reading about experiments in social or moral psychology and marveling about how odd people are. I wanted you to understand these things for yourself. I wanted you to feel in your gut, as they say, what ethical dilemmas are all about. Like the student who came to see me about the essay you had to write, pairing Kant's work with the novel *Invisible Man*. *Invisible Man*, as you remember, describes a man who says people do not see him. They overlook the individual person that he is and see only a black man. The assignment was to write about a time when you were made to feel invisible and a time when you made someone else feel invisible. (I chose this pairing so you would think about how easy it is to do and realize that those who do this are not evil; they are simply human, just as *you* were only human when *you* made someone feel invisible.) The student came to see me during office hours, confused because she did not understand how this assignment related to Kant's work.[13]

"What are you writing about?" I asked.

"I wrote about the time my parents got a divorce. Each of them gave me nice gifts, really great presents. At first, I thought they were trying to make it up to me, for hurting me in the divorce. But then I realized my mother was trying to make my father feel bad by giving me gifts that were better than the ones he gave me, and vice versa. The gifts weren't really about me at all. They were to get back at the other person. It made me feel invisible, just a tool in their divorce."

"Okay," I replied. "So how does this relate to Kant?"

"I'm not sure," she replied.

"What is Kant's theory about?"

"Well, he tells us to ask, before we take an action, whether the world would be better if everyone took acts like this. That's the categorical imperative. You know, if an act falls into this category, then it's a good act and we should do it."

"Okay. Is there anything else in the categorical imperative?" I asked.

She thought a minute. "Well, he tells us not to take an act as a means only, to ..." She stopped, mid-sentence, eyes popping wide open. "Oh my god! That's what he means when Kant says we shouldn't treat people as a means only! That's what my parents were doing! They were treating me as a means to another end. The gifts were only a means to get back at each other; they weren't about making me feel good at all!"

I don't know what happened to this student after she left my class. But I am willing to wager good money that she understands Kant in her bone. She knows how bad it feels to be treated as a means only and, I hope—I believe—she will never do it to anyone else precisely because she experienced first-hand how bad that makes you feel about yourself and about those who do it to you. If only one student gained the wisdom that comes from taking our own moments of suffering and turning them into an empathic regard for the frailty of others, that course was a success.

So I recognize that it is difficult, and risky to ask you to put yourselves into the middle of a real-life ethical situation, and to then ask you to talk about how you felt about it. To ask you about your role in it. I'm so grateful you trusted me and your fellow students enough to share your thoughts about these situations. So many of you were generous enough to convey your honest thoughts and experiences about the ethical dilemmas you confront in your own lives, often with people whom you love and care for even when they let you down by being human. Like the student whose divorced parents gave her presents for the wrong reasons. Or the student in this class—we'll call her Jane—whose sister was gravely ill and the friend Jane asked to drive her to the hospital equivocated just long enough before doing agreeing to do so that Jane was left with mixed feelings about that friend. Jane was brave enough to trust us with this story and to talk about her feelings and discomfort and her own uncertainty about the incident and how to react to the friend now.

We all have some stories like this; it's often the very uneasiness that results from the up-close and personal aspect of thinking about such stories that helps force us to find new ethical ground. Essentially, that's what both this course and this book have been all about: trying to get you to think about the personal issues in your own lives, both the ones that make us feel alive and happy with ourselves, and the ones that come calling late at night and demand to know why we failed someone we loved or were left disappointed by them. The events that make us unhappy or at least uncertain about what to do and who we are. These are often the issues that compel us to grow.

Teachers think a lot about what courses to teach and how best to prepare college curricula. We think about more than just imparting knowledge of a particular subject, as important as that subject matter is. We also think about how best to give students critical thinking skills and about how to help you convert knowledge into wisdom.[14]

If you want to read Kant and Plato and Jeremy Bentham—or Jesus, Mohammed or Moses, if you find the religious route to ethics more copasetic— to find out what you should do, you can come away with certain rules to help you make decisions. (We refer to such ethics, which judge the morality of a position not by the consequences of an action but rather by how well acts corresponds to certain rules, as deontological ethics, or sometime as duty or obligation-based ethics.) It's very useful to have guidelines that are clear. Most of us need these, at some point in our lives anyway. Rules like: "Never lie." Or "honor thy father."

But what if your father abuses you? What if he beats you or verbally belittles you with sarcasm? Is it really right to honor him? What if the father beats up your mother? Your little sister? Should you still pay him respect?[15] And what if the Nazis come to you and ask if you know where Jews are hidden, so they can arrest them and ship them off to concentration camp? Where does the admonition not to lie get you in this case? Is it really ethical to tell the truth to the Nazis, knowing your truthfulness will just result in someone innocent being murdered? Would Kant or Jesus or Mohammed truly want you to do this? Shouldn't we consider the consequences of our acts and not judge acts just by the extent to which they correspond to a rule, no matter how valid that rule seems as a general principle? But then, how can we foresee the consequences of acts? These are the more difficult questions we have to pose for you, and the ones that we faculty members worry about late at night as we wonder whether we have actually given you the ethical life skills to go out into a world that is too often confusing, harsh and perplexing.

We can tell you to trust yourself, but what if you are someone who does not yet have the life skills to trust yourself reliably? I'm not sure I did at your age. I was far too trusting, too naïve, too focused on a world I believed was a rational place, populated with honorable human beings. I had to get whacked around a lot before I toughened up, and even now sometimes—most times?—I'm not sure I get it right. Most of us err in one direction or other. Some are always too cautious, and miss out on lovely opportunities because of our wariness; others are too optimistic, and get disappointed and hurt. If we are lucky, we eventually realize what well may be our innate tendency to one type of behavior versus another, and learn to auto correct, when possible.[16] Above all, as we age, we learn humility and some forgiveness.

So, who am I to try to help you? Isn't it slightly offensive, or at least patronizing and condescending, even to think that you may want or need advice from me? Beyond this, what counsel can be given? Is there some place—the view from nowhere, Thomas Nagel[17] called it—that I can help you find, where you can look objectively at what is going on in your life, and perhaps get a different perspective on the thing that troubles you? But is the view from nowhere where we want to be? Should ethical decisions be made totally objectively, regardless of the context?

You remember our discussion of moral reasoning, and how cognitive psychologists tell us that even the way we think about ethical issues can determine our action?[18] We discussed the Kohlberg–Gilligan debate, which asks whether there is a developmental process of moral reasoning, much as there is a developmental pattern of language acquisition. Kohlberg found objective, dispassionate moral reasoning the highest stage, and based his theory on empirical work done using students from Harvard. Gilligan taught women students in the graduate Education School, back in the days when the Ivy League allowed no women and hence many women went to the Seven Sisters schools, such as Radcliffe. Gilligan's research subjects thus were female students; Kohlberg's subjects were all men. Gilligan's results suggested women followed a slightly different pattern of moral development, finding compassion the highest stage of moral growth. The consequence of these different types of moral reasoning were visibly evident in an actual murder trial of an elderly man accused of killing his aged wife. The wife suffered from terminal cancer and was in great pain. Worse, her doctors held out no hope for a recovery, and all the elderly couple had to look forward to were months, perhaps years, of agony and eventual death. According to both the old man and family friends, the wife begged the husband to help her die. What would you do were you a juror charged with judging this man? Some jurors looked at the case and responded dispassionately, and found the old man guilty. He did kill his wife, after all. He had admitted that. The facts of the case were not contested, and killing someone is against the law. Further, murder seems ethically wrong, at least on the surface, to most of us. Other jurors set the case in a context and found the old man not guilty.[19] These jurors were typically female. As Gilligan's experimental work suggests, it is women who are more likely to fall into this last category. It's a generality, but on the whole researchers find that it is women who hold compassion the highest moral value, not objectivity, as do men and the Anglo-American legal system these men created. (This is Nagel's view from nowhere.)

Years ago, an editor of mine suggested I write a book of essays about ethics. I trusted the editor and thought maybe he had seen something I had not, so every now and then an essay—or an idea for an essay—presents itself to me and I file it away somewhere in the computer, thinking perhaps I may eventually pull together a few thoughts for such a book. In a rash moment, I even got as far as thinking about a title for this book. The title I chose was *Chloe and Nicole and the Elephant in the Parlor* because many of the ethical issues that trouble me the most are the up-close and personal ones, and these often concern my children. This book is the result of that editor's suggestion. A word of explanation, then, at the end of the book, as at the end of a course.

As should be evident by now, Chloe is my much-loved daughter. Nicole is her little friend, age 10 or 12 when I started writing this book. The elephant? That was something I wanted the reader to figure out for themselves. But here's my answer: I think the elephant sitting in the parlor—that huge THING that takes over the room and which we ignore at our peril—is our sense of self. It's who we are. It's who we are when we are with others and who we are when we are alone. My parting hint, wish, teeny bit of wisdom to impart to you, given not to be patronizing or because I believe I have all the answers, but rather because I have come to care for you this last term, is this: "Take good care of your self" for it is your most precious possession. It is what you will have once your beauty and youth and money or position go. It's much more valuable than gold or silver or all the money you will ever possibly earn. For while money indeed can help protect you against many of life's ups and downs, it cannot insulate you from the big losses, like the death of a loved one or the self-doubt that comes with failure.

So think about who you are. Think about it as you take an action, as Kant suggests. But also think of it in terms of how the act will affect you. What will this act do to you? Will it make you a better person? Someone you like, perhaps someone you can even admire? Someone you can live with at the end of the day? Someone you can look at in the mirror in the morning with pride and pleasure, instead of disgust and regret?

Think about that Dutch rescuer of Jews we talked about in class. Marion Pritchard was a young girl about your age, just 18 or 19 when the Nazis occupied Holland.[20] She was a social work student who came out of class one day, much as you come out of class every day and head home. Only this particular day, Pritchard found herself facing the Gestapo, throwing Jewish orphans into a truck, to take them off to concentration camp. She felt paralyzed with shock, uncertain what to do. She stood watching, frozen, doing nothing to help as the Jewish orphans were rounded up by the Gestapo. Stunned, confused, and dazed, Pritchard watched as the Nazis also threw into the truck the Dutch women who tried to save the orphans. Her comment later: "We all have memories of times when we should have done something and we didn't. And it gets in the way during the rest of your life." Partly because of this one harrowing experience, Pritchard later volunteered to hide Jews in her family's country home, rescuing nearly 150 people. Eventually, Pritchard became a psychoanalyst, someone dedicated to helping others think about who we are and how our actions feed back into our sense of self.

I encourage you to remember this young woman, and what she can teach us. I'd like you to think about yourself as others relate to you. How do you feel after you come away from an interaction with them? Do they make you feel good about yourself? Not in some sycophantic way but do you feel they are being straight with you? Honest? Treating you with the respect and dignity you deserve, or are they subtly shading the truth they present to you so you will do something *they* want you to do, something which may not be what you would do were you in possession of the full facts?

We can all think of such instances, some so commonplace they become trivialized. Men sometimes use various tricks to get women into bed with them. Women sometimes try to trap men into marrying them. Or vice versa. Good people who go into politics to make the world better end up making dubious choices because "you have to get elected in order to do good." Bosses and even friends encourage us to shade the truth and our ethics by telling us, "Oh, it's OK. Everyone does it once in a while." We go along to get along.

There are so many ways in which we can sell ourselves short. One of my favorite poems captures this well. The author—a once popular poet named Edna St. Vincent Millay—speaks of how people can betray their loves "through shyness in the houses of the rich or in the presence of clergymen." We can be worked upon "by cynics like chiropractors" or be so "anxious to land a job" that we diminish our loves "by a conniving smile; or when befuddled by drink. Jeered at them through heartache or lazily fondled the fingers of their alert enemies."[21] The antidote to such betrayals, Millay asserts, is to boldly declare that we shall hold fast to the things and the people we love. We should find someone and something that we shall love forever. The poem ends as the author declares:

That I shall love you always.
No matter what party is in power;
No matter what temporarily expedient combination of allied
interests wins the war;
Shall love you always.

In truth, we do not always have someone there to "love us always." Unconditional love is hard to give and hence hard to find in this imperfect world. (As a parent who goofs up all too often, with three children I nonetheless love more than life itself, I can attest to that.) Most of us feel abandoned or adrift at some point. Most of us are lucky if we get one person who ever can look us in the eye, with genuine conviction, and say, "I love you. You are truly wonderful. You deserve the best there is in life. I have your back and support you. Always. Now go, fly, little bird."

I think this is one aspect of what is meant by that parting phrase: "Take care of yourself." I want to explore the origin of that phrase in what I hope will be the one, very small farewell insight I can impart to help guide you after you leave me and my classroom. Just take a minute to think about the origin and meaning of this slightly over-worked expression.

Those of us who lack the wisdom or the poetry to say it any other way fall back on the tried and true. The trite. The kind of expression found in the little poem I read at the beginning of this lecture.

Just in case you ever feel very alone and in need of someone to believe in you, someone to remind you that you deserve the best treatment possible, that you are a human being with worth and dignity and that you should expect and demand this respect from those around you, just as you should give that respect to them, let me say it here.

You have been the splendid company that makes teaching the joy it is. You have enriched my life this past term. How could I not want only the best for you? As we say goodbye and I send you out into the world, I ask you.

Please. Take very good care of your selves.

REFERENCES AND FUTURE READINGS

Anderson, Robert. 1968/1970. *I Never Sang for My Father*. Movie (1970) and play (1968) script.

Bakewell, Sarah. 2010. *How to Live: Or A Life of Montaigne in One Question and Twenty Attempts at an Answer*. Chatto and Windus. 2010; Other Press, 2011. The book uses the life of Montaigne to address what is important in life. The book received the National Book Critics Circle Award (for biography) and the Duff Cooper Prize, awarded for the best work in English or French addressing biography, history, political science or occasionally poetry. The prize honors the British diplomat and Cabinet member Duff Cooper. Since 2013, the prize has been known as The Pol Roger Duff Cooper Prize, to honor the financial support by Pol Roger.

Ditto, P. H., Pizarro, D. A., Tannenbaum, D. 2009. "Motivated Moral Reasoning". In B. H. Ross (Series ed.) and D. M. Bartels, C. W. Bauman, L. J. Skitka and D. L. Medin (eds.). *Psychology of Learning and Motivation*, vol. 50: "Moral Judgment and Decision Making" (pp. 307–338). San Diego, CA: Academic Press.

Edmonds, Dave. 2013. *Would You Kill the Fat Man? The Trolley Problem and What Your Answer Tells Us about Right and Wrong*. Princeton, NJ: Princeton University Press.

Elliott, Jane. 1970. *The Eye of the Storm*. Boston: PBS Frontline.

——— 2001. *The Angry Eye*. Boston: PBS (Public Broadcasting Station) WGBH.

Ellison, Ralph. 1948/1995. *Invisible Man*. Vintage Books/Random House.

Gaskell, Elizabeth Cleghorn. 2011. *Cranford*. Oxford: Oxford University Press.

Greene, Graham. 1948. *The Heart of the Matter*. London: William Heinemann.

Greene, Joshua D. 2009. "Dual-Process Morality and the Personal/Impersonal Distinction: A Reply to McGuire, Langdon, Coltheart, and Mackenzie". *Journal of Experimental Social Psychology*, vol. 45, no. 3: 581–84.

———— 2013. *Moral Tribes: Emotion, Reason, and the Gap Between Us and Them.* New York: Penguin Press.

————. 2014. "Beyond Point-and-Shoot Morality: Why Cognitive (Neuro)science Matters for Ethics." *Ethics*, vol. 124, no. 4: 695–726.

Greene, Joshua D., R. Brian Sommerville, Leigh E. Nystrom, John M. Darley, Jonathan D. Cohen. 2001. "An fMRI Investigation of Emotional Engagement in Moral Judgment". *Science*, vol. 293, no. 5537: 2105–8.

Greene, Joshua D., Cushman, F. A., Stewart, L. E., Lowenberg, K., Nystrom, L. E. and Cohen, J. D. 2009. "Pushing Moral Buttons: The Interaction Between Personal Force and Intention in Moral Judgment". *Cognition*, vol. 111, no. 3: 364–71.

Hardy, Thomas. 1874. *Far from the Madding Crowd.* New York: Harper & Brothers

Harmon, Glennice L. 1948. "They Ask Me Why I Teach". *NEA Journal*, vol. 37, no. 1: 375.

Kahneman, Daniel. 2011. *Thinking, Fast and Slow.* New York: Farrar, Strauss and Giroux.

McGuire, J., Langdon, R., Coltheart, M. and Mackenzie, C. 2009. "A Reanalysis of the Personal/Impersonal Distinction in Moral Psychology Research". *Journal of Experimental Social Psychology*, https://doi.org/10.1016/j.jesp. 2009.01.002.

Millay, Edna St. Vincent. 1931/1934.1939/1958. *Collected Poems.* New York: Harper Perennial.

Monroe, Kristen Renwick. 1996. *The Heart of Altruism: Perceptions of a Common Humanity.* Princeton, NJ: Princeton University Press.

Nagel, Thomas. 1986. *The View from Nowhere.* Oxford: Oxford University Press.

Pedersen, Anne, Iain Walker, Mark Rapley and Mike Wise. 2003. "Anti-racism—What Works? An evaluation of the Effectiveness of Anti-racism Strategies'. Prepared by the Centre for Social Change & Social Equity. Murdoch University. March 2003, pp. 78–80.

Peters, William. *A Class Divided: Then and Now* (first edn.). 1987. Yale University Press.

Ringel, M. M. and Ditto, P. H. 2019. "The Moralization of Obesity". *Social Science & Medicine*, vol. 237: 112399.

Steele, Claude and Joshua Aronson. 1995. "Stereotype Threat and the Intellectual Test Performance of African Americans". *Journal of Personality and Social Psychology*, vol. 69, no. 5: 797–811.

Stewart, Tracie L. 2003. "Do the 'Eyes' Have It? A Program Evaluation of Jane Elliott's 'Blue-Eyes/Brown-Eyes' Diversity Training Exercise 1". *Journal of Applied Social Psychology*, vol. 33, no. 9: 1898–1921.

Tajfel, Henri. 1959. "Quantitative Judgment in Social Perception". *British Journal of Psychology*, vol. 50, 16–29.

————. 1969. "Cognitive Aspects of Prejudice". *Journal of Social Issues*, vol. 25, 79–97.

————. 1974. "Social Identity and Intergroup Behaviour". *Social Science Information*, vol. 13, 65–93.

————. (ed.). 1978. "Differentiation Between Social Groups". *Studies in the Social Psychology of Intergroup Relations.* London: Academic Press.

————. 1981. "Human Groups and Social Categories". *Studies in Social Psychology.* New York: Cambridge University Press.

————. 1982. "Social Psychology of Intergroup Relations". *Annual Review of Psychology*, vol. 33, 1–39.

————. 2010. *Social Identity and Intergroup Relations*. New York: Cambridge University Press.

————. and John. C. Turner. 1979. "An Integrative Theory of Intergroup Conflict". In William G. Austin and S. Worchel (eds.). *The Social Psychology of Intergroup Relations*. Monterey, CA: Brooks-Cole.

————. and John C. Turner. 1986. "The Social Identity Theory of Intergroup Behavior". *Psychology of Intergroup Relations*. Chicago: Nelson-Hall.

Tajfel, Henri, M. G. Billig, R. P. Bundy and Claude Flament. 1971. "Social Categorization and Intergroup Behaviour". *European Journal of Social Psychology*, vol. 1, no. 2: 149–78.

NOTES

ACKNOWLEDGMENTS

1 I am taking liberties here. John Stuart Mill—indeed one of my favorite philosophers—never gave explicit advice to children, at least as far as I know. But he did publish a wonderful essay, *On Liberty*, in 1859, in which Mill argued that society may intervene only when individual acts concern others; society may not mediate acts that affect only the individual him or herself. This assumes that we can distinguish between what are known as self-regarding and other-regarding acts. One of the major criticisms of Mill's theory centers on the fact that *all* acts can have some effect on others. (The illustration my political theory professor noted was brushing one's teeth, an act which may seem to influence just me but which in fact can have repercussions for other people, such as my dentist.) In my own thinking, and cognizant of the need to sometimes explain myself to children who may need a simple rule to guide their lives, I pirated the Mill distinction, recrafting it to derive a simple maxim for the children. As I write this, I am reminded that while I was in grad school, I dated an English economist, a Milton Friedman student who left his Cockney roots, convinced of the intellectual superiority of the Chicago School of Economics. At some point, my young man explained Friedman's concept of externalities, arguing that government should stay out of people's private sphere. I thought a moment, then replied that I understood. "This is like Mill's self-regarding/other-regarding distinction."

"No," my young man replied. "It's Friedman's idea."

I laughed, assuming any good Englishman would have heard of John Stuart Mill. "I think Mill got it first."

Ignoring my sarcasm and undeterred by what he should have known was a chronological impossibility that Friedman might just possibly have heard of or even read John Stuart Mill, and hence been influenced by Mill's thought, my young man insisted the idea had originated with Friedman. In fact, the concept of externalities originates with two British economists, both of whom surely read Mill: Henry Sidgwick (1838–1900) and Arthur Pigou (1877–1959). Sidgwick first formally articulated the concept and Pigou formalized it. In general, an externality is defined as the cost—or the benefit—that affects a party who was not involved in choosing to incur that cost or benefit. Air pollution is one frequently cited example, in which a firm's pollution fouls the air of people uninvolved in the decision to create the product that then results in the pollution. This externality is a by-product of the company's decisions to produce their product, and the consumers who purchase this product. Their acts thus create an obligation for the company to pay for the external cost to others in the form of the pollution it creates, and to pass that cost along to the consumer.

2 I am grateful for Chuck's encouragement but he certainly should not be held responsible for the product his encouragement produced.

3 I have changed the name of the babysitter, as I have most of the people mentioned in the book, some of whom are composites.

4 The astute reader may note that Nik's name is spelled without a c. When he was five Nick—then spelled with a c—changed the spelling of his name, prompted in part by reading *D'Aulaire's Book of Greek Myths* (Ingri d'Aulaire and Edgar Parin d'Aulaire 1992) and partly by Nicholas's father's pride in his Greek ancestry.

5 *Aesop's fables*, the D'Aulaires' books on myths (1992/2002, 2006, 2016), the Singers's (2005) literary anthology, and the Bible are just a few illustrations of this. In this instance, my use of homey, motherly stories constitutes an attempt to let students know that we can be professionals and family people too; there were few role models for me, as I began my career and I want my students to know it is possible to be both a parent and a scholar. There is a less lofty reason as well. The motherly stories are repayment for all those economics/econometric courses in which the professor had just about explained a complex phenomenon so that I could grasp it and then he—it was always a man—went into a sports metaphor. "It's as if the Federal Reserve had acted as a tight running end and fumbled the ball on the 40-yard line," the professor would explain. All the boys in the class would nod their heads knowingly; I had NO idea at all what they were talking about since, as my example probably illustrates, I know nothing about sports of any kind!

PREFACE

1 The title is a quote from Joan Didion. "We tell ourselves stories in order to live. We live entirely by the impression of a narrative line upon disparate images, the shifting phantasmagoria, which is our actual experience" (Didion 1979).

2 This lovely phrase occurs at the end of a beautiful documentary on Joan Didion, *The Center Will Not Hold* (Dunne et al. 2017). I recommend the documentary and Didion's own work to readers, especially *Blue Nights* (2011).

3 One of my favorite t-shirts says: *In a world where you can be anything, be kind.*

4 One of my students was a first-generation college student, raised by two immigrant parents so poor they had to work two jobs each just to support the family. In a course called "The moral of the story" we discussed how people learn ethical precepts via stories. I asked the class about their favorite stories, and raised the topic of bedtime stories. The student told me he never had any bedtime stories, because his parents were always too tired to read them. Because of their financial need, he said his entire life had been focused on money and getting ahead. But then he said he read Michael Sandel's *What Money Can't Buy: The Moral Limits of Markets* (2012), and it changed his life.

INTRODUCTION: THE MORAL OF THE STORY

1 An excellent anthology that uses excerpts from great pieces of literature to teach ethics is Peter and Renata Singer's *The Moral of the Story* (Wiley-Blackwell, 2005). The anthology eschews the kind of personal stories emphasized here but raises a wide range of ethical subjects and themes to suggest that literature can add a richness to the discussion of real-life moral dilemmas and questions. Harold Bloom addresses ethical issues, especially dying, in his last book (2020).

   Martha Nussbaum's *The Fragility of Goodness: Luck and Ethics in Greek Tragedy and Philosophy* (2nd Edition, Cambridge University Press, 1986) is another wonderful book, drawing on literary texts from ancient Greece to discuss the moral lesson in plays, Platonic dialogues and myths, such as that of Phaedra or Hecuba.

2 Just this morning, a former student brought her 2-year-old daughter and her new baby to show me. She asked what advice I had on how to teach her daughters to be good to other people, especially when other people might not be good to them in response.

3 Usually when students write to catchup, it is not unrelated to a need for a recommendation. There was nothing of that in Jessie's email. She simply knew I would want to know she was doing well.

CHAPTER 1: WALNUT

1 The scholar in me of course had to check on the origin of this quote. Doing so produced a multitude of cities cited. Shaw supposedly nominated Ireland, where Shaw believed everything happens 50 years later. Heine—among others—nominated Holland. Both Mark Twain and Will Rogers suggested Cincinnati was the place to be, although the grace period was then only two years. The only quote I could find for Bismarck said Mecklenburg and not 30 years. Since this is a memoir, however, not a piece of scholarly work, I decided to stick with my recollection; it's my memory and it does not need to be accurate in this instance. Mother used to chide me when I would tell my children my funny family stories. "You're getting them all wrong," she would protest. Always anxious to get her to record her thoughts on paper—knowing she wrote far better than do I and had many lively stories to relate—I would reply: "History belongs to the writers, so *you* write it down, or else I will, and then it will be my version that sticks." She always refused, and so it is my memory that constitutes the official record.

2 I am indebted to Bernie Grofman for this lovely word.

3 *Hara-kiri* is Japanese ritual suicide by disembowelment. It involves plunging a short blade into one's abdomen and pulling the blade so the abdomen is slit open. Although it sounds gruesome, the act, my father explained, is one intended to allow the soldier to die with honor rather than be captured by the enemy and, presumably, be tortured. It also is performed by soldiers who feel they have brought shame on themselves. As Daddy explained this to his horrified 12-year-old daughter, *hara-kiri* was probably the Japanese general's attempt to die with some dignity, and my father interpreted the general's giving him the records as a sign of great respect and honor, one my father treated with high regard.

4 I use the words my grandfather used—hobos, cripple, etc.—even though those may offend some people now. I apologize for being politically incorrect but believe it is important to quote people properly, as doing so does capture the spirit of that time, including the derogatory words sometimes used then. I do not advocate such derogatory terminology or the behavior they encouraged, but it is important not to sanitize the past since doing so can inhibit our ability to understand why people were offended by such terms and how ugly and degrading this language can be and was experienced as such.

5 Tommy remained close to my mother, who once took him, my brother and me with her to a tap-dancing class in which Mother had enrolled. In those days Tommy had a bit of a tendency to exaggerate but that night at dinner, when asked what he had done that day, he quite truthfully and as a matter of fact reported that he had gone to watch Aunt Trudi at her tap-dancing class. His father—usually mild-mannered and affable—pounded the table. "That does it, young man!" Uncle Tom laid down the law. "No more lying and exaggerating! That's it!" Mother was so embarrassed when she heard this story that she quit her tap dancing.

6 As I write, I have a blooming African violet near my desk, a gift from my friend, Barbara.

7 Years later, Aunt Beverly and Mother wrote an anonymous column for *The Walnut Leader*, filled with reminiscences. Everyone in town loved the old stories from the past, especially Grandpa Bob, who told friends he thought perhaps he must have met the authors—signed Sally Forth and Tagalong—at some point, since they seemed to recount so many stories he remembered. I don't believe Mother ever told him his daughters were the authors.

8 The popularity of *Finding Your Roots* with Henry Louis Gates, Jr. and *Who Do You Think You Are?*, both genealogy documentary series, are excellent illustrations of this yearning.

9 *The Ingenious Gentleman Don Quixote of La Mancha* (*El ingenioso hidalgo don Quijote de la Mancha*) is a Spanish novel published in two volumes by Miguel de Cervantes Saavedra in 1605 and 1615. It tracks the adventures of an other-worldly Don Quixote, who believes he is a medieval knight, defending justice and the weak, but who ends tilting at windmills he mistakes for villains. When I took my junior year in Geneva, I traveled to Spain for Christmas break, and sent my parents two figures: one of the Don and the second of his faithful servant, Sancho Panza, who is the practical one who cares for and protects his master. The packages were not designated for a particular parent, just sent with a card that each parent was to choose one figure. Daddy opened Don Quixote, a choice Mother always found apt, likening herself to Sancho Panza, with her feet solidly on the ground, faithfully caring for her somewhat other-worldly and idealistic husband. *Don Quixote* is considered one of the most influential works from the Spanish Golden Age of literature and, indeed, in the entire Spanish literary canon. It is also often considered one of the earliest novels in modern Western literature.

10 *The American Scholar* is published by the Phi Beta Kappa Society. Daddy was elected his senior year in college, but Mother was invited her junior year. She was tremendously proud of her grandson, Nicholas, when he was elected to Phi Beta Kappa at UCLA. Nik, of course, didn't realize what an honor this was and rather casually tossed off the fact that he had been invited to "some party" for Phi Beta Kappa to attend at graduation but that he assumed no one would be interested, so he'd decline the

invitation. Up until that moment Nik had not even thought to mention that he had been elected to the honorary society, something neither of his parents ever attained. We definitely went to see Nik being honored, his grandmother perhaps proudest of all.

11 **Kristi to Mom.**
In a message dated 2/19/2010 5:21:48 a.m. Central Standard Time:
Couldn't sleep so got up and ate pie—I know. I know—and then for some reason was moved to bang this out. Hope you like it. Remember it's not fact; it's memoir. Hugs, K.

Mom to Kristi.
This is a delightful memoir and I enjoy reading and rereading it because it gives me a glimpse into what you have carried with you from an experience I was responsible for weaving into your childhood. The summer visits you and Jamie and I made to Walnut were motivated chiefly by my desire to cling to a childhood and youth that was behind me. When I married Jim and followed him to Collinsville, I turned my back on Walnut, but family ties remained. And perhaps an essential bit of my own personal identity that I was even then trying to establish and still confounds me. (Only now the little girl of those days has, in her work, shown me what I have been seeking!) Besides, I told myself and others who asked, that I was going to let my children see a simpler life and learn the community and affection that family held.

So, what did Kristi see; what did she learn? A light heart, personal freedom, affection for others, whatever their frailties? Provincialism and physical discomfort in the heat and humidity of the prairies she gives short shift through the prism of adult experience. Probably no one thing, full and complete, ever to be isolated and identified, all, singly, just a blip in Kristi's life experience. I shall still wonder always why your Communist friend at NYU called you a "real American". Was it Walnut's glimpse of the past?

I am struck that you have a real facility for writing more personal prose. Perhaps once the latest book goes to press, you will try your hand at some more personal stories. There is a need for memoirs to record the past before it disappears from human memory or becomes condensed and analyzed by the experts. I love the way you describe your emotions in a foray through the "Confederated Store." It is so true.

Your story blends right in with my thoughts about the book about Midwestern historians. There is a kernel of truth about the mindset of historians born and bred in the Heartland as compared to Schlesinger and others from the East or West. And yet most of them ended up at Ivy League schools. Their adult examinations of history must have been affected by later education and experience. I end up digging out Andre Maurois's essay on the *Three Ghosts of America* (1931). From historians and philosophers to politicians and voters, aren't we all a kind of Duke's mixture of puritan, pioneer and robber barons' conflicting beliefs and motivations? Ambivalence, thy name is Man.

More of the book later. And in the name of verisimilitude for your Walnut thoughts, let's correct some of the minor facts in case your memoirs fall into the hands of Walnut natives. Jack McCarthy's grocery moved across the street when the Federated Store replaced the old general store and stayed there until his widow became librarian of the new, improved library. The pizza parlor replaced the A&P store that went out of business when automobiles and "hard" roads made it easy to drive to supermarkets in larger cities. I believe when you were in college, an up-to-date men's clothing store actually opened where McCarthy's grocery had been. And strangely enough, though the high school and most of the businesses are gone, the population of Walnut has remained at 1,500 persons since 1930. Still, a memoir it is and precious to me.

Love, Mother.

P.S. The reason for the memoir is easy. Grandpa Bob knew the importance of a piece of pie, and he approved when you finished off the last of his gooseberry. Lesser things—a line of music, a whisper of perfume—can trigger memory. Katherine Grayson died today at 89 and I remembered your brother Jamie had a crush on her in the movies.

Kristi to Mom.
Consultant to the rescue, indeed! Thanks. I am off to the gym right now, then to fetch Chloe and am going to do more personal writing after she leaves tonight. I decided this weight on my heart every time she leaves for her father's—and I reopen the narcissistic wound left from the divorce—can perhaps best be funneled into some writing. We all have our things that "save" us, and I think memory is mine. I dislike sleeping pills and prefer to work in the middle of the night when I can't sleep. As your friend, Ernie Schusky says, there is no law that sleep has to be done between midnight and 8:00 a.m. Nicole seems better. Chloe is doing better with sleep. I have a nice movie to watch tonight, and the laundry is being done so I think things are okay. Then, too, I have a long natter to look forward to with my dear mother tonight. Many hugs, and love, of course, K.

12 This essay was written in 2010, long before Donald Trump entered the race for president in 2015, so my remarks are not directed against him in particular. I do find strong elements of nostalgia in his support, however, with its emphasis on a national restoration that will return us all to a safer, grander world in which "the other"—all those people who are "different"—cannot threaten us because we have a strong leader to protect us. I suspect many Trump supporters fear the government is not doing enough to defend their jobs or wages, fear being downsized and taxed to provide social benefits for people they consider undeserving strangers. As with other situations when political leaders exploit our nostalgia for a simpler time—as was the case in Weimar Germany—many worried about the impact of national disaster—such as the Reichstag fire or an October terrorist attack on the 2016 election. Ironically, we came perilously close to experiencing this situation on January 6, 2021.

13 I realize that home is not always such a pleasant memory for everyone but I believe the yearning for such security is a part of our DNA. It's like the view we have of parents. We know they are imperfect, and recognize that some people have dreadful parents. Yet the canonical expectation most of us carry says that parents should love us and treat us well. When that expectation is not met, we become angry and bitter. I suspect the longing for good memories of home resembles that expectation.

14 My daughter, Chloe, now 27 as I write this in 2021, lives in Mother's home on Pine Lake, safely sheltered away from the COVID pandemic that hit in 2020, while Chloe was a grad student at Washington University in St. Louis. Knowing she was safe in a home in the country, instead of in a small apartment in a large, often racially charged city like St. Louis, made me feel more at peace about a daughter I could not see for over a year. I think it would have pleased her grandmother greatly to know that her home, so lovingly designed by mother and her new husband, later sheltered her beloved granddaughter.

CHAPTER 2: J. O.

1 John was the eldest brother, followed by Karl, my father (James Oliver, Jr.), and Tom, then finally a girl named Elizabeth. Both Daddy and Karl were runners and, after they turned 50 and competed in races for senior runners, used to hold hands as they came across the finish line, so both could finish first. Karl's daughter, my cousin Kay, tells me Karl suffered from *polycythemia vera*, a rare bone marrow disease that leads to an abnormal increase in the number of blood cells. The red blood cells are mostly affected. Unlike my memory, Kay says she knew nothing of a propensity of this disease among Basques but did remember hearing it occurred more among Ashkenazi Jews. If we were of Basque origin, we could easily be Sephardic Jews. So far, however, neither Kay nor I find any independent verification for any ancestral link to either group.

2 John Sevier was born in 1745 and died in 1815.

3 Irving Dilliard was born in Collinsville and loved the town so much he always refused to move to St. Louis County, where most of the top brass at the *St. Louis Post-Dispatch* lived. Irving was a character, scrupulous to a fault and passionate about first amendment rights and the law and the press. He and my father loved to argue constitutional law, and Irving was a good friend of William O. Douglas and Paul Douglas. So upset about civil and human rights, the teetotaler Irving got drunk with Felix Frankfurter on August 23, 1927, the night Sacco and Vanzetti were executed. Irvine later edited Learned Hand's papers and took personal umbrage when Richard Nixon—no favorite or Irving's, who left town rather than write the *St. Louis Post's* editorial endorsing the Eisenhower/Nixon ticket—purchased and lived in Learned Hand's home. After retiring from the *St. Louis Post-Dispatch*, Irving was a Nieman Fellow at Harvard and taught for many years at what is now known as Princeton University's School of Public and International Affairs.

4 My cousin Judson, Uncle John's son, said he took a political science course at the University of Maryland in which J. O. was described as "an ideal legislator," a model of a good public servant.

CHAPTER 3: FORGIVENESS AND THE THIN RED LINE

1 Nancy and I struggled through the Trump years, when she entered local politics and became a strong Trump supporter. We continued our friendship, however, usually just agreeing to disagree, and left it like that. When COVID-19 came and Nancy did not get vaccinated, and after my vaccinated daughter got a break-through case of COVID-19 in May 2021, I became less tolerant of these political differences, deeply upset at the thought that my daughter could have died because others refused to be vaccinated. Nonetheless, I called Nancy that summer, when I learned she had contracted a second case of COVID-19, and she called me late in September to offer consolation when she learned a dear friend of mine was dying of cancer.

2 Martin 2012.

3 There is relatively little work in evolutionary biology that addresses forgiveness. One is *Beyond Revenge: The Evolution of the Forgiveness Instinct* by Michael McCullough (2008). *Beyond Revenge* argues that despite the popular belief that revenge is a disease, both revenge and forgiveness have been adaptive for our species. McCullough draws on

cultural, neurological, psychological, social, and religious mechanisms to ask what conditions are most likely to encourage forgiveness rather than revenge. As we would expect from an evolutionary biologist, McCullough's explanatory mechanism remains long-term adaptation as a species.

This same emphasis on species adaptation underpins a closely related field: evolutionary psychology, a theoretical approach that examines psychological behaviors from an evolutionary perspective. In particular, evolutionary psychology tries to determine those human psychological traits that are evolved adaptations, that is, they are a result of natural selection or sexual selection in human evolution. Evolutionary psychologists argue that it is those behaviors or traits that occur in all cultures which may be evolutionarily helpful adaptations. Some of these include the ability to infer others' emotions, the ability to discern kin from non-kin, to identify and prefer healthier mates, and to cooperate with others. Forgiveness and revenge—usually treated hand in hand—fall into this category but have not yet been studied extensively.

4 I am certainly not a student of comparative religions, so I may be wildly distorting the written work here but as I understand it, there are some critical differences in religious attitudes toward forgiveness. For Jews, a person who has caused harm needs to sincerely apologize. At that point, then the wronged person is compelled to forgive. But even minus an apology, forgiveness is considered a pious act. (*Deuteronomy* 6:9).

Christian teachings on forgiveness follow a similar theme, making forgiveness an admirable act, as noted in the *Lord's Prayer*: "And forgive us our trespasses, as we forgive those who trespass against us" (*Matthew* 6:9-13). Forgiveness seems even more important for Christians than for Jews, however, with Christianity holding what seems a more idealized view of forgiveness as an ennobling act, as expressed in Christ's words during his suffering and crucifixion: "Father, forgive them, for they know not what they do." (*Luke* 23:34). Christ also instructs his followers "to love your enemies and turn the other cheek" (*Matthew* 5:9 & *Luke* 6:27-31). The medieval Christian view toward forgiveness moves one step beyond this, linking forgiveness to eternal life. St. Francis of Assisi admonishes Christians "not so much seek to be consoled as to console. To be understood as to understand. To be loved as to love. For it is in giving that we receive. It is in pardoning that we are pardoned. And it is in dying that we are born to eternal life." This is known as *The Peace Prayer*, by St. Francis of Assisi.

Again, to an untutored eye, this Christian view seems different from the Jewish concept of *Teshuva* (literally "returning"), which is a way of atoning and one that requires the cessation of the harmful act, regret over doing that act, confession and true repentance. Thus Jews link the genuine repentance for the wrongs you have committed with the ability to forgive others for what they have done to you. The importance of forgiveness, and the linking of forgiveness with repentance, is noted in the importance accorded Yom Kippur, the Day of Atonement when Jews are admonished to perform *teshuva*. Two of the most relevant Jewish passages on forgiveness are: "It is forbidden to be obdurate and not allow yourself to be appeased. On the contrary, one should be easily pacified and find it difficult to become angry. When asked by an offender for forgiveness, one should forgive with a sincere mind and a willing spirit." (*Mishneh Torah*, *Teshuvah* 2:10) The second critical text is: "Who takes vengeance or bears a grudge acts like one who, having cut one hand while handling a knife, avenges himself by stabbing the other hand." (*Jerusalem Talmud, Nedarim* 9.4)

This view links forgiveness to acknowledgment of the wrong; it introduces the concept that you cannot be forgiven your wrongs unless you forgive those who wronged you. Christianity does not require that link. Christianity seems to view forgiveness as something that will bring you reward in heaven, something that pleases God. The consequences of forgiving for the life on earth are not made so central. Nor is the act of forgiveness linked to the acknowledgement by the wrong doer that a bad act was, in fact, committed.

We find a similar move from the Christian emphasis on the ennobling aspect of forgiveness—and its link to eternal salvation—to a more pragmatic view of forgiveness in Islam, which makes central the impact of forgiveness's impact on the one who forgives. Inspired by Adam's thesis on forgiveness after 9/11, I read more about forgiveness in Islam. Here two interesting facts stuck out. First, the word Islam itself is derived from the Semitic word for "peace." Second, forgiveness is a prerequisite for genuine peace. True, the *Quran* allows for violence, but only to defend faith, property or life. In Islam, as in Christianity, forgiveness is the better course of action whenever possible: "They avoid gross sins and vice, and when angered they forgive." (*Quran* 42:37). In terms of clemency, we try admonishing the faithful that (42:40): "[a]lthough the just penalty for an injustice is an equivalent retribution, those who pardon and maintain righteousness are rewarded by God. He does not love the unjust." This reflects the Christian view that forgiveness pleases God but is more explicit in advocating forgiveness because forgiveness is something that brings peace to those who forgive, not just something that pleases God.

There are many other world religions which include teachings on forgiveness. My goal is not to summarize these but rather to ask what guidance these other religious examples of forgiveness might provide me, and to understand why contemporary culture in the US seems to assume forgiveness is a good thing. Here I found it enlightening to examine the Eastern religions' views on forgiveness. In general, these Eastern religions seem more psychological in emphasis, moving toward the kind of view we find in Islam, in which forgiveness will bring inner peace, the kind of peace that comes from freeing those who have been wronged but can find forgiveness from the anger that might cause them ongoing pain even after the harm has been done.

For Buddhists, forgiveness helps avoid the unhealthy emotions that would otherwise cause harm to our mental well-being. The hatred and anger carry lasting effects on our karma ("actions"); forgiveness thus creates emotions with a wholesome effect for us. This resonates with the Islamic linking of forgiveness to peace for the person who can forgive. Buddhism questions the reality of passions that give rise to anger through meditation and insight. "After examination, we realize that anger is only an impermanent emotion that we can fully experience and then release." (*Healing Anger: The Power of Patience from a Buddhist Perspective* by the Dalai Lama illustrates this attitude toward the Buddhist value toward releasing anger.) Other Buddhist quotes also capture this view that retaining anger harms us: "Holding on to anger is like grasping a hot coal with the intent of throwing it at someone else but you are the one who gets burned." The Buddha: "You will not be punished for your anger, you will be punished by your anger." And finally: "It is natural for the immature to harm others. Getting angry with them is like resenting a fire for burning" (*Shantideva).*

For Buddhists, then, the value of forgiveness is the good effect it will have on us. Sikhs also view forgiveness as a remedy to anger. The road to forgiveness here is not to please God but rather via compassion. When aroused by compassion, we can forgive an offender. It is this compassion that spawns peace, humility, tranquility, and cooperation in human interactions. The role of a deity enters insofar as the act of forgiveness itself is considered a divine gift; it is not the product of human agency and to take personal credit for the compassion that leads to forgiveness will impede our spiritual progress. Some verses from the Guru Granth Sahib, the Sikh scriptures, capture the Sikh view of forgiveness: "To practice forgiveness is fasting, good conduct and contentment." (*Guru Arjan Dev*, 223) "Where there is forgiveness, there God resides." (*Kabir*, page 137) "Dispelled is anger as forgiveness is grasped." (*Guru Amar Das*, 233)

The Sikh teachings on forgiveness thus resonate with Buddhism insofar as both link forgiveness closely to anger and to the view that anger harms us by taking away our inner peace. It seems also to link anger to unfulfilled desires. It is when a person fails to fulfill his or her desires and wants, that anger can well up. Our egos can easily feel slighted, embarrassed, belittled or in some other way be offended. For Sikhs, as we learn to discipline our mind through meditation on the Word, our ego and anger naturally turn to compassion and forgiveness. Since anger and forgiveness are considered opposites, the human mind can contain only one of them at a given time. This seems to return us to the concept of the impact on us from our forgiveness, or a failure to forgive.

5 With apologies to scholars of religion, I am greatly overly simplifying here in trying to convey a general sense of the differences for the lay reader. In fact, I find Islam also moving toward this view.

6 As discussed earlier, that forgiveness-is good because it frees us of our bitterness, our anger and our resentment is a theme also found in Eastern religions, such as Buddhism.

7 I find little literature on the ennobling aspect of forgiveness. It does not seem immediately obvious to me that we should necessarily feel better about ourselves if we forgive someone who harms us. Certainly, a forgiveness that is forced upon us by cultural or religious pressures via creating in us a feeling that we must forgive, could well make us feel more resentful.

8 If putting up with behavior, from friends or loved ones, when that behavior feels hurtful, degrading or just plain unkind to you is something you can find it in your heart to do, I applaud you. (This seems an extreme Christian—even martyr-like—view.)

This concern with the impact of forgiveness on the one who forgives introduces us to another equally important aspect of forgiveness, one that also involves questions of self-esteem and one that introduces us to a close cousin of forgiveness: reconciliation, or at least a *modus vivendi* with the person who hurt you. I will return to this shortly. But regardless of how we view forgiveness itself—whether we adopt what I think of as an instrumental view of forgiveness—how is my failure to forgive going to affect me as a person?—and a concern with forgiveness as it affects our self-esteem by keeping us in abusive relationships—true forgiveness still seems to involve the four factors discussed above.

9 This discussion leaves unanswered many questions. How do we absolve someone of their offence(s)? Would this process not vary from person to person? From situation to situation? When and where does this take place? In some distant future once the hurt has lessened and the event settles into perspective? Does forgiving someone mean we extend

compassion to them as a person? Or resume normal relations as though the offending act had never occurred? Is it righting the wrong within our sense of self, our conscious mind, our beliefs or in what we might think of as our hearts? How do we determine when these conditions are satisfied? Empirical work is needed on these questions.

10 Martha Nussbaum presents her usual insightful discussion of ethical issues, focusing here on forgiveness, trust and anger in her 2016 book, where she links trust and its loss to one's sense of self. Her work underlines my belief that forgiveness must be proceeded by an acknowledgment by the offender that wrong was done; if it is not acknowledged, it is as if the person who hurt us is not seeing us, is ignoring us, which explains the link between forgiveness and self-esteem I describe in this chapter. See Martha Nussbaum, *Anger and Forgiveness; Resentment, Generosity, Justice.* Oxford University Press, 2016.

11 I discuss these in the next chapter, "I Got Nothing!" Do we have an obligation to tell the person they have hurt us? Certainly if we wish to maintain the relationship, or hope to do so. Such communication seems critical for good human relations. Doing so, however, is a separate issue from forgiveness; telling someone they have hurt us seems central to the possibility of maintaining a good relationship and, in addition, it may be one of fairness.

While we shouldn't feel compelled to forgive just because it's good for our soul's well-being, neither should we have to forget even if we forgive. Nor does the act of NOT forgiving necessarily have to condemn us to bitterness within us. If failure to forgive does necessarily entail our holding onto bitter feelings, this need not necessarily be a bad thing, insofar as it protects us from further mistreatment. Retaining the anger necessary for self-protection seems preferrable to a kind of forced forgiveness that condemns us to self-loathing and lack of self-respect.

12 I gave a talk at Caltech for a conference on forgiveness. Most of the other speakers advocated forgiveness, and I began my talk by saying I was going to be the odd man out. I summarized my views and afterwards had a young woman come up with a follow-up to a question she had posed during the discussion period. The follow-up made it clear to me that she was in an abusive relationship and wanted advice on whether it was all right to leave. "Should she not stay and try to forgive the person?" she asked. "Or was it OK to leave, and not forgive the person who was continually harming her?" I am not sure I gave her the answer she wanted—or needed—to hear. But her question underlined the importance of having someone raise the possibility that forgiveness should be secondary to self-protection.

CHAPTER 4: "I GOT NOTHING!"

1 Wendy Sherman, former US Undersecretary of State for Political Affairs (September 2011–October 2015) noticed the difficulties in resolving hostilities that arise from long-standing grievances, and that these often worked against the underlying interests of the nation. Her study of the conditions that lead to political forgiveness, and the process by which such forgiveness is achieved, is published in a Belfer Center for Science and International Affairs report: "On Political Forgiveness: Some Preliminary Reflections." Her conclusions suggest that remembrance is a powerful agent of forgiveness and that political forgiveness is not always a linear process, in which

the wrongdoer extends an apology that is then accepted, and then the two nations develop and improve their ties using as the foundation of future work their mutual national interests. This finding also emphasizes the importance of future interactions but makes forgiveness more a strategy, a function of a self-interested calculation of national interest, rather than what I would call genuine forgiveness.

2 See Monroe 1996, Chapter 1 for a fuller discussion.

3 Otto's story is contained in *The Hand of Compassion* (Monroe 2004), a title that came from a quote by Otto in describing his altruistic activities. "The hand of compassion was faster than the calculus of reason."

4 I realize they still do matter to many people, and I respect that, although I personally think religion is a silly thing to let come between people.

5 I am grateful to Aaron Sorkin for the story and, indeed, for the entire series of *The West Wing.*

CHAPTER 5: "IT'S AN IMPORTANT POLITICAL PROBLEM. I SHOULD KNOW ABOUT IT." AGENCY

1 Chloe was not the only ISPP baby. Dorotka Reykowska, daughter of Janusz and Zula Reykowski, also had logged many miles as an ISPP child. At a meeting in Barcelona, a large group of ISPP scholars went out to dinner. Many of them—Danny Bar-Tal and Ervin Staub in particular—had known Dorotka for many years, watching her grow from a little girl to a beautiful and superbly competent young lady who took beautiful charge of her somewhat other-worldly father at international conferences. We all were at a long table in a restaurant in Barcelona that year, and Dorotka had just gotten engaged. Ervin Staub raised his glass and proposed a toast. "I believe someone at this table has just gotten engaged and I would like to wish her every happiness." Everyone looked at Dorotka, whose face was slowly flushing; everyone except the 12-year-old Chloe, that is, who was happily enjoying her gazpacho, not paying any attention at all to the adults. Staub continued: "So I would like us all to drink to the future happiness of the newly-engaged young lady: Chloe." Everyone roared. Dorotka relaxed, and Chloe was totally taken aback but unfazed.

2 The college was founded in 1592 but most of the buildings appeared to be eighteenth century to my untrained eye. In checking, I find most were built in the eighteenth and early nineteenth centuries.

3 See the chapter on Tony in *Ethics in an Age of Terror and Genocide* (2012) for Tony's fascinating story and the chapter on Beatrix for that of his cousin.

4 See the chapter on Florentine for the most extreme illustration of a Nazi in tune with the *zeitgeist.* Monroe (2012).

CHAPTER 6: NICOLE'S FATHER IS NOT GERMAN! THE MORAL SALIENCE OF DIFFERENCE

1 The full title of this piece was originally "The immutability of differences, the framing of our discussion so differences, and the social construction of their moral and political salience," surely a title that would put off even the most dedicated general reader. Those interested in a fuller, academic version, written with Rose McDermott and published

in *PS: Political Science and Politics.* January 2010: 77–81, may consult this article. I am grateful to Rose and to *PS* for allowing me to reprint parts of it here.

2 Monroe 2004.

3 I am speaking of academia in North America here, not the broader world, in which—I fear—anti-Semitism remains all too alive. We now also find anti-religious bias in the form of anti-Muslim sentiment, far too much of which manifests itself within the US academy, as in the world at large.

4 Athletic abilities do often take on moral salience and have become interwoven with race in the United States.

5 Seminal work by Benedict Anderson (1983) provides powerful illustration that the very concept of nationalism emerges from a kind of shared hallucination, or a communal agreement that participants simultaneously adhere to in constructing their notion of community or nation. Benedict credits the printing press with a critical role in nationalism since groups of people read material in a common language and then began thinking in terms of "an imaginary community."

6 *Finding Your Roots*, by Henry Louis Gates, Jr., presents wonderful discussions of the complexity of the racial line in America, dating back to slavery. Season 2, Episode 9 is just one of many thoughtful episodes.

7 There is a lot of work on equality that is both pathbreaking and controversial. Consider what has become a hot-button item in America today (2021): critical race theory (Lerer 2021: 1). Initially critical race theory was developed by legal scholars and civil-rights activists trying to understand the intersection of law and race, and to challenge liberal approaches to justice and race. (The main American legal scholars were Derrick Bell, Alan Freeman, Kimberlé Crenshaw, Richard Delgado, Cheryl Harris, Charles R. Lawrence III, Mari Matsuda, and Patricia J. Williams.) The foundational assumption underpinning critical race theory holds that subtle, complex, and ever-changing institutional and social dynamics, and not necessarily intentional, explicit prejudice can lead to racism. Another core concept concerns what is called intersectionality, the extent to which race interacts— or intersects —with other identities, such as class or gender, to result in a kind of double-whammy of prejudice. At least initially, then, critical race theory was developed to demonstrate how socially constructed categories based on race or culture can intertwine to create forms of oppression and inequality. The current political controversy over critical race theory focuses on schools that teach kindergarten to 12-year-old students, and how we discuss with young students the historical patterns of racism in the United States. Critics do not like the idea of telling young people that racism is so entrenched in law and our basic political institutions that the legacies of slavery, segregation and Jim Crow continue to produce an uneven playing field for people of color, even today (Lerer 2021). This analysis treats racism not simply as a matter of bigotry on the part of an individual but also as something that has become institutionalized and systemic in America, deeply woven into our most basic institutions and implicit assumptions. Personally, I find this basic concept simple enough to explain to a child but contemporary critics argue that teaching critical race theory is inculcating children into the belief that the United States is a racist society from its inception, that it accuses all white Americans of being racist, and divides people according to race into oppressors and oppressed. I could not find any instance of critical race theory being taught to grade school children, and all the fuss seems a political red herring, not a reality to fear.

8 In my father's day, every educated person spoke German, the language of art, music, physics, philosophy, etc. Most educated people ended up studying in Germany, which was at the forefront in most academic disciplines. How such a society sank into the barbarism of the Nazi period remains a great mystery, as well as a tragedy.

9 Adorno *et al* (1950). See *The Authoritarian Personality* (1950).

10 For the best introduction to social identity theory, see Tajfel and Turner 1979 or Tajfel 1982.

11 Tajfel and his students tend to reject individualistic explanations of group behavior, instead arguing that we choose from a wide range of our complex identities, highlighting any one identity at any one moment. The social context will influence this choice, sometimes evoking personal identities, in which case the individual will relate to others in an interpersonal manner, depending on the other's character traits and any personal relationship existing between the individuals. But under other conditions, Tajfel argues that a social identity would become more important. In this case, behavior will be qualitatively different and will be group behavior. See the Tajfel works cited at the end of this chapter or *Ethics in an Age of Terror and Genocide* (Chapter 8) for a fuller summary of social identity theory.

12 Tajfel spent most of his career at Bristol, where he conducted his famous minimal group experiments and headed what later became known as the Bristol School of Social Psychology, much as Nicole's father chaired the Art History Department at UC Irvine.

13 This distinction mirrors the common debate in international relations between realists who focus on relative gains and liberals who emphasize absolute gains..

14 See *Neighbors: The Destruction of the Jewish Community in Jedwabne, Poland* by Jan T. Gross (2001, Princeton University Press).

15 The Battle of the Blackbirds, also known as the Battle of Kosovo, occurred on June 15, 1389, when the Serbian Prince Lazar Hrebeljanović fought an invading Ottoman army under Sultan Murad Hüdavendigâr. The battle was fought near Pristina, capital of modern-day Kosovo. Few reliable accounts remain but historians generally believe both armies were wiped out, and both leaders killed. But because the battle depleted Serbian manpower, Serbian principalities not already conquered by the Ottoman empire came under Ottoman rule in the following years.

    As the Balkans erupted into hostility after the death of Tito (1980), the significance of the Battle of the Blackbirds played an increasingly symbolic role, primarily since it represented sacred ground for the Serbs, much like Valley Forge or Gettysburg for Americans. To others—such as the Albanians—the fourteenth-century battlefield and its monument constituted painful reminders of the sectarian animosities and violence that have dominated the Balkans for some seven hundred years, and of Serbian repression in particular. As NATO became more involved in the Balkan wars, soldiers who had never heard of this 600-year-old battle found themselves standing round-the-clock guard over the site of the fourteenth-century Battle of the Blackbirds. Many countries have similar, long-standing anger about events that occurred far in the past; this is just one illustration.

16 The movie *Hotel Rwanda* demonstrates this beautifully. Based on the true story of the hotel manager—Paul Rusesabagina—who saved over a thousand Tutsis during the

Rwandan genocide of 1994, Paul is classified as a Hutu because his father was Hutu. But Paul's mother was Tutsi, as was Paul's wife, Tatiana.

17 A further body of literature underlines the claim that discussions of differences in American political science need to move away from the existing paradigm, which assumes that existing political cleavages are somehow immutable, and ask instead why certain cleavages and differences are accorded ethical and political salience. The 2008 election should alert us to the extent to which such a conceptual move is critical if we are to recognize the extent to which the human psychology is far more complicated than many traditional political discussions of racial identity might suggest. This literature focuses on the psychological dynamics driving coalitions and alliances.

Recent experimental evidence suggests the possibility that humans categorize race, at least in part, as a byproduct of an unrelated psychological mechanism designed to detect the nature of coalitions and alliances. In a clever study conducted by Robert Kurzban and colleagues (Kurzban, Tooby and Cosmides 2001), subjects confronted a task where coalitional status was uncorrelated with race. Under such conditions, race effects were quickly "erased" in the space of an hour's task, in favor of preferred memory for alliance structures. In this study, researchers used the "who said what" paradigm to show subjects in interaction between individuals of different races. These individuals displayed cross-cutting cleavages by wearing T-shirts of different colors designed to mark particular teams or groups. So, for example, white people wore both green and blue shirts, as did black people. When later asked who said what, subjects showed differential ability to notice and remember who said what based on the color of shirts as opposed to the color of skins, indicating the primary nature of the psychological coalitional-tracking mechanism. These researchers argued that because individuals were less likely to encounter others who did not look like them in the ancestral past, racial categorization developed as a byproduct of a psychological process designed primarily to detect out-group members because it was so uncommon to encounter members of another so-called race. When individuals did meet such people, they were most often out-group members, signaling their incorporation into a different alliance structure. When it becomes clear that race no longer indicates such coalitional status, race-based categorization can remarkably quickly remand to secondary status in attention and memory.

Another important aspect of this study shows that this finding does not result merely as a consequence of clever experimental design. Rather, the Kurzban study also demonstrated that the effect of sex could not be erased in the same way. Gender continues to trump coalitional status regardless of manipulation, thus suggesting that encoding by sex remains a primary psychological adaptation (Kurzban, Tooby and Cosmides 2001), most likely related to strong reproductive incentives. The implications of the Kurzban experiments for evaluating the impact of race and gender in the 2008 election are intriguing. Pollsters were surprised at the number of voters who admitted to racial prejudice, but nonetheless reported they were voting for Obama because they thought he would be the better person to get the country out of the then economic mess. Is this the "team" aspect that Kurzban, Tooby and Cosmides found, where people use race as a code for strangers when they are not sure who might hurt them, but then drop their racist views once they conceptualize members of the other race as friends or as team players who can potentially help them? And does the resilience of sex as a fundamental category of differentiation explain why more Democratic primary voters said they would not vote for a woman than for a man in 2008? How critical a factor was this in the 2016 election? The linkages between voting and the deep-seated psychological mechanisms underlying attitudes toward in-group/out-group members need to be examined more closely but the preliminary evidence might suggest that it is harder for a woman to succeed than for a black man.

18 Sanders insisted that he is proud to be Jewish but that his religion is not relevant to his political views, that church and State should be separate. In what proved to be an extraordinarily divisive political year, the media made little of the fact that the Jewish Sanders did well in Muslim areas.

19 The suggestion that our psychological mechanisms of categorization and racial encoding may, in fact, not be so blunt derives from two interrelated lines of research. (Please note that I use the language of the researchers in describing their experimental results. I do not myself believe Chinese, Africans and Europeans constitute different races. We are all members of the human race.)

First, Elizabeth Phelps has studied racial stereotyping, prejudice and discrimination using functional Magnetic Resonance Imaging (MRI) technology. The amygdala, the part of the brain associated with emotion in general, and fear in particular, does indeed tend to show greater response to faces of a different race than one's own (Hart *et al.* 2000). In other words, it may not be the linkage between race and fear that causes prejudice and stereotyping, but rather the novelty of difference itself that precipitates a particular kind of reactivity. Indeed, there is evidence that the amygdala shows greater activation to out-group members in general, not just those from different racial groups (Cunningham *et al.* 2004, Johnson and Fredrickson 2005). In this way, faces of other races, because they are visually dissimilar, make some individuals more likely to respond to other racial groups with fear (Ohman and Mineka 2001). Indeed, recent evidence indicating that conservatives have a stronger physical response to threat itself, as measured through galvanic skin response and strength of eye blinks in reaction to threatening stimuli, suggests some individuals may in fact be more genetically prepared to experience fear in the face of any threat (Oxley *et al.* 2008). If this process does occur, then unlike the classical conditioning model presented above, racial bias could represent an overgeneralization of a kind of prepared fear response, whereby certain types of novel stimuli are more likely to be perceived as threatening.

Indeed, familiarity does appear to alter the amygdala's response to certain races' faces. For instance, white people do not show the same level of amygdala reaction to famous or familiar black faces, such as Bill Cosby (before his fall from grace), Tiger Woods or now possibly Barack Obama. In addition, Phelps *et al.* (2001) find that inter-racial dating reduces fear activation in the face of out-group members more broadly; when someone is dating a person of another race, they do not demonstrate the same degree of hostile or fearful responses that are generated among those with same-race partners.

A second line of research comes from Susan Fiske's work into person perception and stereotyping. Fiske finds that between 80 to 90 percent of how individuals respond to others derives from our assessment of two main characteristics: warmth and competence. Particular combinations and interactions between these characteristics result in predictable emotional reactions to individuals and groups. For our purposes, the relevant category emerges from the intersection of judgments that categorize relevant others as low warmth and high competence. This evaluation of others creates envy; the empirical work suggests this category encompasses Jews, Asians and rich professionals.

Fiske argues that while prejudice produces distinct brain activation patterns, behavioral manifestations of prejudice need not necessarily result (Fiske *et al.* 1999). Rather, social context affects the link between brain and behavior, just as the constituent elements of prejudice and discrimination remain socially defined (van den Bos 2007). Fiske and her colleagues make an argument that understanding prejudice requires making sense of the psychological processes by which people come to code and categorize potential threats from dissimilar others.

These lines of research, drawn from psychology, indicate that the human psychological architecture concerning reactions to race may be more complicated than ordinarily conceived in discussions of American politics. In particular, our reactions to out-group members may not derive solely from processes of social learning and acculturation, but also may build on psychological mechanisms designed to respond to out-group members in defensive ways. Racial categorization has often signaled, quickly and easily, such out-group status, and thus becomes an often-inaccurate marker of such coalitional membership. Thus, race becomes entrained as part of the process of alliance categorization. Individuals who seek in-group supporters may exclude racial out-group members because of their improper calibration between racial and coalitional status in others. This does not make such a process right or correct, but rather offers an opportunity by which racial prejudice might be overcome by emphasizing the commonality in all humans, noting their shared endeavors toward justice, and emphasizing the political and moral salience of empathy and compassion, instead of hatred and division.

20 *Tales of the South Pacific* is a Pulitzer Prize–winning book of short stories about World War II published by James A. Michener in 1947. Based on Michener's own experiences while a lieutenant commander in the navy on Espiritu Santo in the New Hebrides Islands (now called Vanuatu), the book outlines the difficulties when two different cultures interact. The movie *South Pacific* appeared, based on the book, as a 1949 Broadway musical and, in 1958, as a film. While the musical won several Tony Awards and was a blockbuster, it nonetheless drew strong criticism, even hostility and controversy. Its romantic tension drew on what was then seen as an interracial romance, a strong taboo at the time. Hammerstein gave an interview in 1958 (*The Mike Wallace Interview*) and noted that both of the two love stories involve prejudice. Nellie Forbush is a Navy nurse who falls in love with a Frenchman. When she realizes he once was married to a Polynesian woman and has two children with her, Nellie runs away, breaking off the romance. She later realizes how stupid her prejudice was. "What we were saying was that ... all this prejudice that we have is something that fades away in the face of something that's really important," Hammerstein told Wallace.

Hammerstein cleaned up the basic stories from the original book, making the play far less dark and more palatable for American tastes at the time. In the original story, Emile de Becque has eight "mixed-race" and illegitimate daughters by four different women, none of whom he married, when he meets the nurse Ensign Nellie Forbush.

In the musical, he has two legitimate mixed-race children by a woman whom he had married and who had—conveniently for the plot line—died. Despite this sanitizing, when the play toured nationally, *South Pacific* received strong criticism, especially in the American South. Two Georgia state lawmakers found "You've Got to Be Taught" repugnant, holding that a song "justifying marriage between races was offensive." One of the Georgia legislators, Rep. David C. Jones, wrote in a letter, "We in the South are a proud and progressive people. Half breeds cannot be proud."

21 See Cunningham *et al.* 2004, Fiske *et al.* 1999, Hart *et al.* 2000, Johnson and Fredrickson 2005, Ohman and Mineka 2001, Phelps *et al.* 2001, van den Bos *et al.* 2007.

22 In this regard, the transgendered movement will be an especially important one to watch.

23 I owe the term "community of concern" to Marion Smiley. For an excellent description of this concept and its importance for how we treat people, see Smiley (1992).

CHAPTER 7: SCIENCE FICTION FANTASY, MORAL IMAGINATION AND THE ABILITY TO CONCEPTUALIZE YOUR WAY OUT OF A PROBLEM

1 Octavia Estelle Butler, born on June 22, 1947, died on February 24, 2006. A distinguished American science fiction writer, Butler won both the Hugo and the Nebula awards. One of the best-known women in the field, in 1995 Butler became the first science fiction writer to receive the MacArthur Fellowship, often known as the Genius Award. Butler used the conventions of science fiction fantasy to question the existing culture of gender, race and power, using these devices to subtly encourage the reader to rethink, reinterpret and review the current world from a fresh perspective. For Butler, it seems fair to say that the world of science fiction is a world of possibilities and that science fiction encourages the moral imagination.

2 Of course, we can choose not to exercise our imagination and many people do just that. They choose to stay within the confines of their own experience, not asking what it would be like to have been born into a different circumstance. This lack of moral imagination can result in their failing to hear the cries and suffering of others, leaving them unable to be inspired and aspire for a better world than the one they know through their own personal experience. The inability of otherwise good people to be able to imagine and empathize with others also carries moral consequences, just as the ability to understand the perspective of others relates to growth in our moral development.

3 The origins of this quote are not clear, nor is the quote itself. According to some sources, Kennedy said: "There are those that look at things the way they are, and ask *why*? I dream of things that never were, and ask *why not*?" Kennedy later stated that he was quoting George Bernard Shaw. In *Back to Methuselah*, Shaw has a serpent say: "You see things; and you say, 'Why?' But I dream things that never were; and I say, 'Why not?'" John F. Kennedy used this phrase in a 1963 (June 28th) visit to Ireland. In addressing the Irish Dail: "George Bernard Shaw, speaking as an Irishman, summed up an approach to life, 'Other people,' he said, 'see things and say why? But I dream

things that never were and I say, why not?'" In an address on Youtube, Edward Kennedy further paraphrased the quote in his eulogy to Robert Kennedy (June 8, 1968): Some men see things as they are and say *why?* I dream things that never were and say *why not?* (Eulogy in CBS news video) https://www.youtube.com/watch?v=8ADeazX9blw.

4 A 2021 Public Broadcasting Service (PBS) documentary on Hemingway, by Ken Burns and Lynn Novick, makes the point that the brilliance of Hemingway's writing lay in its ability to convey the feeling, not just the facts, of what an event or an emotion was like.

5 Full points to my ex-husband for his enlightened attitude and generosity. He supported my career, always treated it as equal to his own and I am most grateful for that.

6 After I had written this piece, I saw an article by Charli Carpenter, "Rethinking the Political Science Fiction Nexus: Global Policy Making and the Campaign to Stop Killer Robots." The description of the piece reads: "A burgeoning literature in IR asserts there is a relationship between pop cultural artifacts and global policy processes, but this relationship is rarely explored using observational data. To fill this gap, I provide an evidence-based exploration of the relationship between science-fiction narratives and global public policy in an important emerging political arena: norm-building efforts around the prohibition of fully autonomous weapons. Drawing on in-depth interviews with advocacy elites, and participant observation at key campaign events, I explore and expand on constitutive theories about the impact of science fiction on 'real-world' politics." For the full article, see *Perspectives on Politics*, vol. 14, no. 01:pp. 53–69. Published online by Cambridge University Press, March 21, 2016.

CHAPTER 8: PASSION

1 I told this story at Nicholas and Leah's rehearsal dinner, noting that I had been wrong. Life could get even better than this. That Alex had made me a mother, Nicholas had made us a family, and Chloe had made all our dreams come true. And now we had Nik's beautiful Leah in our family, so things can always get even better. A good thought to remember.

2 Chloe's memories of bedtime differ slightly from mine. She reminds me that it was always I who fell asleep first, usually as I sang to her each night. Eventually, she relates, and I have to concur, I would conk out entirely, arms wrapped around Chloe so the poor child could not move. She said she'd just lie there thinking, listening to me breathe, and eventually, the warmth and the regular rhythm of my breathing would lull her to drift off herself. But Chloe also told Nicole—who had a very firm and fast bedtime, and one much earlier than Chloe's—that she didn't actually have a bedtime. "We just wander around until I fall asleep," she told her best friend. Perceptions vary!

3 I should note that this emptiness is increasingly rare as I now see my chicks happy in their own lives. I suspect that for most mothers, however, the twinge of loss comes and goes. I have been immensely fortunate in having some amazing students—some grad students, some summer interns or Tobis Fellows—who have become so dear to me they are like children, or at least cherished family members.

When I taught a course at the New York University (NYU) School of Law I was surprised to find no one stayed after class the first seminar the first week. The second week, one young woman remained behind but, when I asked if she had a question, she replied no, and left. The third week this same woman hung about a bit and then, when asked if I could help her with anything, remarked that "This is a very different course." I told her honestly that it really wasn't a law course. I noted that the then dean believed lawyers needed a course in social statistics, so the lawyers could understand the increasing use of statistical data in legal cases. "No, that's not what I mean. You don't brutalize us." I was a bit taken aback and asked why should I want to do this.

"Well, all our other professors do it and we're all terrified of you. We think you're being so nice that you are just luring us out and then will slam us once we start to trust you."

I had to explain that this is not what happens in social science, that we operate on a kind of guild system, in which students get trained and welcomed into the club. In fact, we often become dear friends of our faculty members, as I did with Joe Cropsey, Lloyd and Susanne Rudolph and David Easton.

I'm not sure the young woman believed me but developing friendships with your students truly is one of the joys of teaching, and a saving grace during the social isolation of COVID-19.

CHAPTER 9: CAT

1 In fairness, I should note that I can probably be an extremely difficult person to live with and that my ex-husband is a very good man and a devoted father.

CHAPTER 10: BEST FRIENDS FOREVER

1 Rebecca West (December 21, 1892–March 15, 1983), also known as Dame Cicely Isabel Fairfield and as Dame Rebecca West, was a British author, literary critic, and journalist who wrote in many genres. Among West's major works are *Black Lamb and Grey Falcon* (1941), which gives an account of West's train trip to Yugoslavia in 1937, in which West discusses the history and culture of Yugoslavia along with the seriousness of Nazism.

2 Monroe *et al.* 2015.

3 *The Hand of Compassion: Portraits of Moral Choice during the Holocaust.* Princeton University Press, 2004 or *The Heart of Altruism: Perceptions of a Shared Humanity.* Princeton University Press, 1996.

4 One such person is Gary Becker, University of Chicago Nobel laureate in economics. The first version I could find of Becker's economic analysis of marriage is found in an out-of-print volume from the National Bureau of Economic Research Volume, titled: *Economics of the Family: Marriage, Children, and Human Capital Volume.* Authored and edited by Theodore W. Schultz in 1974, Becker's chapter title is "A Theory of Marriage", pp. 299–351. Becker essentially argues that we marry using a cost-benefit analysis and try to find someone who will add to our utility. While this concept seems

bizarre to me, I must admit there are other people I have known to whom it evidently does make sense. When I got engaged, one of the lawyers in my fiancé's Wall Street law firm apparently asked him what I did for a living. Upon being told that I was a professor at NYU, the young woman—also an associate at the law firm—somewhat scoffingly told my fiancé: "She's going to dilute your income."

CHAPTER 11: WRETCHED, SLACKER DISNEY CHILD

1 Nani means "mother's mother" in Hindi and shortly after Prem Chadha came to work for us she announced that she was Alex's Nani. She didn't seem to treat me the way a mother would treat a daughter, however, and I once asked her—after a conversation in which her husband described his thoughts on reincarnation—what she believed. Nani was always diplomatic, kind, extremely sensitive and never wanted to upset anyone by disagreeing. But when pushed a bit gently, she told me she thought we had been related in another life, that perhaps we were sisters. That explained a lot about how Nani related to me, and that was how we continued to interact for the rest of Nani's life. I hope Nani was right that we were related in another life; I just hope it is a future one, not a past one. This book is dedicated to Nani and to my mother.
2 I have changed the name of both the teacher and the child.

CHAPTER 12: CHLOE, NICOLE AND THE ELEPHANT IN THE PARLOR: THE LAST LECTURE AND SOME FINAL THOUGHTS ON ETHICS AND CHARACTER

1 I have been blessed by having many students become dear friends, from Adrienne Berczeller, Donna Laughlin and Laura Scalia at NYU to Andrada Costoiu, Jessica Gonzalez and Monica DeRoche at UCI. One of the great side-benefits and unanticipated joys of teaching.
2 After Grandpa Bob died, I helped my mother and Aunt Beverly find poetry for the funeral, drawing on some of the books in the Walnut house as inspiration. I found one poem I thought seemed appropriate for Grandpa, who at 91 has lived a long, rich life. "What do you think of this one?" I asked them. "I especially like the lines: *Twilight and evening bell, And after that the dark! And may there be no sadness of farewell, When I embark*; It's by Alfred, Lord Tennyson and is called *Passing the Bar*. Do you think Grandpa would have liked it?" My mother and aunt looked at each other and gave me what I realized were knowing smiles, as they related how every school child in Grandpa's generation had been forced to memorize this poem, and so Grandpa would certainly have known it.
3 "They Ask Me Why I Teach" was written by Glennice L. Harmon, and published in 1948, in the *NEA Journal*.
4 I am grateful to Ken Arrow for sharing this phrase with me.
5 Years ago a colleague recounted how he had worked for an elderly businessman turned philanthropist when the gentleman established a lecture series at the local university. The evening Ken described featured a lecture by a Yale art historian/

archaeologist speaking on Etruscan vases. Armed with over 200 slides of various Etruscan vases, the professor was happily presenting an animated and quite detailed talk on the beautiful variations in each ever-so-slightly different vase. The lights were low, the food at dinner had been good and the drink plentiful, lulling many in the audience to sleep. All was well until my friend noticed the octogenarian philanthropist heading out the door. Concerned, Ken hightailed it after him.

"Is there a problem, sir?" Ken asked.

"Nope! Just gotta take a crap."

Ken immediately backed off. But the philanthropist stopped and turned around, imparting what I find a great piece of wisdom.

"You know, the rest of us, we get up in the morning. We go to the office. We work, we slave, we make a buck. We come home, we eat dinner, watch TV, bang the wife, and go to bed." The philanthropist shook his head slightly, gesturing toward the speaker, so engaged in his Etruscan vases he had failed to notice the sleeping audience or his exiting host. "Him," the philanthropist announced profoundly, "He's got something else to think about!"

6 Years ago, I taught a Thursday class where I mentioned the Anne Frank House in Amsterdam. The next class meeting was Tuesday, when a student told me how much she had loved the Frank House. She told how she had gone home after class on Thursday, told her parents about our class discussion and her father—a pilot, flying to Amsterdam the next day—had taken her to Amsterdam that weekend. An equally touching illustration of the joy of teaching comes from a cousin of Grandpa Bob's, who related that her husband, Warner Fite, Stuart Professor of Ethics at Princeton from 1917–1935, turned to her after watching Adlai Stevenson's acceptance speech when he ran for president in 1952, and said: "It's good to know Adlai was listening."

7 One year a young man wrote a note on his final exam, prefacing it with a reminder that he was graduating and had already been admitted to law school so really didn't care much about his grade in my class. But he did want to tell me that he had loved one of the books assigned: *How to Live: Or A Life of Montaigne in One Question and Twenty Attempts at an Answer* by Sarah Bakewell. He had not previously known much about Montaigne and Bakewell had inspired him to read the original essays, written—and revised— between 1570 and 1592. (The essays were first published in 1580.) My student just wanted me to know that he had ordered all of Montaigne's essays and was going to spend his spring break reading them.

One young man from Orange County had fallen in love with the work of an essayist writing in France in the 1570s. I counted that course a great success.

8 What is now referred to as the "trolley problem" originated with Philippa Foot, an English philosopher. Foot used the trolley story to ask: Why do we find it acceptable to let a trolley heading for five people be re-directed to kill one person instead, while we as a society oppose the idea of killing one healthy man to take his organs in order to use them to save five other people who probably will otherwise die. The trolley problem was developed more fully and popularized by Judith Jarvis Thomson of MIT (Edmonds 2013) among others.

9 See in particular work by Joshua D. Greene, professor of psychology at Harvard. Greene uses behavioral experiments, including functional neuroimaging (fMRI) to inquire about moral judgment and decision making. Greene is one of a generation of social

psychologists asking about moral psychology and moral cognition. Greene's research group focuses on what they call a dual process theory of moral judgment, in which the human brain contains competing moral subsystems. The first subsystem is emotional and intuitive; it is the center where the brain makes deontological judgments. This subsystem would tell us that it is wrong to push the fat man off the bridge. The second subsystem, however, is more rational and calculated. Psychologists believe it contains the place where utilitarian judgments are made and would, in the trolley problem, argue in favor of pushing the fat man off the bridge in order to save the lives of others. See Greene *et al.* (2001: 2105–8.) Greene's later work tackles larger issues of group morality. See Greene (2013). Some of Greene's initial work turned out to be controversial. In 2009, McGuire, Langdon, Coltheart, and Mackenzie (2009) reanalyzed a particular finding of Greene's experiment, dubbing it "overturned;" Greene later (2009) wrote that he agrees that the particular finding is now "overturned." But Greene also argues that McGuire *et al.* conflated two findings and that the important finding about dual-process theory should stick. Greene *et al.* (2009) refine the controversial part of Greene *et al.* (2001). Leaving aside this debate for the moment, Greene's work remains important because he brings together his (and others') previous experimental studies supporting the dual-process theory and, notably, proposes a *central tension principle* which holds that "characteristically deontological judgments are preferentially supported by automatic emotional responses, while characteristically consequentialist judgments are preferentially supported by conscious reasoning and allied processes of cognitive control" (Greene 2014: 699). The groundwork for this is done in *Moral Tribes* (2013), but the argument is more concise in Greene (2014).

10 The Tajfel studies are described earlier in this book (Chapter 6) and in *Ethics in an Age of Terror and Genocide* (Monroe 2012).

11 Elliott's class experiment has become famous. It shows, in Elliott's words, how "what had been marvelous, cooperative, wonderful, thoughtful children turn into nasty, vicious, discriminating, little third graders, in a space of fifteen minutes." One of her classes was filmed in 1970, and is featured in *The Eye of the Storm*. A PBS Frontline special filmed a reunion of this 1970 class, and includes charming portraits of the grown-up adults viewing themselves as children and commenting on how this experiment changed their lives. Eventually, Elliot quit teaching to speak full time against discrimination, mostly by conducting the same simple exercise throughout the world. See also her work with college students in a 2001 documentary, *The Angry Eye*.

12 Work on stereotype threat is just one such fascinating area. As best I can ascertain, the term "stereotype threat" was first introduced by Claude Steele and Joshua Aronson (1995). The term stereotype threat describes what psychologists since then have identified as the psychological experience of a person—let's call her Joan—asked to perform a task—in which Joan believes, or is made to believe—that people like her usually do not perform well. The theory suggests that the existence of negative stereotypes regarding a specific group will contribute to group members feeling anxious about their performance. This, in turn, then may hinder their ability to perform to their full individual potential. (For example, Joan would ordinarily do well on the math test but does not do well precisely because she is told that "people like her" are not good in math.) The opposite of stereotype threat is stereotype boost, a

phenomenon occurring when positive stereotypes about their social groups encourage people to perform better than they otherwise would have done.

Joan may stop seeing herself as "a math person" after she experiences a series of these situations in which she feels stereotype threat. Joan's response is often described as a psychological coping strategy that allows Joan to keep her self-esteem in the face of failure. Both Jane Elliott's work and work on stereotype threat underline the importance of how others view and treat us, and how critical others thus are for our own sense of self-esteem and well-being.

13 I relate this story in a slightly different format in the Introduction.

14 A friend in math said she has colleagues who will give a pop quiz each week to make sure the students do the reading, the homework and learn the material. Her reservation about this strategy is that this tactic results in students who learn the material and can regurgitate it on exams but have not really gained the ability to think critically about anything.

15 We discussed some of this in Chapter 5. I also recommend a movie called *I Never Sang for My Father*, starring Gene Hackman as the son and Melvyn Douglas as the extremely difficult father. The extent to which we may have a deep-seated need for parental love, despite our knowledge of how many parents are incapable of giving such love, is captured beautifully at the end of the movie, when the son says: *What did it matter if I never loved him, or if he never loved me? … But, still, when l hear the word Father …. It matters.*" Anderson (1968: Page 62).

16 For a fascinating discussion of the thought process, its rationality and lack thereof, see Kahneman (2011).

17 *The View from Nowhere* (Nagel 1986), addresses a long-standing issue in philosophy: the extent to which people possess the unique ability to view the world with detachment. That is, are we able to think about the world in a manner that transcends our particular individual interests and experiences? (Hence the place designation of "Nowhere.") Yet we also work out of our own personal view of the world, one reflecting our individual knowledge, lives and interests. How are we then to reconcile these two standpoints, or ask if they can be integrated? This is discussed by Nagel and was reflected in the social psychological experiments by Gilligan and Kohlberg. Nagel effectively argues that the excessive objectification—found in law—has afflicted recent and contemporary analytic philosophy, where it has resulted in implausible forms of reductionism in the philosophy of mind. While Nagel does not decide where the two viewpoints can be reconciled, he does suggest that the two viewpoints learn to live alongside each other. Care ethics and feminist ethics are two notable schools that address this same tension.

18 See work by Gonzalez (forthcoming) and by Ditto *et al.* (2009) on the ethical importance of how we think.

19 Something close to this phenomenon is reflected in a long-standing truth recognized by trial lawyers: jury nullification, which refers to situations when members of a jury acquit the defendant even though they believe the defendant is guilty. The reasons driving jury nullification are many, several of which might be at work in the case of the old man who engaged in a requested mercy killing of his wife. Jury members may find the crime does not justify the extreme punishment. They may believe the particular law itself is not just. They may find the prosecutor has misapplied the law in this particular instance. They may be favorably prejudiced toward the defendant.

Or jury nullification might reflect more general frustrations with the criminal justice system. Effectively, for some reason, the jurors do not like their options and so, given no recourse, find an obviously-guilty person not guilty.

My father, a Circuit Court Judge, used to tell the story of Hugo Black, a Supreme Court justice who came from rural Alabama. Black's story—at least in my father's rendition—begins with a poor farmer whose mule goes lame just as the crops ripen and need to be picked. The poor farmer therefore goes to his neighbor, a rich farmer, and asks if he can borrow a mule, just long enough to bring in his crops. The rich farmer says, "Sure, as long as you sign a piece of paper saying that if you do not have the mule back by 5 p.m. on the dot that I get your farm."

The poor farmer says, "What? Are you crazy?" The rich farmer sticks to his demands, so the poor farmer eventually gives up and leaves.

The next day, the rich farmer gets up, notices his mule is gone and goes to the sheriff, certain that the mule has been stolen by his poor neighbor. The rich farmer thus demands the poor farmer be arrested for stealing his mule. The sheriff tries to calm the rich farmer, appealing to his sense of neighborliness and community spirit, to no avail. The rich farmer is adamant. "I want that man arrested and I want him tried for stealing my mule. And I want a circuit judge to hear the case before a jury."

Again, the sheriff appeals to the rich farmer's sense of friendship and community spirit. Again, to no avail. So, with reluctance, the sheriff goes to the poor farmer's. Upon finding the mule, the sheriff is compelled by duty to arrest the man. The sheriff puts the poor farmer in jail, where he must wait for the circuit judge to arrive. When the judge arrives, a jury is impaneled and the evidence presented. A fair man but one bound by the law, the circuit judge instructs the jury carefully. "This is a simple case. If you find the evidence presented here leads you to conclude that the defendant stole the mule, then he is guilty; if he did not steal the mule, however, he can be found not guilty. Do you understand? A simple factual case. No complicated law."

The jury members all nodded their agreement. They understood the judge's instructions.Back after 15 minutes, the jury announced its verdict. "Not guilty but he has to return the mule."The defendant is elated. The judge is aghast. "No, no, no. If he has the mule, he has to be found guilty. You can't say he is not guilty but has to return the mule. That doesn't make sense." The judge then repeats the prior instructions. "Now, do you understand? Simple facts. Nothing complicated in terms of law. Just follow the evidence."Once again, the jury nods its assent. They are happy to comply. This time the jury is out for nearly 30 minutes. Eventually, however, they do return to render their new verdict. "Not guilty, and he can keep the mule!"

20 Pritchard is featured in a beautiful movie, made by a nun concerned about what her church had not done during the war. *The Courage to Care* interviews people who rescued Jews during World War II, asking why they risked their lives for strangers. Nominated for an Academy Award, the film captures an essential aspect of rescue behavior and altruism. A survivor named Emanuel Tanay brilliantly sums this up: "These were not people making choices on reflection. They just had to do it because that's the kind of people they were." Identity was key.

21 "Modern Declaration" by Edna St. Vincent Millay (1931/34/39/1958).

REFERENCES

Anderson, Robert. [1968]/1970. *I Never Sang for My Father.* Play 1968. Movie 1970. Directed by Gilbert Cates. New York, United States.

Bakewell, Sarah. 2010. *How to Live: Or A Life of Montaigne in One Question and Twenty Attempts at an Answer.* Chatto and Windus. 2010; Other Press. 2011.

Becker, Gary. 1974. "A Theory of Marriage". *Economics of the Family: Marriage, Children, and Human Capital Volume.* Edited by Theodore W. Schultz. Chicago: University of Chicago Press.

Bettelheim, Bruno. 1976. *The Uses of Enchantment: The Meaning and Importance of Fairy Tales.* New York: Vintage Books of Random House.

Bloom, Harold. 2020. *Take Arms Against a Seas of Troubles: The Power of the Reader's Mind over a Universe of Death.* New Haven, CT: Yale University Press.

Brooks, David. 2015. *The Road to Character.* New York: Random House.

Bstan-'dzin-rgya-mtsho, Dalai Lama XIV, Thupten Jinpa and Śāntideva. 1997. *Healing Anger: The Power of Patience from a Buddhist Perspective.* Ithaca, NY: Snow Lion Publications.

Butler, Octavia E. 2020. *Unexpected Stories.* Burton, MI: Subterranean Press.

Cervantes Saavedra, Miguel d. 1949. *The Ingenious Gentleman Don Quixote of La Mancha.* Translated by Samuel Putnam. New York: Viking Press.

———. 1991. *El Ingenioso Hidalgo Don Quijote De La Manca.* Madrid, Espana: Akal.

Chua, Amy. 2011. *Battle Hymn of the Tiger Mother.* New York: Penguin.

Conrad, Joseph. 1899. *The Heart of Darkness.* London: Blackwood's Magazine.

Cunningham, William, Marcia Johnson, Carol Raye, Chris Gatenby, John Gore and Mahzarin Banaji. 2004. "Separable Neural Components in the Processing of Black and White Faces". *Psychological Science,* vol. 15, no. 12: 806–13.

Carpenter, Charli. 2016. *Perspectives on Politics,* vol. 14, no. 01: pp. 53–69. Published online by Cambridge University Press, March 21, 2016.

D'Aulaire, Ingri and Edgar Parin d'Aulaire. [1992]/2002. *D'Aulaires' Book of Greek Myths.* New York. Delacorte Press.

———. 2006. *D'Aulaires' Book of Trolls.* New York: New York Review, Children's Collection.

———. 2016. *D'Aulaires' Book of Norwegian Folktales.* Minneapolis, MN: University of Minnesota Press.

163

Dick, Philip K. 1954. *Orbit Science Fiction* (September–October 1954, No. 4). Götzis, Austria: Hanro Corporation.

Didion, Joan. 1979. *The White Album*. New York: Simon & Schuster.

———. 2011. *Blue Nights*. New York: Vintage Books of Random House.

———. 1968. *Slouching Towards Bethlehem*. New York: Farrar, Straus and Giroux.

Digeser, Peter. 2001. *Political Forgiveness*. Ithaca, NY: Cornell University Press.

Ditto, P. H., D. A. Pizarro, D. Tannenbaum. 2009. "Motivated Moral Reasoning". In B. H. Ross (Series ed.) and D. M. Bartels, C. W. Bauman, L. J. Skitka and D. L. Medin (eds.) *Psychology of Learning and Motivation*, vol. 50: "Moral Judgment and Decision Making" (pp. 307–38). San Diego, CA: Academic Press.

Duggal, Kartar Singh. 2004. *The Holy Granth Sri Guru Granth Sahib*. New Delhi: Hemkunt Publishers.

Dundes, Alan. 1991. "Bruno Bettelheim's Uses of Enchantment and Abuses of Scholarship". *The Journal of American Folklore*, vol. 104, no. 411: 74–83.

Dunne, Griffin, Annabella Dunne, Mary Recine and Susanne Rostock. 2017. *Joan Didion: The Center Will Not Hold*. Netflix Documentary.

Edmonds, Dave. 2013. *Would You Kill the Fat Man? The Trolley Problem and What Your Answer Tells Us about Right and Wrong*. Princeton, NJ: Princeton University Press.

Elliott, Jane. 1970. *The Eye of the Storm*. Boston: PBS Frontline.

———. 2001. *The Angry Eye*. Boston: PBS (Public Broadcasting Station) WGBH.

Ellison, Ralph. 1952. *Invisible Man*. New York: Random House.

Fiske, Susan T., Amy J. C. Cuddy, Peter Glick and Jun Xu. 1999. "A Model of (Often Mixed) Stereotype Content: Competence and Warmth Respectively Follow from Perceived Status and Competition". *Journal of Personality and Social Psychology*. Copyright 2002 by the American Psychological Association, Inc. 2002, vol. 82, no. 6: 878–902.

Foot, Philippa. 1978. *Virtues and Vices and Other Essays in Moral Philosophy*. Berkeley: University of California Press/Oxford: Blackwell.

———. 2001. *Natural Goodness*. Oxford: Clarendon Press.

———. 2002. *Moral Dilemmas: And Other Topics in Moral Philosophy*. Oxford: Clarendon Press.

Galsworthy, John. [1922]/2008. *The Forsyte Saga*. Oxford: Oxford University Press.Oxford World's Classics.

Gardner, Robert H. and Carol Rittner. 1985. *The Courage to Care*. Documentary.

Gardner Feldman, Lily. 1984. *The Special Relationship between West Germany and Israel*. Winchester, MA: Allen & Unwin.

———. 2012. *Germany's Foreign Policy of Reconciliation: From Enmity to Amity*. Lanham, MD: Rowman & Littlefield Publishers.

Gaskell, Elizabeth Cleghorn. 2011. *Cranford*. Oxford: Oxford University Press.

Gilligan, Carol. 1981. *In a Different Voice: Psychological Theory and Women's Development*. Cambridge, MA: Harvard University Press.

Gonzalez, Jessica. Forthcoming. "Moral Cognition: An Introduction to the Field". Chapter 10 in *Science and Ethics*, Kristen Monroe (ed.).

Greene, Graham. 1948. *The Heart of the Matter*. London: William Heinemann.

Greene, J.D. 2009. "Dual-Process Morality and the Personal/Impersonal Distinction: A Reply to McGuire, Langdon, Coltheart, and Mackenzie." *Journal of Experimental Social Psychology*, vol. 45, no. 3: 581–84.

Greene, Joshua D. 2013. *Moral Tribes: Emotion, Reason, and the Gap Between Us and Them.* New York: Penguin Press.

Greene, J.D. 2014. "Beyond Point-and-Shoot Morality: Why Cognitive (Neuro)science Matters for Ethics". *Ethics*, vol. 124, no. 4: 695–726.

Greene, Joshua D., R. Brian Sommerville, Leigh E. Nystrom, John M. Darley, Jonathan D. Cohen. 2001. "An fMRI Investigation of Emotional Engagement in Moral Judgment". *Science*, vol. 293, no. 5537: 2105–8.

Greene, J. D., Cushman, F. A., Stewart, L. E., Lowenberg, K., Nystrom, L. E. and Cohen, J. D. 2009. "Pushing Moral Buttons: The Interaction Between Personal Force and Intention in Moral Judgment". Cognition, vol. 111, no. 3: 364–71.

Gross, Jan T. 2001. *Neighbors: The Destruction of the Jewish Community in Jedwabne, Poland.*, Princeton, NJ: Princeton University Press.

Harmon, Glennice L. 1948. "They Ask Me Why I Teach". *NEA Journal*, vol. 37, no. 1: 375.

Hart, Allen J., Paul J. Whalen, Lisa M. Shin, Sean C. McInerney, Hakan Fischer, Scott L. Rauch. 2000. "Differential Response in the Human Amygdala to Racial Outgroup vs Ingroup Face Stimuli". *NeuroReport*, vol. 11, no. 11: 2351–54.

Hellman, Lilian. 1973. *Pentimento.* New York: Little Brown.

Hilton, James. 1934. *Goodbye, Mr. Chips.* London: Hodder and Stoughton.

Holy Bible. 1968. New York: American Bible Society.

The Jerusalem Talmud. Talmud Yerushalmi. Seder Nezikin. Masekhtot Shevi'it Ve-'avodah Zarah. 2011. Translated by Heinrich W. Guggenheimer. Berlin: De Gruyter.

Johnson, Kareem and Barbara Fredrickson. 2005. "We All Look the Same to Me: Positive Emotions Eliminate the Own Race Bias in Face Recognition". *Psychological Science*, vol. 16, no. 11: 875–81.

Kahneman, Daniel. 2011 *Thinking, Fast and Slow.* New York: Farrar, Strauss and Giroux.

Kernis, Michael H. (ed.). 1995. *Efficacy, Agency, and Self-Esteem.* New York. Springer.

Koestler, Arthur. 1943. *Arrival and Departure.* New York: MacMillan.

Kohlberg, Lawrence. 1981. *Essays on Moral Development, Vol. I: The Philosophy of Moral Development.* San Francisco, CA: Harper & Row.

Kurzban, Robert, John Tooby and Leda Cosmdies. 2001. "Can Race Be Erased? Coalitional Computation and Social Categorization". *Proceedings of the National Academy of Sciences*, vol. 98, no. 26: 15387–92.

Lee, Harper. 2002. *To Kill a Mockingbird.* New York: Harper Perennial.

———. 2016. *Go Set A Watchman.* New York: Harper Perennial,

Lerer, Lisa. 2021. "The Issue Riling Up Virginia Voters: What's Taught in the Schools". *New York Times*, October 13, 2021: 1.

Lewis, Sinclair. 1920. *Main Street.* New York: Harcourt Brace.

Lijphart, Arend. 1977. *Democracy in Plural Societies: A Comparative Exploration.* New Haven, CT: Yale University Press.

Maimonides, Moses. 1997. *Mishneh Torah.* Translated by Eliyahu Touger. New York: Moznaim.

Mann, Thomas. [1901]/1994. *Buddenbrooks: The Decline of a Family.* Translated from the German by John E. Woods. New York: Random House.

Martin, Adam Bryant. 2012. "Forgiveness in an Age of Terror: The Political Psychology of Forgiving the Perpetrators of the 9/11 Attacks". Diss., University of California, Irvine.

Maurois, Andre. 1931. "The Three Ghosts of America". *Scribner's Magazine*. August 23, 1931.

McCullough, Michael E. 2008. *Beyond Revenge: The Evolution of the Forgiveness Instinct*. San Francisco, CA: Jossey-Bass.

McGuire, J., R. Langdon, M. Coltheart and C. Mackenzie. 2009. "A Reanalysis of the Personal/Impersonal Distinction in Moral Psychology Research". *Journal of Experimental Social Psychology*, https://doi.org/10.1016/j.jesp.2009.01.002.

Michener, James. [1947]/1984. *Tales of the South Pacific*. New York: Fawcett.

Mill, John Stuart. 1859. *On Liberty*. London: John W. Parker and Son.

Millay, Edna St. Vincent. 2011. *Selected Poems*. New York: Harper Perennial Modern Classics; Illustrated edition (March 8, 2011).

Monroe, Kristen Renwick. 1996. *The Heart of Altruism: Perceptions of a Common Humanity*. Princeton, NJ: Princeton University Press.

———. 2004. *The Hand of Compassion*. Princeton, NJ: Princeton University Press.

———. 2008. "Cracking the Code: The Moral Psychology of Genocide". *Political Psychology*, October 2008.

———. 2012. *Ethics in an Age of Terror and Genocide*. Princeton, NJ: Princeton University Press.

———. 2015. *A Darkling Plain: Stories of Conflict and Humanity during War*. With Chloe Lampros-Monroe and Jonah Pellechia. New York: Cambridge University Press.

Montaigne, Michel de. 1580. *Essais de messire Michel de Montaigne ... livre premier et second* (first edn.). Bourdeaus: impr. de S. Millanges. Retrieved June 1, 2017—via Gallica.

Munsch, Robert. Illustrated by Sheila McGraw. [1986]/1995. *Love You Forever*. Boston, MA: Firefly Books.

Nagel, Thomas. 1986. *The View from Nowhere*. Oxford: Oxford University Press.

Nussbaum, Martha C. 1999. "Virtue Ethics: A Misleading Category?". *The Journal of Ethics*, vol. 3, no. 3: 163–201.

———. 2000. *Women and Human Development: The Capabilities Approach*. New York: Cambridge University Press.

———. 2001. *Upheavals of Thought: The Intelligence of Emotions*. New York: Cambridge University Press.

———. 1986/2001. *The Fragility of Goodness: Luck and Ethics in Greek Tragedy and Philosophy* (second edn.). New York: Cambridge University Press.

——— 2016. *Anger and Forgiveness; Resentment, Generosity, Justice*. Oxford: Oxford University Press.

———. 2018. *The Monarchy of Fear: A Philosopher Looks at Our Political Crisis*. New York: Simon & Schuster.

———. 2019. *The Cosmopolitan Tradition: A Noble but Flawed Ideal*. Cambridge, MA: Harvard University Press.

Ohman, Arne and Susan Mineka. 2001. "Fears, Phobias and Preparedness: Toward an Evolved Module of Fear and Fear Learning". *Psychological Review*, vol. 108, no. 3: 483–522.

Oxley, Douglas R., Kevin B. Smith, Matthew V. Hibbing, Jennifer L. Miller, John R. Alford, Peter K. Hatemi and John R. Hibbing. 2008. "Political Attitudes are Predicted by Physiological Traits". University of Nebraska—Lincoln DigitalCommons@ University of Nebraska—Lincoln Faculty Publications: Political Science Department of 9-19-2008.

Pedersen, Anne, Iain Walker, Mark Rapley and Mike Wise. 2003. "Anti-racism—What Works? An Evaluation of the Effectiveness of Anti-racism Strategies". Prepared by the Centre for Social Change & Social Equity. Murdoch University. March 2003, pp. 78–80.

Phelps, Elizabeth A., Kevin J. O'Connor, J. Christopher Gatenby, John C. Gore, Christian Grillon and Michael Davis. 2001. "Activation of the Left Amygdala to a Cognitive Representation of Fear". *Nature Neuroscience*, vol. 4, no.4: 437–41.

Quindlen, Anna. 1994. *One True Thing.* New York: Random House.

The Qur'an: A Modern English Version. 1998. Translated by Majid Fakhry. London: Garnet Publishing.

Ringel, M. M. and P.H. Ditto. 2019. "The Moralization of Obesity". *Social Science & Medicine*, vol. 237: 112399.

Rosten, Leo. 1937. *The Education of Hyman Kaplan.* New York: Harcourt Brace.

Rousseau, Jean-Jacques. 1992. *Discourse on the Origin of Inequality.* Translated by Donald A. Cress. Indianapolis, IN: Hackett Publishing.

———. 2002. *The Social Contract and the First and Second Discourses.* Translated by Susan Dunn and Mary Gitz. New Haven, CT: Yale University Press.

Sandel, Michael. 2012. *What Money Can't Buy: The Moral Limits of Markets.* New York: Farrar, Straus and Giroux.

Schulman, Tom. 1989. *Dead Poets Society.* Film. Directed by Peter Weir.

Shakespeare, William. 1992. *Macbeth.* Wordsworth Classics. Ware: Wordsworth Editions.

———. 1994. *King Lear.* Wordsworth Classics. Ware: Wordsworth Editions.

Shantideva. 2006. *The Way of the Bodhisattva: A Translation of the Bodhichary ̄avat ̄ara.* Translated by Padmakara Translation Group. Boston: Shambhala.

Singer, Peter and Renata Singer. (eds.). 2005. *The Moral of the Story: An Anthology of Ethics Through Literature.* (first edn.). New York: Wiley-Blackwell.

Smiley, Marion. 1992. *Moral Responsibility and the Boundaries of Community: Power and Accountability from a Pragmatic Point of View.* Chicago: University of Chicago Press.

Staub, Ervin. [1989]/1992. *The Roots of Evil: The Origins of Genocide and Other Group Violence.* New York: Cambridge University Press.

Steele, Claude and Joshua Aronson. 1995. "Stereotype Threat and the Intellectual Test Performance of African Americans". *Journal of Personality and Social Psychology*, vol. 69, no. 5: 797–811.

Stewart, Tracie L. 2003. "Do the 'Eyes' Have It? A Program Evaluation of Jane Elliott's 'Blue-Eyes/Brown-Eyes' Diversity Training Exercise 1". *Journal of Applied Social Psychology*, vol. 33, no. 9: 1898–1921.

Theodor W. Adorno, Else Frenkel-Brunswik, Daniel Levinson and Nevitt Sanford. 1950. *The Authoritarian Personality, Studies in Prejudice Series, Volume 1.* New York: Harper & Row.

Thomson, Judith Jarvis. 1986. *Rights, Restitution, and Risk: Essays in Moral Theory.* Cambridge, MA: Harvard University Press.

———. May 1985. "The Trolley Problem". *Yale Law Journal*, vol. 94, no. 6: 1395–415.

Thompson, Flora. 1945. *Lark Rise to Candleford, a Trilogy.* New York: Oxford University Press

Tajfel, Henri. 1959. "Quantitative Judgment in Social Perception". *British Journal of Psychology*, vol. 50, 16–29.

———. 1969. "Cognitive Aspects of Prejudice". *Journal of Social Issues*, vol. 25, 79–97.

———. 1970. "Experiments in Intergroup Discrimination". *Scientific American*, vol. 223, 96–102.

————. 1974. "Social identity and intergroup behaviour". *Social Science Information*, vol. 13, 65–93.

————. (ed.). 1978. *Differentiation Between Social Groups: Studies in the Social Psychology of Intergroup Relations*. London: Academic Press.

————. 1981. "Human Groups and Social Categories". *Studies in Social Psychology*. New York: Cambridge University Press.

————. 1982. "Social Psychology of Intergroup Relations". *Annual Review of Psychology*, vol. 33, 1–39.

————. 2010. *Social Identity and Intergroup Relations*. New York: Cambridge University Press.

Tajfel, Henri and John. C. Turner. 1979. "An Integrative Theory of Intergroup Conflict". In William G. Austin and S. Worchel (eds.). *The Social Psychology of Intergroup Relations*. Monterey, CA: Brooks-Cole.

————. 1986. "The Social Identity Theory of Intergroup Behavior". *Psychology of Intergroup Relations*. Chicago: Nelson-Hall.

Tajfel, Henri, M. G. Billig, R. P. Bundy and Claude Flament. 1971. "Social Categorization and Intergroup Behaviour". *European Journal of Social Psychology*, vol. 1, no 2: 149–78.

van den Bos, Wouter, Samuel M. McClure, Lasana T. Harris, Susan T. Fiske, Jonathan D. Cohen. 2007. "Dissociating Affective Evaluation and Social Cognitive Processes in the Ventral Medial Prefrontal Cortex". *Cognitive, Affective, & Behavioral Neuroscience*, vol. 7, no. 4: 337–46.

Warren, Robert Penn. 1953. *All the King's Men*. New York: Modern Library.

West, Rebecca. 1941. *Black Lamb and Grey Falcon*. London: MacMillan.

Williams, Bernard. 1972. *Morality: An Introduction to Ethics*. New York: Cambridge University Press.

————. 1981. *Moral Luck: Philosophical Papers 1973–1980*. New York: Cambridge University Press.

————. 1985. *Ethics and the Limits of Philosophy*. Cambridge: Harvard University Press.

————. 1995. *Making Sense of Humanity*. Cambridge: Cambridge University Press.

INDEX

CPSIA information can be obtained
at www.ICGtesting.com
Printed in the USA
BVHW041114210523
664588BV00001B/6